DREAM ON:

A Dream Interpretation and Exploration Guide for Women

Phyllis R. Koch-Sheras,
E. Ann Hollier, Brooke Jones

Prentice-Hall, Inc., Englewood Cliffs, New Jersey 07632

Library of Congress Cataloging in Publication Data

Koch-Sheras, Phyllis R.
Dream on.

"A Spectrum Book."
Includes index.
1. Women's dreams. 2. Women—Psychology. I. Hollier,
E. Ann. II. Jones, Brooke. III. Title.
BF1099.W65K6 1983   154.6'3'088043   83-10974

This book is available at a special discount when ordered in
bulk quantities. Contact Prentice-Hall, Inc., General
Publishing Division, Special Sales, Englewood Cliffs, N.J. 07632

This book is dedicated to Tana, Gail, and Chris,
for whom it was begun, and to Daniel and Sarah,
with whom it was finished.

1 2 3 4 5 6 7 8 9 10

ISBN 0-13-219493-7 {PBK.}

ISBN 0-13-219501-1

Editorial/production supervision by Cyndy Lyle Rymer
Manufacturing buyer Doreen Cavallo
Cover/jacket design by Hal Siegel

Prentice-Hall International, Inc., London
Prentice-Hall of Australia Pty. Limited, Sydney
Prentice-Hall Canada Inc., Toronto
Prentice-Hall of India Private Limited, New Delhi
Prentice-Hall of Japan, Inc., Tokyo
Prentice-Hall of Southeast Asia Pte. Ltd., Singapore
Whitehall Books Limited, Wellington, New Zealand
Editora Prentice-Hall do Brasil Ltda., Rio de Janeiro

Contents

Preface

Dream On is both a dream guide and a women's book. It directly addresses women's special strengths and issues, and it offers dreamwork as a creative way of dealing with the changes women are experiencing in their lives today. Women have a great need, as well as an opportunity now, for self-discovery as they confront challenges very different from those of their mothers and grandmothers. Through dreamwork, women can discover the knowledge and direction they need to make sense of the changing roles and self-images that accompany these challenges.

This book goes beyond the traditional focus of using dreams solely to solve personal problems; rather, it emphasizes how you can use dreams to recognize and develop your hidden abilities and strengths. Using the techniques presented here, you can explore and enjoy talents you may never have realized you possessed, and you can benefit from the solutions they offer to the personal dilemmas in your waking life.

It is also important to recognize the social context out of which women's problems often arise. This book emphasizes the need for changing the environment around you in order to resolve your "personal" problems. You will learn how you can use your dreams to change and enrich your relationships, education and inspire others, enhance your spiritual community, guide professional decisions, and even implement social and political reforms.

In this book we address all women, and we have included the dreams of women from all stages and phases of existence: traditional and non-traditional, homemaker and executive, single and coupled, living alone and in families, heterosexual and lesbian, daughters, mothers, and grandmothers, from ages eight to eighty. Following most of the dreams is the dreamer's individual commentary about the dream. We use each dreamer's comments so she can tell you in her own words how she used her dreams to expand self-awareness, develop hidden talents and resources, and change her life as well as the lives of others.

Though we focus on the special needs, strengths, and interests of women in this book, we hope that men will also read and profit from it. Dreams and dreamwork may be a more natural and accessible avenue to personal growth for many women, but men can also use dreamwork to guide them in the evolution of their inner truths. Both men and women need to understand and integrate the personal and social changes that are sweeping through women's lives today, since men's roles and images must inevitably change as well. We believe this book can help men understand the contemporary female experience in a new way, and men as well as women can recognize their own struggles for authenticity and sensitivity in the dreams of the women presented here. Through a greater understanding and empathy for one another, we can work together to create a new vision for the future.

Dream On provides a guidebook for achieving this vision through dreamwork. The "journey" begins by dispelling some common myths about dreams and by showing you how to understand your dreams. Once you have become familiar with the language of your dreams—how they speak to you and how to communicate back to them—you can embark on a self-guided tour of the new worlds open to you through dreamwork using any of the wide variety of techniques provided here. Finally, the book addresses some of the pressing issues faced by women today, and demonstrates how women of different ages and backgrounds have dealt with these issues with the help of their dreams.

As you continue on your dream journey through this book, you will become more aware of the process of discovering yourself—a process that never ends. As long as you live, you will dream, and as long as you use what your dreams bring, you will enhance your life and the lives of those around you. Issues in your life will come and go, but the process of living and learning about them through your dreams is never-ending.

For us writing this book was very much like the process of working on a dream: a labor of love and self-exploration. Each chapter, like any dream, required confronting ourselves, clarifying our beliefs and values, and struggling to convey them clearly and honestly. As we worked together to give expression to our ideas and to write about our own dreams and those of others, we learned something new about ourselves that helped the writing process as well as our own personal growth. We also discovered *each other* in new and exciting ways, drawing strength from the common ground we share, respecting and integrating our differences in order to come together in a celebration of dreams—the natural resource that literally lies sleeping in all of us.

Our greatest excitement is now to share all we have discovered with you, the reader. We hope that you will experience the same sense of creative discovery and excitement as you bring your dreams into your own waking life and the lives of others.

ACKNOWLEDGMENTS

The authors gratefully acknowledge the following people for their assistance, advice, and support, and for so willingly contributing their dreams and comments to make this book a reality: Martin Albert, Daniela Alexander, Maxine Atlas, Su Autrand, Jane Barnes, Woody Black, Tana Bradley, Mrs. N. Jerry Brownstein, Sharon Davie, Dick Delanoy, Kay Deaux, Jacqui des Marets, Jo DesMarits, Helen Eitelberg, Lisabeth Fisher, Phyllis Frame, Jeanne Van Gemert, Amy Gorn, Melinda Guttman, Jo Hollier, Momzelle Hollier, Elizabeth Howard, Roger Howe, Karen S. Ireland, Janice Koch, Mrs. Morton Koch, Sherry Kraft, Todd Leuders, Lori Lichtenwalner, Jean Lightner, Chris Luckman, Brian Manire, Linda Manire, Dick McLeester, Michael McLaughlin, Kay McNett, Rachel Mead, Lucille Michie, Nick Morgan, Ellie Pancoe, Ralph O'Brien, Debbie Phelps, Swami Radha, Henry Reed, Robin Robello, Corina Ross, Daniel Sheras, Peter Sheras, Betty Siegner, Sally Amazon Smith, Bharbreh Strauss, Ann Swingler, Deborah Strzbeck, Miriam Trogdon, Robert Van de Castle, Ruth Weeks, Gail Waldron, Steven Worchel, and many others. Dreamers' names and those of others mentioned in their dreams have been deleted or changed in the text to protect their privacy.

We also want to acknowledge you, the reader, for using this book to explore your inner self. We would be interested in hearing about the results of your explorations. You can write to us care of General Publishing Division, Prentice-Hall, Inc., Englewood Cliffs, New Jersey 07632. We look forward to hearing from you. Have a pleasant dream journey!

part one
DREAMS: THE ROAD TO SELF-DISCOVERY

Introduction:
Why Dreams for Women?

> ...The feminine genius is the genius of self-creation. The outer
> world will never be as crucial for its flowering as the inner world.
>
> —May Sarton[1]

There are two reasons why we have written this book especially for you.
The first has to do with the status of dream books today, and the second
with the status of women.

First, a number of popular books exist that offer various approaches
to working with dreams, and interestingly enough, many of these are
written by women. Further, most people with a serious interest in dreams
are women. Yet, none of the available books on dreams addresses women's
lives directly; none focuses squarely on the issues facing women today;
and none illustrates how women of widely different lifestyles, values, and
goals have found fresh perspectives for exploring these issues through their
dreams. While there are books about dreams written *by* women, there have
been none, until now, written *for* women.

Secondly, in terms of women's status, we live in a society which, to
its own detriment, largely ignores the special skills and perspectives women

have to offer—skills that are *different* from those of most men. The differences between men and women have been touted for so long to keep women in the position of second-class citizens that it is tempting for women to deny that these differences exist, as a way of defending ourselves. Yet to stress the similarities between women and men to the point of ignoring the special strengths of each is to throw the baby out with the bathwater. Rather than protest that there are no differences between women and men, we would do well to explore the specific strengths and resources that are available to us because of them.

Our culture tends to value such "masculine" qualities as independence, competitive spirit, dominance, and rational, linear thought, while dismissing as unimportant those qualities labeled as "feminine"—nurturance, sensitivity, emotional and physical expressiveness, desire for intimacy or affiliation with others, and intuitive perception. Recently, however, psychologists and feminists have begun pointing out what many of us have known all along—that these qualities, while different from those of most men, are desirable traits that both men and women would do well to develop.[2] These qualities—so many of them a vital part of dreams and dreamwork—are necessary to complement and balance the masculine traits our culture values so highly. Without them, independence becomes self-centered indulgence, success becomes defined in terms of money and power, and rational, scientific thought results all too often in "good ideas" that profit a few while ravaging the earth and exploiting and dehumanizing others.

Our values and priorities must be reexamined. A growing emphasis on such reassessment is already evident in current women's writing. Many women writers are urging us to turn our attention inward, to develop the imaginative, intuitive, and psychic skills we all possess, and to recognize how valuable these are to us. According to psychotherapist Jean Baker Miller, author of *Toward a New Psychology of Women:*

> We have reached the end of the road that is built on the set of traits held out for male identity—advance at any cost, pay any price, drive out all competition and kill them if necessary. . . .We must return to a basis of faith in affiliation—and not only faith but recognition that it is a requirement for the existence of human beings.[3]

In this time of rapid technological and social change, this need to look inward, to discover our own guiding principles and the personal meaning in our experiences is especially pressing for women. For the first time in history, we can see glimpses of a future in which every individual can grow and develop as a whole person, free of the socially imposed definitions of "masculine" and "feminine." We as women are now freer to explore new possibilities and define ourselves as we choose. It's an exciting time to be a woman!

As we seek new perspectives and roles to replace the old ones, often we fall into the trap of either emulating or condemning men—neither of which provides a solid base for personal growth and change. Instead, we need to *integrate* our emotional, nurturant, and intuitive abilities with those "masculine" qualities long denied to women. This puts today's women in a unique position. As we move into male-dominated fields, we can take this new synthesis with us. Thus, women have a vital contribution to make in laying the groundwork for the society of the future.

This process of self-discovery and integration is difficult for women, because the tools at hand for this task are often inadequate. While women have used consciousness-raising groups and political activism to change the existing power structure, these alone cannot fully help us understand or direct the corresponding inner changes we experience as we strive to define ourselves on our own terms. We must repeatedly reexamine and break up the "gestalt"[4] of our old self-images to remain authentic to ourselves and others. Such self-definition demands a constant flow of fresh perspectives that responds to our changing inner needs and offers us needed insights at each stage of our development.

This is where our dreams can help. Everyone dreams; and we are all influenced by our dreams, whether we are aware of them or not. The potent images of dreams and waking fantasies offer us the raw materials necessary to discover and define ourselves. All we need to do is make intelligent use of them. Through these channels we can then get a fresh, personal, and creative perspective on ourselves and the world around us, one that allows us to step outside our customary viewpoints in seeking solutions to the issues we face. Not all the solutions suggested by our dreams will be either desirable or feasible. Yet, unrestricted by the rules and laws of our conscious waking lives, the images in our dreams and fantasies can provide us with the knowledge and direction we need to discover our own strengths and resources, and our own truths.

As we begin to risk exploring the alternatives now open to us, a new generation of women is being formed, which lives and works out of what the philosopher Mary Daly calls this "new space" of inner strength and resourcefulness.[5] Through dreamwork, we can learn the skills and self-confidence we need to join them, to begin living out of an understanding of our own nature and potential for creative growth.

chapter one
Reclaiming Our Dream Selves: The Feminine Principle

TRAVELING TO THE CENTER: RECLAIMING OUR INTUITIVE SELVES

How would you like to have a friend who is always there when you need her? How would you like an eager and available guide who knows you so intimately she can point out your strengths and weaknesses, offer practical solutions to everyday problems, advise you when to move ahead and when to be patient, and stimulate your imagination? Such a helper would offer you humor and support, give advice on how to maintain your equilibrium, issue progress reports on your growth and development, and, above all, guide you to the core of your being—your center of personal power—where you can discover your own truths.

"Sounds too good to be true!" you say. "Who *wouldn't* want such a friend?"

The fact is you *already* possess such an ally. There is no fee for this wonderful service and no special place to go for it—it is with you all the time! This personal guide can be found in your dreams, the gateway to the center of your creative unconscious. Your dreams can, with some encouragement, do all the things mentioned above and more.

6

This idea may seem strange to you. Perhaps you didn't know that you dream every single night; or, maybe you had not realized that dreams were "good for something." Your dreams cannot solve *all* of your problems, but there are many ways to benefit from dreamwork—the process of remembering and making use of your dreams—once you discover what your dreamlife has to offer and how you can put it to use.

Through our dreams we journey to our "center"—exploring that core of important feelings, ideas, and information that lies beyond our conscious awareness and might otherwise remain hidden from us. This is illustrated by the heroine of a popular novel who becomes aware in a dream of some feelings about her husband that might have been too painful or frightening to admit consciously. She acknowledges these feelings in a letter to her mother following the dream.

INDIFFERENCE

[I dreamed I] was dead and had been for three days, but Rob continued to sit across from me at dinner, sleep beside me through the night and kiss me good-bye in the morning—without even noticing I had ceased to breathe.

His indifference in the dream so paralyzed me that I pretended to be asleep when he left for the office this morning. . . . And the dream suggests, that in my heart I suspect even more. . . . Am I the only wife to feel so wasted, so unused, so alone? I would not put this question to anyone but you, dearest Mama. And indeed I would feel I were betraying Rob by even thinking it, if my dreams had not already betrayed my doubts.[1]

This dream example shows how paying attention to your dreams can play an important role in leading you to self-discovery, frightening and puzzling though it may be at times. This process of discovery is essential if women are to continue to grow and evolve. In the words of author and poet Adrienne Rich, the search for "truthfulness anywhere means a heightened complexity . . . But it is a movement into evolution."[2]

For this search—this "movement into evolution"—to be meaningful and authentic for us as women, it must be consistent with our own needs and strengths, which are often very different from those of men. Women have a "broader or at least a different base" than men, from which we operate in making sense of ourselves and the world.[3] Our differences in cognitive functioning have been extensively documented:

[Men] seem to be less dependent on situational variables . . . more narrowly focused, less distractible. Females, by contrast, are sensitive to context, good at picking up information that is incidental to a task that's set them, and distractible, which is *also* to say un-blinkered by the demands of a particular goal.[4]

Women also tend to use more nonverbal channels of communication to collect information, and we are generally more effective in expressing our emotions, verbally and nonverbally, than are men.[5] There are exceptional women and men who do not reflect these feminine or masculine traits and there is much overlap in the range of abilities and sensitivities of each gender. However, when looking at women or men *as a group,* a pattern of differences emerges that clearly biases men more toward behavior of one sort and women more toward behavior of another. It is not a matter of which behavior pattern is "better," but rather, how best to capitalize on these differences for our individual and mutual benefit.

It may be our greater sensitivity to emotions and nonverbal com-munication—our so-called "women's intuition"—that often leads women to evaluate information and make judgments differently from men. Psychologist Carol Gilligan, after extensive research on the development of moral reasoning in women, suggests that women's "greater orientation towards relationships and interdependence implies a more contextual mode of judgment and a different moral understanding ... [thus] women bring to the life cycle a different point of view and order human exper-iences in terms of different priorities."[6] Because this orientation or knowl-edge in women has been considered "intuitive" or "instinctive," it has been neglected or devalued by men and women alike. Both the picture language of dreams and many approaches to dreamwork tap these non-verbal and intuitive sources of information. Women express a greater interest in dreams than men do, and this may be because dreaming is one form of the intuitive mode of experience to which women are more attuned.

In this book you will find many techniques—representing many different modes of experience—that will show you how to use your dreams to recognize, confront, and overcome conflicts in your changing images of yourself and others. You will also find a structure for discovering and developing your unknown latent abilities as well as methods for integrating these abilities with the strengths you already possess. By getting to know the hidden allies in your dreams, you can reclaim and celebrate an im-portant and valuable natural resource that is always available to you.

A COMMON MEETING GROUND

The treasures of the dreamworld are available to you regardless of your age, sex, race, or social class. No capital, specialized equipment, or sophisticated knowledge is necessary to explore your dream universe. All you need to begin is the desire and the will to embark on this journey into inner space. The rewards of dreamwork will follow as your skills increase through practice. This "open door policy" of the dreamworld makes it possible for women of many ages, backgrounds, and environments to come together on a common meeting ground. Some kind of commonality is essential for women, because when problems such as those confronting women today have their origins in the culture at large, there is no ultimate individual solution; it is only collective effort that can bring about lasting and fundamental change.

One way to begin exploring new paths together is through *social dreamwork,* that is, sharing and working on our dreams with others. (See Chapter Eight for further discussion of social dreamwork.) By sharing and learning from our dreams with our friends, families, children, and co-workers, we can provide the mutual support and guidance we continually need. While this is true for anyone, it may be especially beneficial for women who are more relationship-oriented than men.

Not only can social dreamwork bring women together, it can also help us to acknowledge and accept the important and necessary differences among us. We would do ourselves and other women a disservice to expect these differences to be overcome, for the search for individual truth through dreams leads to a wide variety of personal meanings and values. Through dreamwork, we can learn to recognize and support one another's unique characteristics and abilities, and better understand lifestyles that differ from our own. In fact, sharing and working with dreams can be a testing ground where new and creative ways of accepting, expressing, and making use of individual differences can be explored.

The following dream and comments illustrate how one woman used social dreamwork to achieve a new understanding of individual differences in the process of working creatively with other women.

THE TRIAD
I'm designing a creative sculpture or production. I include various presentations on a similar theme. There are three structures—dif-

9

ferent kinds of "pencil sharpeners" that I shape in different ways. I feel confident and assured as I tell people what I want and how I think it would work best. Some women disagree with me, but I calmly explain what I believe. They listen and go along with it.

In working on this dream, I decided to make a drawing of the sculpture. I recognized myself as the central figure of the sculpture, with two female figures on either side of me, whom I saw as the two co-authors of the book I was writing. I shared my dream and drawing with my co-authors and came to see each of us as having our own special function in "sharpening points" and making unique statements consistent with our personalities and styles. I saw the base of the sculpture as our common ground—rounded and full, strong, solid and lasting. The base (the book) could not exist or be balanced without all three figures: each part complemented and supported the other. As with Sisterhood, our book had room for and required differences as well as similarities, conflict as well as cooperation.●

Figure 1-1.
The Triad
(by Phillis Koch-Sheras).

The book referred to above is *this* book, and the dreamer was one of the authors. The "Triad" dream reflects the difficulties involved in integrating the working and writing styles of three different women; yet it also shows how the authors have been able to come together through the avenue of dreams to create and share something vital out of the combination of their experiences.

● *This symbol will be used throughout the book to signify the conclusion of the dream commentary.*

In the same way, ideas and insights that come out of working with your dreams can enrich your life and relationships at home, at work, and at play. The road to self-discovery and creative change is not always an easy one. Dreamwork can help you appreciate the small victories along the way and remind you that it is often the going, not the getting there, that matters most.

TAKING NEW PATHS:
DIRECTIONS FOR SOCIAL CHANGE

Our dreams are primarily mirrors of ourselves, reflecting the outer world as it is perceived through the filter of our thoughts, feelings, and perceptions—conscious and unconscious. However, the questions for which we seek answers often have a cultural, as well as a personal, context. Our cultural perspective determines which situations we view as problems, and our problems themselves often arise because we cannot or will not fit into the mold that other people or social customs demand.

In seeking solutions to our personal dilemmas through dreamwork, we need to understand the social fabric out of which these issues may arise. In turn, when we change ourselves through dreamwork, we also affect the world of the people around us. Thus, personal and cultural changes are not at odds; they are *natural partners.* Social change may be swept along by political activism such as the women's movement. However, such change only becomes a reality because many individual women *live these changes in their own lives.* This process is different for each woman, as each of us experiences the conflicts and challenges of current women's issues in a unique way and reacts to them out of a different fund of experiences and values.

Throughout this book you will find examples of dreams and dreamers' comments that show how dreamwork techniques have been used by women of many different backgrounds, lifestyles, and values to deal with important issues in their lives—motherhood, work, intimacy, family relationships, aging, and more. We will also show how women have used dreamwork to enrich their lives and bring about changes in their communities by working with dreams—both their own dreams as well as others—in schools, businesses, religious or spiritual groups, and political activities.

Dreamwork alone, however, is not enough to bring about change. Your most profound insights are useless without the resolve to *act* on them and the persistence to try out new ways of being. It is important to remember here that even the most sweeping social changes are still the results of many *individual* acts. Publicly or privately, intentionally or not, you are the instrument that brings about change. As you explore your inner self through dreamwork, you will become more aware of the power you have to shape and direct the changes in your own life. You will also become more aware that, as you change yourself, you create the possibility for change in others.

BE YOUR OWN GUIDE

In using dreams to achieve both personal and social change, we enter into the often complex and confusing inner world of the unconscious. Adrienne Rich talks about the necessity and difficulties of this process for women today—our "drive to self-knowledge":

> ... At this moment ... there is the challenge and promise of a whole new psychic geography to be explored. But there is also a difficult and dangerous walking on the ice as we try to find language and images for a consciousness we are just coming into, and with little in the past to support us.[7]

When we find ourselves on thin ice, it is tempting in our confusion and fear to rely on someone else—some authority or expert who supposedly knows the way—to give us the support and answers we need. We may even come to believe that what this authority tells us is "the truth." We have played dependent and passive roles for so long that many of us find it difficult to believe in ourselves—in our own abilities and self-knowledge, our own truths. We as women must encourage each other to find our own truths and personal meanings in our experiences, and, in so doing, learn to understand and direct our own lives. For this reason, it is important to trust yourself to *be your own guide* in working with your dreams. You are *already* your own guide in your dreams: You alone determine the plot, the scenery, the characters, the mood of your dreams. Because you are the creator of your dreams, some part of you already knows the meanings and messages hidden in your dream symbols. Through self-guided dreamwork, you can come to know these hidden truths about yourself. It will be easier then to understand what guides your thoughts and actions in both your waking and dreaming lives, enabling you to discover what you really want and how to get it.

"Easier said than done!" you may be saying to yourself now, especially if your dreams are still relative strangers to you. You may genuinely feel that you would like someone to *tell* you what your dreams mean, at least at first. However, while there are many aids in the chapters ahead that will help you in exploring your dream universe, the only one who really knows what your dreams mean is *you.* You are the only one who can decide which methods are the best ones for discovering yourself, in both your dreamlife and waking life. Thus, we offer you many approaches to work with your dreams, and we encourage you to try them out at your own pace, fitting them to your interests and needs. As you make your dream odyssey, you will find many signposts and guidelines along the way. You will also encounter other dream travelers who will share their experiences. The direction and distance you travel are completely up to you.

WORKING WITH DREAMS:
THE AGONY AND THE ECSTASY

While it may be exhilarating to explore your dreams in this time of women's awakening consciousness, it can also be disorienting and painful. You may become aware of some feelings—joy, anger, and frustration—that you hadn't recognized before. At the same time, you may discover ways to use these dream feelings productively in your waking life.

This was the experience one of the authors had in juggling the time to write this book along with a marriage, career, and new motherhood. When she had the following dream, her life seemed disorganized and too busy for any nurturance or relaxation. She comments on how this dream helped her to regain a sense of control over her life and take more care to meet her needs.

THE AGONY AND THE ECSTASY

I'm seeing two clients at once. I notice that one of them, Maria, is quiet and pouting. Then my class comes into my office. I dismiss them, saying "You should have a lot of work to do." No one leaves. Someone says Bernard Gunther was here but he left, and I feel badly that I missed him. The class finally leaves. I stay and talk to Maria about her passivity. We leave together. As we're walking I see Bernard Gunther carrying a briefcase, several books, and papers. I pass him and go on to my other office.

When I first thought about this dream, I had no idea who Bernard Gunther was. As I began working on the dream, however, I suddenly remembered that he was the "guru" of the Sensitivity Movement, teaching the benefits and joy inherent in everyday lives. I then heard him say, "Remember the ecstasy in your life and take the time for it." That helped me realize that, like Maria, I had been ignoring the need—and opportunities— for more joy and nurturance in my work and in my home life. I resolved to integrate these things into my life so there would be more "ecstasy" and less "agony"!●

Keeping a balanced perspective is important in dealing with both your dreaming and waking life. It is easy at times to lose sight of your purpose and goals and the joy to be derived from them, especially when you are in the midst of your own struggles. Adrienne Rich makes this point dramatically in this description of a dream she once had.

> THE BLUES
> I dreamed I was asked to read my poetry at a mass women's meeting, but when I began to read, what came out were the lyrics of a blues song. I share this dream with you because it seemed to me to say something about the problems and the future of the woman writer, and probably of women in general. The awakening of consciousness is not like the crossing of a frontier—one step and you're in another country. Much of women's poetry has been of the nature of a blues song: a cry of pain, of victimization . . . charged with anger. I think we need to go through the anger, and we will betray our own reality if we try . . . for an objectivity, a detachment.[8]

Even when we feel confused and exhausted by the process of self-discovery and social struggle, we must remind ourselves that

> Women are only beginning to uncover our own truths; many of us would be grateful for some rest in that struggle, would be glad just to lie down with the shards we have painfully unearthed, and be satisfied with those. . . . The politics worth having, the relationships worth having, demand that we delve still deeper.[9]

Delving into your dreams for those truths can be an end in itself, needing no explanation, no justification, and no grand, immediate insights. The treasures are there, hidden in the mystery and complexity of your dreamworld, and the discovery will come as long as you continue to search. Working with your dreams provides you with a structure for dealing with your subjective experience in a productive way. If you feel confused as you begin your search, that's understandable. Nonetheless, however dark or dangerous the road ahead may seem, you alone must take the first step on your journey into the world of dreams. There you will discover the knowledge—your personal truth—that can guide you further.

chapter two

Sleeping Beauty Revisited: Facts and Fairy Tales About Women's Dreams

Sleeping Beauty slept for 100 years of her life. We spend one third of our lives sleeping. Unlike Sleeping Beauty, you need not be at the mercy of a Prince Charming to wake you up to reality. You can break the spell of misinformation and myths surrounding sleep and dreaming by informing yourself about the factors that commonly affect your dreams, and making this information work for you. Separate the facts from the fiction so that you aren't taking any fairy tales with you on your dream journey!

YOU DREAM EVERY NIGHT

Dreaming is a universal human experience. You dream several times during the night, as well as during naps. In fact, you produce well over 1000 dreams a year. The tendency to forget dreams is so common, however, that many people are convinced they dream only occasionally or not at all. Actually, these "non-dreamers" are just *non-recallers*. For many, dream memories evaporate quickly upon waking; yet, anyone can acquire or improve their ability to remember dreams, even those of us who rarely recall them.

Dreams are not "caused" by hunger, thirst, indigestion, or illness. These bodily states may influence what you dream about, and can result

Figure 2-1. Dreams are not caused by the things you eat, although dream content can be influenced by indigestion. Reproduced with permission from Winsor McCay, *Dreams of the Rarebit Fiend* (Dover Books, 1973), p. 11.

in higher dream recall by causing frequent awakenings. The dreams themselves, however, are a natural part of your night life whether you ordinarily remember them or not.

Two different kinds of mental processes occur while you sleep. These alternate throughout the night in a regular cycle that is as automatic as breathing. One kind of thinking occurs during the part of your sleep cycle known as REM (rapid eye movement) sleep, when your eyes dart about rapidly behind your eyelids. During REM sleep, your thoughts generally are very vivid, emotional, and dramatic, and include visual images that play out a fairly coherent story. If awakened during or just after REM sleep, you will remember a dream about 80 percent of the time. If you are awakened during some other part of the sleep cycle, you are much less likely to remember anything at all. If you do, it is likely to be shorter, more fragmented, and less vivid, visual, emotional, and bizarre. Because of these differences, there is some controversy over whether to call what goes on in non-REM sleep "dreaming" or not. What you recall if awakened at this time will tend to be more like your thoughts of waking life and less vivid than the usual dream.

REM periods occur at regular 90-minute intervals while you sleep, alternating with other, non-REM stages of sleep. In a normal night's sleep, you spend a total of about one and a half hours in REM sleep. If you woke up after every REM period you might be able to recall as many as six dreams in a single night!

YOU NEED TO DREAM

Dreaming plays a vital role in your well-being. It is important for certain mental processes, such as reasoning and memory, and for your physical and emotional functioning. Without dream time, your thinking would become disorganized. You deal more effectively with problems after you have "slept on them," so even your forgotten dreams are valuable. However, you gain much more from your dreamlife if you pay attention to it. For example, people who remember and work on their dreams as part of therapy make better progress and are less likely to drop out of therapy prematurely than those who do not.[1] Thus, dreams play an important role in integrating information, solving problems, and resolving conflicts—and you do not need to be in therapy to put this resource to work for you in your everyday life.

WHY YOU FORGET YOUR DREAMS

Although we dream throughout the night, we do not remember most of these dreams unless we wake up during the night. We usually remember only our last dream in the morning. There are a number of "dream pirates" busy at work to keep us from remembering even these morning dreams. You can outwit these pirates, however, if you check your waking life for the following factors.

Cultural Factors and Personal Motivation

In many cultures, dreams have always been viewed as a valuable source of information and guidance. To understand our own culture's attitude toward dreams, we need only look at the connotation the word "dreamer" brings to mind. It suggests the impractical visionary or the loafer. Thus, we are often told that dreams are silly, troublesome, and unimportant: "Dreams . . . are not real . . . they are hallucinations, mental enactments of desires . . . They happen only in your head!" says the hero of a novel.[2] Most parents instill the notion in their children that dreams, especially nightmares or "bad dreams," are best forgotten. "Go to sleep dear, it's just a dream," is a phrase often repeated to children Fantasizing—or anything non-rational for that matter—is usually considered a waste of time and less valuable than objective or practical matters. With no encouragement from the culture around us to focus on our dreams, it is little wonder that so few of us are motivated to remember them. Even confirmed non-recallers often begin to remember dreams, however, once they learn how valuable their dreams can be.

Personality Factors

The dreaming mind, although clever and imaginative, does not always practice tact, good taste, and other social niceties. Often the exaggerated bluntness in them hits home with painful clarity and forces us to confront parts of ourselves we would rather ignore. One way to avoid things we don't want to see, feel, or do is simply to forget them. The degree to which we do this, of course, varies from individual to individual. We have met "non-dreamers" who suddenly remember dreams after reading a book on the subject or meeting dream enthusiasts, and these people may lapse back into forgetfulness once they encounter negative feelings or meet a less agreeable side of themselves in a dream. Good recallers are more in touch with their anxieties and insecurities in waking life and more willing to express them; whereas poor recallers tend to avoid confronting unpleasant situations and inner fears.

How You Wake Up

Some ways of waking up are more conducive to recalling dreams than others. If, upon waking, you toss and turn, bolt out of bed, or think about the day's anticipated activities, you are likely to lose many valuable dreams. Going over the dream or writing it down before going back to sleep or getting out of bed will help to fix it firmly in your mind. In Chapter Four we will discuss some wake-up practices that encourage dream recall.

When You Wake Up

If you wake up during or just after a REM period, you are very likely to remember a dream. REM sleep takes up more of your sleep cycle the longer you sleep, so if you wake up at the end of a full night's sleep, chances are good that you will awaken from REM sleep and remember a dream. This is especially true if you wake up naturally, although you may remember a dream you were having when awakened by some other means such as an alarm clock. If you awaken from non-REM sleep, however, your dream recall will be quite low. If you wake from a dream in the middle of the night, wake up completely and write it down before going back to sleep, or the dream is likely to be lost forever.

What You Remember

Long, vivid dreams with great emotional impact are more easily recalled than shorter ones with little emotional content. Thus, a person who remembers dreams only occasionally is more likely to remember a nightmare than a less emotional dream, while good recallers remember a wider variety of dreams.

Age and Dream Recall

We spend less and less time in REM sleep as we age. Five-year-olds, for example, spend about 25 percent of their sleep time in REM sleep; young adults spend about 22 percent; and the aged spend about 18 percent. For this and other reasons, our dream recall often diminishes as we grow older.

Gender and Dream Recall

Women tend to be better dream recallers than men, probably because women focus more on inner processes. However, there is wide variation among members of both sexes. Pregnant women, for example, have better dream recall than other women. A woman's menstrual cycle seems to affect her recall ability as well, with recall at its peak just before menstruation.[3]

Other Factors

Insufficient sleep may lead to drowsiness upon waking, reducing dream recall. There are also a number of other factors that inhibit recall, not only by leaving you groggy upon waking, but also by disturbing the sleep cycle and inhibiting REM sleep. These include drugs such as amphetamines, sleeping pills, alcohol, and marijuana, as well as emotional factors such as anxiety and depression.

YOUR DREAMING BODY

Rapid eye movements, mentioned earlier, are not the only changes in your body during dream sleep. While you are involved in your nightly dream adventures, your body is acting out a drama of its own: Your brain metabolism is stepped up, and there is an increased flow of blood, causing your brain temperature to rise; your breathing and pulse quicken and become more irregular. Your body also experiences an increase in oxygen consumption, gastrointestinal secretions, and adrenal hormones in your blood. Your nipples become erect and your vaginal temperature rises along with the increased flow of blood to that region of your body. A number of women have reported experiencing mild vaginal contractions when waking from dreams.

WOMEN'S DREAMS DIFFER FROM MEN'S

The waking interests, goals, and personalities of men and women often differ from one another. Not surprisingly, the dreams of women and men reflect these differences in their content and themes. Following are some of the differences documented on dreams collected in the 1940s.[4]

TABLE 2-1. Gender Differences in Dream Content

WOMEN'S DREAMS	MEN'S DREAMS
Take place in familiar, indoor settings	Take place in unfamiliar, outdoor settings
Show attention to color, clothing, jewelry, face, eyes, household objects, flowers, rooms	Show attention to autos, tools, weapons, money, hair, qualities of size, speed, intensity
Have more single, familiar characters—mothers, family members, babies, children	Have more groups of unfamiliar characters, identified by occupational roles
Show subtle forms of aggression, sensitivity to rejection. Aggressive encounters occur more with same-sex members. Men are more often the aggressor, women the victim	Show overt forms of aggression
Report sexual encounters with familiar partners	Report sexual encounters with unfamiliar partners
Show more verbal activity and emotional reactions; more aesthetic and moral judgments, more concern with time	Show more sex dreams, more failure and success themes
Have fairly equal number of male and female characters	Have twice as many male as female characters
Animal dreams contain more references to mammals	Animal dreams contain more references to birds and non-mammals

Another difference in men's and women's dreams is that women have more nightmares than do men, at least up until age 50. Women also report many more psychic dreams than men do.

The Effects of Menstruation and Pregnancy

Bodily states can play a major role in shaping your dreams. You probably know or have sensed already that your hormonal balance changes continually through the menstrual cycle, as well as during pregnancy, influencing your moods and abilities. But did you know that these same factors also influence your dreams?

Dreams occurring during menstruation depict more babies, children, and mothers; the dreamer is likely to be more friendly to other females in her dreams, although others, especially males, may not be as friendly toward her. Whether these changes in dream content are biological or cultural in origin, they seem to reflect the sense of identification women feel with other women during this time, and perhaps a feeling of being less attractive to males. Another characteristic of menstrual dreams is the increased number of references to enclosed spaces such as rooms, and to anatomy, possibly suggesting the dreamer's awareness of the womb and uterine function at this time.

Here is a sample menstrual dream containing a number of these characteristics.

BAY OF ANIMALS
A male friend and I are standing on the beach of a small bay. Many animals start chasing us in all directions on the beach. The male animals turn into boars and the females into deer. I'm afraid of all of them, especially the boars. A deer finally catches up with me. I'm afraid she's going to bite off my arm, but instead she nuzzles up and rubs her chin against me affectionately. Now three of the boars turn into men. They throw a lasso around my friend and me. The men take us to their shack and hold us captive. We eventually talk them into letting us go, although the men address themselves mostly to my male friend and ignore me.

Since the dreaming mind appears to tap information about our bodies, it is not surprising that some women dream of pregnancy and mothering very shortly after conception. This may happen even when a woman is not trying to conceive and doesn't consciously know she is pregnant. Other women may not dream about their pregnancy until the fourth or fifth month of gestation, when their condition becomes more of a physical reality. Pregnancy themes are common in a woman's dreams late in her pregnancy. The woman's own mother may also appear in her dreams with increasing frequency as delivery approaches.[5]

At first the unborn child may appear vague and formless in dreams, but as pregnancy progresses, the baby takes on a more definite identity.

Most "dream babies" are born magically and are able to walk and talk right away. A woman may dream that her baby is born deformed or dead, or she may find herself giving birth to a litter of animals. Following is a dream reported by a woman in her ninth month of pregnancy, revealing her fears about childbirth.

MY BABY!

I am sitting on the floor at an encounter group meeting. I look down and think I see a baby inside my uterus. I look again and see the baby outside of me, still attached to the cord and crying. I notice that one of the baby's eyes is much larger than the other. I scream for help. Mom comes, but she doesn't know what to do. I get very angry at her. I start running around the room, screaming "Help!" I want my husband. Someone reminds me that he has gone out of town and can't be reached. I'm angry and scared. The baby has stopped crying and may not be breathing. I start to cry and hold the baby, rocking him and saying, "My Baby!"

Analysis of such dreams as this one indicates that ". . . most women seem to harbor secret fears that they are carrying the equivalent of Rosemary's Baby."[6] Despite the reluctance of many women to discuss these dreams, they are indeed quite common. How unfortunate that obstetricians and other health care workers do not know or pass along this information to pregnant women. Doing so might save them much needless guilt and anxiety.

THE CONTENT
AND THEMES OF YOUR DREAMS

Now that you know something about how and why you dream, you may be wondering *what* and *who* you dream about. The findings of dream researchers indicate that our dreams are shaped by many factors, including our sleep environment and bodily states, events in our waking life, and even our attitudes toward our dreams.

Sleep Environment and Bodily States

How and where you sleep can affect the content of your dreams. Sirens, barking dogs, train whistles, and other stimuli in your immediate environment may weave themselves into your dream fabric, as the following dream and comments show.

WE BURN YOU WITH OUR FIRE
I'm in a fort with a lot of soldiers. We are completely encircled by
angry Indians who are moving closer and closer with flaming torches
raised above their heads. They move in unison toward us, step by
step, chanting "We burn you with our fire, we burn you with our
fire!" I am so terrified I can hardly move. I look at the torches and
wonder why they want to burn us.

When I awoke from this dream, the house was filled with smoke. I had put
a pot of beans on the stove and had forgotten about them when I went to
lie down for a nap. ●

Physical sensations have been found to affect the content of dreams.
Experimental subjects who are sent to bed thirsty or who get water sprin-
kled on their faces while dreaming tend to have dreams about water.
Bodily information in dreams can also include warnings of threatened or
failing health. Dreams often provide clues to potential or existing health
problems that we may be unaware of otherwise.

Even when you trace dream elements to bodily or external stimuli,
it is important to examine these symbols because of the part they play in
the *meaning* of your dream. In the "Fire" dream above, for example, the
dreamer could have translated that same smell of smoke into something
completely different—perhaps a dream of charging into a burning house or
of lighting a cigarette. How you choose to translate a stimulus will tell you
something about yourself.

Concepts of Waking Reality

One striking example of how dreams reflect our waking concepts of reality
can be seen in the differences between the dreams of women and men discussed earlier. Many of the differences reflected there were waking-life
concerns and values typical of women and men in the early 1940s, when
that information was collected. If a similar study were done today, dream
content would reflect changes in perspectives and lifestyles that have
taken place for women and men since then. For example, women's dreams
now reflect far less preoccupation with marriage, and women are becoming
more assertive, even aggressive, in their dreams. Now women more often
describe their dream characters in terms of occupational status—formerly
a male trait.[7] Another theme becoming more common in women's dreams
is that of making love with another woman. While this theme may symbolically represent a change in women's views of themselves (that is,

greater self-love), it may also represent an area of their sexuality many women want to explore.

Women's attitudes toward their dreams are changing along with the changes in dreams themselves. For example, while women used to be disturbed at the idea of assuming "masculine" roles or identities in their dreams, this has changed. Women now accept such dreams more readily, perhaps because of an increasing willingness to value and integrate waking life qualities once considered strictly "masculine" or "feminine." It is important to keep in mind that your dreams change as your waking outlook on life changes.

Attitudes Toward Your Dreams

Perhaps the most important factors that shape your dreamlife are your attitudes, beliefs, and expectations toward your dreams. A narrow set of attitudes about dreams will result in a small dreamworld. For example, people in therapy whose only knowledge about dreams comes from information provided by the therapist will produce dreams that correspond neatly to the therapist's own expectations. Moreover, people who believe they don't dream create a "dreamless" reality for themselves by not remembering their dreams at all.

The opposite also holds true. As you become acquainted with greater possibilities for your dreamlife, your dream universe expands outward in all directions. In dream workshops we have seen this happen literally overnight. At one dream workshop, a woman confessed that she had never heard other people's dreams before and was surprised to hear the women around her reporting dreams about animals. She had never had an animal dream in her life and doubted that she ever would. That night the main character of her dream turned out to be a Siamese cat. Another woman at the same workshop stated that all her dreams were "realistic" and never contained elements of fantasy. In her dream that night, she found herself waving her arms and splashing magic colors all over a wall. Both these women had glimpsed the growth potential of their dreamlives, and each was greatly excited about making dreamwork a regular part of her life.

Like these two women, you will fiind that as you expand your awareness about dreams in general and delve deeper into your own dreamworld, your dreamlife will grow. In turn, as your dreams become more accessible and meaningful to you, *you* will grow. Read on and discover for yourself what your dreams have in store for you!

chapter three

Dream Landscapes: A Picture Is Worth a Thousand Words

DREAM SYMBOLS

Your dreams speak to you in a kind of picture language and, as the saying goes, "a picture is worth a thousand words." Your dreaming mind, like an artist, reaches into every nook and cranny of your storehouse of memories, some known and some unknown, choosing exactly the remembered image it requires for its most perfect form of expression. Such dream images, or symbols, stand for or bring to mind various ideas and events, and they often represent issues or parts of yourself that you are concerned with in waking life. Understanding what these symbols represent to you is the first step toward grasping the meaning of your dreams.

Dream Characters as Symbols

The characters in your dreams represent more than they may seem to at face value, even when they are very much like the people you know in waking life. Let's take a look at some common dream characters and what your "dream portraits" may be telling you about these people—and yourself.

You as a dream character. The main character in your dreams is usually *you*, whether you experience yourself as an active participant, as an observer, or both. Almost always, the character you think of as yourself in the dream is the one you identify with the most—the part of you that you are most familiar with, or perhaps the part of you that you most readily accept. If you experience the dream from multiple points of view, or in the role of more than one character, this could mean that you accept, or at least recognize, several different viewpoints or differing parts of yourself, as the following dream and comments show.

ONE HELL OF A WOMAN

A woman is being chased by a man. I'm watching, but when I look closely I see that she is me! Just as she is about to be caught and destroyed, a magnificent woman about three stories tall comes out of nowhere. She's dressed all in black, with black wings and a black cape and boots. She is me, too, although we don't look alike. She steps forth and snaps her fingers. A flood of warm white light emanates from her womb and bathes the crouching woman below her. The same light repels the man, and he runs away, never to return.

In this dream I portray my inner drama of getting down on myself for what I have done or have not done and carrying this self-degrading act to an extreme. Then, the most powerful part of me comes to the rescue and straightens things out. This dream made me aware of how often I play out this scenario and how silly it is. I did some fantasy dreamwork where I integrated the three characters visually and created an image to help me integrate these parts of myself in the future. ●

Experiencing your dream from an unusual point of view like this can, in itself, offer some clues for understanding the dream. Like a game of charades, your dreaming mind may be acting out your view of yourself and others.

Familiar people as dream characters. Other characters in your dreams may be less easily understood. You probably often dream about characters who resemble someone you know in waking life. Family members appear in our dreams frequently, as do our close friends, lovers, and coworkers. As we saw in Chapter Two, the appearance of familiar people in our dreams is especially common in women's dreams.

The familiar people in your dreams will often represent their waking life counterparts—at least as you see them. Their dream appearances may serve to help you understand and work on your relationships with them in waking life. At the same time, these characters may have a symbolic meaning. They may represent someone else, past or present, whom they resemble in some way, or their actions may suggest an abstract idea, such as authority, freedom, or nurturance. There also may be similarities between these dream characters and aspects of your own personality. Many times the people and even the animals in our dreams represent parts of ourselves we may be less familiar with or less willing to accept fully. Thus, it is helpful to examine your dream characters in various lights to reach a fuller understanding of their meanings.

Casual acquaintances as dream characters. Because our dream characters are often people who are important to us, the appearance of casual acquaintances in dreams may be puzzling. It is unlikely (though not impossible, of course) that dreams of the mail carrier, television repairperson, or a familiar face on the street actually reflect some aspect of your relationship with that person in your waking life. So you may ask, "What roles do these persons play in my dreamlife?" Most often, a closer look will reveal that these acquaintances *remind* you of someone you *are* emotionally connected with in some way. A likeness in hair color, facial features, profession, or other traits can link the mere acquaintance with a key relationship—past or present—where some "unfinished business" probably lies. The dream character, in this case, can serve as a cue that those unresolved feelings are still operating in your unconscious as well as in your waking life. For example, sexual feelings we may be uncomfortable acknowledging toward an important person in our lives may be expressed toward a less intimate character in our dreams, as in the following dream.

JUSTIN
I am making love with Justin, who is the head of one of the programs at the nursing school I attend.

I wondered why I would dream about making love to Justin, since I am not attracted to him. In exploring my associations to him, I realized how much he reminds me of my cousin, Al, whom I'd always been sexually attracted to. I had picked up vibes from him that the feelings were mutual, but we had never pursued this, probably because we are related.●

A casual acquaintance in a dream can also be symbolic of some trait in ourselves. The following dream about suicide shows how the intense feelings of a divorced and recently remarried woman were embodied in the dream appearance of a casual acquaintance.

SUICIDE

Several of my students have decided to commit suicide. I go to meet them at the river to try to convince them to reconsider. They all jump in. I go in with them and swim along. One by one and in couples they decide to get out of the water and save themselves. One of the women is Jane Tanner. I am very pleased.

Jane Tanner is a student of mine whom I know only casually. She represents to me, however, a very significant part of myself—the young, divorced, frail-looking, weak-sounding woman who is also very strong, resilient, and intelligent. I had this dream during a visit to my hometown where I had grown up and gotten married. Jane is the depressed, fearful, self-destructive part of me that I felt during my first marriage and divorce, as well as the strong, resourceful part of me that survived that time and chose to go on living. ●

Dreams of famous people. For most of us, the world of public affairs or show business takes a back seat in our dreams to people and events closely connected to our daily lives. When dreams about famous personalities do occur, such characters usually represent qualities in ourselves or in others close to us.

When you have dreams about famous people, resist the temptation to write them off as merely wish fulfillment or compensation for leading such a dull life. Go over events of the previous day that might have brought them, or something they stand for, to mind; ask yourself if anyone you know resembles this famous person, or what aspect of yourself she or he may be reflecting, as in the following example.

DELIVERANCE

Burt Reynolds is in a doctor's office being examined. He's being extremely brave and courageous about the whole thing. When the exam is over, the doctor leaves for a moment, then returns delivering a candy bar the size of a surfboard. He hoists it onto the table and tells Burt it's his treat for being so brave.

I had this dream after deciding to undergo some minor surgery. I'm usually a real baby about trips to doctors, and I think my dream was reflecting my own bravery at this decision.●

Composite characters. Some dream characters can embody characteristics of two or more people in your life. Such "composite characters" seem to be the dreaming mind's way of emphasizing an important point. The first question to ask when a composite character appears in your dream is, "What do the persons embodied in this character have in common?" Composite dream characters can also represent a state of transition, conflict, and change. Here a woman relates a dream about a composite character, expressing her conflicting feelings about two relationships, one just ending and the other just beginning.

THE BEST OF BOTH WORLDS

A nude woman walks toward me with her arms outstretched, and I am pleasantly surprised but suddenly confused to discover that she is divided right down the middle—Cathy is on the left side and Tara is on the right! We make love in the living room.

When I had this dream, I wasn't sure where my real affections lay. In one way, I could feel myself wanting to hang onto what Tara and I had together—something that represented security to me. The right side of the woman was Tara, and I think of my own right side as being the more "secure" part of myself (I am right-handed and see much better with my right eye). My new relationship with Cathy, on the other hand, seemed especially promising in terms of my learning new things about life and about myself. I felt pulled between the security of the past and the free excitement of a new kind of lifestyle with Cathy in the future, and I wanted them both! The fact that we made love in the living room was symbolic to me of a living style or lifestyle change, as well as a transition between the two relationships.●

Dream helpers. Dream helpers or guides often appear in your dreams to lend support or to suggest new directions and options for your waking life. These helpful dream friends generally represent a need you are feeling, consciously or unconsciously, for increased assistance, approval, cooperation, love, nurturance, or information.

Some dream helpers are especially powerful and moving figures who seem to transform you by the very fact that they appear in your dreams.

They are usually unknown to you in waking life, are often exotic characters such as witches or wizards, or they have unusual qualities such as great beauty or the ability to work magic. These characters, called *archetypes,* symbolize universal ideas and themes that represent some of the most powerful parts of your personality: wisdom, intuition, nurturance, fertility, and spirituality. The following dream shows how an archetypal figure provides needed information and guidance for the dreamer.

Figure 3-1. Archetypal figures often possess unusual qualities, such as great beauty, wisdom, or supernatural abilities, or they may resemble mythological beings, by E. Ann Hollier

THE SAGE

I am in a motel making love with a man and a woman. I kiss the woman and press my breasts against hers. Suddenly I find myself on some concrete steps in the middle of a shopping mall! I look around and see people all around me and feel utterly foolish. Then I look up and notice an altar where there sits an Asian woman wearing robes of red brocade and huge, dark sunglasses and looking very regal. She addresses me carefully and slowly: "Continue to do what you do without regard for what others think. To do so will bring you luck." I ask, skeptically, "Good luck or bad luck?" She smiles and replies, "*Good* luck."

I had this dream when I was struggling to break away from relationships with men and develop satisfying lesbian relationships. The Oriental woman represented a stronger, more intuitive part of myself—the "hidden I" portrayed by the wise woman whose eyes are hidden by large sunglasses. This dream character gave me support and encouragement that was lacking in my daily environment at the time.●

Occasionally, a dream helper may appear in an unexpected or disguised form such as a robber or trickster. Thus, you need to examine such characters carefully, rather than looking at them in black-and-white terms and dismissing them as necessarily harmful or destructive. They may have some important function to perform or message to deliver that is hidden behind their frightening appearance, as the following dream illustrates.

RUBBER SPIDERS

I am in a prison where the prisoners are being subjected to a most unusual form of torture—being violently beaten with a large rubber spider. The guards performing the torture are huge, with tattered green skin like mummy wrappings. They have no mouths or noses on their faces, perhaps no eyes either, although they can see.

This dream occurred during a period of great creative productivity, during which I could hardly eat or sleep and felt driven by the need to set my ideas down on paper. I associated the spiders with my creativity, as they are spinners of beautiful webs. I did some fantasy dreamwork in which I had one of the guards show me how to use the spider. The rubber melted and ran all over the floor and walls, forming pictures and words as it flowed. I realized then that the guards represented my ability to express myself. Like my creative work, they were half-formed beings. They appeared as punishing jailers because I had begun to feel trapped and punished by the difficult, demanding task of giving a form to my ideas. My dream helped me adopt a more positive attitude toward this process.●

Dream Objects and Settings As Symbols

Your dream characters are not the only things in your dreams that represent ideas, problems, or parts of yourself. The objects and settings in your dreams can also have symbolic meanings which you can unlock by exploring your associations to them.

Your associations to some symbols may be unique, based on events in your life that give a specific image or symbol particular meaning. Many symbols also have cultural meanings, representing similar ideas for most people sharing the same customs or language. There are even universal symbols, like archetypes, that are shared by all humankind. In addition, any one symbol can hold multiple meanings, embracing the personal, cultural, and universal. To illustrate how rich in meaning your dream pictures can be, think about all the possible meanings that *water* might have in a dream.

People have universally looked upon water as a vital fluid essential to all life. It nourishes plants and quenches the thirst of animals and people: it even cradles us in the womb before birth. Water also forms natural boundaries between lands, separating the known from the unknown, and provides in itself a home for creatures that often seem foreign to us. Thus, in our dreams, water can represent such qualities as life force or vitality and nurturant or creative tendencies. It can also represent the mystery within us, the unconscious that lies beyond the known terrain within our own minds. Water is also universally viewed as a potentially destructive force, and dreams of storms, tidal waves, and floods might represent our fear of the potential or actual release of forces within us that are not under our control.

In our own culture, we often refer to water to describe emotions and experiences. We speak of someone as being "wet behind the ears" or "all wet," of "laundered" money, a "watered-down" version, of being "swamped" with work or "flooded" with calls. These figures of speech can appear in our dream pictures as visual puns when we dream of water. Cultural influences can affect our associations in other ways as well. For example, we would be less likely to regard a dream of a flooding river as a positive dream, than, for example, the ancient peoples of the Nile who depended upon the yearly floods to fertilize their fields and irrigate their crops.

Water can have specific meanings for us individually as well. For instance, a farmer might be most aware of the life-giving qualities of water, while a sailor would more often think of water in terms of another, mysterious world. Someone just "diving into" a new project might dream of water with a completely different set of associations. You can probably add several unique associations of your own to the symbol of water, based on your experiences with water in the past.

UNDERSTANDING YOUR DREAM SYMBOLS

Perhaps you are feeling by now that there is a meaning hiding behind every object in your dreams. And there is! You don't need to let this discourage you from learning your dream language, though. How do you decide what a particular symbol means in a specific dream when there can be so many different ways of looking at it?

There are three kinds of clues to look for: First, look at your own *waking associations* to the dream object or character for some ideas. Second, consider the *context* in which the symbol appears. Third, your *feelings and attitudes* toward the symbol, both in the dream and after you wake up, as well as later while working with the dream, can tell you a lot about which meanings are most likely.

Waking Associations

As a first step, you can always gain insight into a dream symbol, even without other clues, by examining your waking associations to the symbol. Begin by examining how the symbol behaves and how it makes you feel, both in the dream and in waking life. Try to relate your thoughts to personal, cultural, or universal associations to the symbol. Then look for similarities between these qualities and recent events, thoughts, or feelings in your waking life; also consider any similarities to characteristics of yourself and others. Since dreams appear to be related most often to events of the previous day, pay special attention to any possible similarities between what you've said, thought, done, and felt the day before the dream, and the symbols and events in the dream.

Fortunately, a dream will often put the same message across in several different ways, so even if you miss some of the associations, you can find other clues to help you. The following dream illustrates how different forms of the same message can be combined into a neat, compact dream image.

COFFEE

I'm riding in a car with a friend at night. We hear sirens and then see ambulances, police cars, and fire engines approaching. The sirens grow louder and louder, until the noise is almost deafening. I shout, "What do you suppose all the alarm is about?" My friend turns to me and replies, "Pat Coffey."

Pat Coffey is a health-minded acquaintance of mine, so the dream seemed to be suggesting that I'd been drinking more coffee than was good for me lately. *Pat* is also the name of a coworker who consumes caffeine despite an ulcer and repeated warnings from doctors. I also thought about the use of the word *Pat*, in the sense of *aptly*. My query about the alarm was thus answered with, aptly, coffee. I took the hint and switched to decaffeinated Java. ●

All of the useful information contained in a dream may not be immediately obvious. It is important, therefore, to hold the door open to future associations you may have to the dream or to a particular dream symbol.

Context

Suppose a woman walked up to you and said "Thanks a lot," then walked away. What would you suppose she meant by it? Even though you know what the words mean, you probably wouldn't be able to decide whether she was being grateful or sarcastic unless you had more information: her tone of voice, the expression on her face, and what you had done to cause her remark. Dreams are like that, too. A lot of pieces go together to make up the whole picture. Though you may know in a general way what one dream symbol or event represents, you may not properly understand what it is trying to tell you unless you look at it in context.

In interpreting a symbol, the context of your dreamlife includes such things as other aspects of a particular dream (such as the dream setting and the other symbols that appear in it), other dreams of the same night that may be related, the appearance of the same symbol in past dreams, your past experience with that object, person, or event in waking life, the events in your current waking life, and your feelings toward the symbol. All these factors can serve as clues to you, the dream detective, in deciphering the meaning of your dream symbols.

The context in which dream symbols appear will differ from dreamer to dreamer, and it may vary from one dream to the next. As your feelings and the circumstances of your waking life change, so does the nature of your dreamlife. For this reason, although past experience with a symbol can give you important clues to its present meaning (see Chapter Eleven), it is important not to jump to conclusions about your dream symbols, or to assume that what is true about a symbol in one dream is *necessarily* true in another. Be sure to look at the whole dream picture when working with your dreams.

The context of your dreams and dream symbols also includes such factors as your attitude toward your dreams and your beliefs about them, as well as the influences of other people or the culture around you. To show you just how dramatically this broader context can affect your dreams, let's look at a culture where dreams play a much more active role.

A dream culture. The Senoi Indians live deep in the mountains of Malaysia. Little was known about them until anthropologist Kilton Stewart began to publish astonishing reports about the extraordinary harmony of their lives.[1] They never fight or steal from each other, rarely get angry or upset, and show no signs of mental illness as we know it. Dr. Stewart believed that their peaceful existence was due to the central role dreams play in their daily lives. The Senoi believe that the dream world, while different from the waking world, is equally real, and Senoi children learn from early childhood to shape and direct their dreams, much as we are accustomed to directing our daily lives. They are taught to face and conquer danger in their dreams, turn dream enemies into helpers, and get gifts from them to bring back with them to the waking world. The day begins for the Senoi with dream sharing and is filled with activities directed by their dreams, from dream instructions about where to hunt for the day's catch, to new insights, or songs and dances from their dreams to share with one another.

Without knowing anything about psychology as such, the Senoi have discovered a way of tapping and directing their creative and intuitive abilities to a degree most of us never reach. Perhaps it is because they learn to overcome inner conflicts, symbolized by the dangers and enemies of their dreams, that they are at peace with themselves and one another, seldom troubled for long by the inner turmoil that we take so much for granted.

More recently, some question has been raised about the authenticity of anthropologist Stewart's claims. However, clinicians, dream therapists, and other people involved in dreamwork have found the Senoi model extremely useful in understanding their dreams and incorporating dream knowledge into their waking lives. In particular, although we live in a culture that, by and large, considers dreams useless and unimportant, we can create a "dream context" by seeking out other people who are interested in dreams and believe in their importance. We can learn to recognize and use our ability to make our dreams work for us, to help us grow as individuals and as women, and to enrich our daily lives with their gifts. In this context, our dreams become a powerful tool and an important resource.

Dream Emotions

An important aspect of a dream, which may be lost with an over-emphasis on symbols and their meanings, is its emotional content. Dreams are very often emotionally charged, so looking at your dream feelings may offer the key to a deeper understanding of the message behind the dream symbols. Paying attention to your gut reactions—both in the dream state and in waking dreamwork—balances the intellectual process of interpretation.

It is human nature to feel several contradictory emotions about the same situation. Dream emotions depict some part of our feelings, often those ignored in waking life. A dream in which emotion plays an important part may be telling us to temper or balance our waking emotions about a particular situation as a way of getting a more realistic perspective on the situation. In the following example, we see how an intense dream emotion helped to convey an important message.

THE LIE

I am with some other people in an office. A machine in the office is pouring out water and will not stop. We are certain that the end of the world is near and that we will all drown in the flood. Suddenly we are standing in a box or very small boat in a tiny rivulet running through an open field. We look at each other, thinking how ridiculous the whole thing is.

I had this dream shortly after being made a supervisor at my job. A new person that I liked very much had just come to work there. In lavish detail, she told me about her husband working overseas. Some time later, she confessed that she had fabricated the whole story so I would give her extra vacation time for an overseas trip. I was angry and bewildered at hearing this, and my frustration and resentment began to interfere with my ability to work with her. I had neglected, however, to take into account the fact that this woman valued our friendship enough to clear up the false story. My dream pointed this out by saying I was, in effect, making a mountain out of a molehill. After weighing my waking feelings with the dream message, I was able to put the situation into perspective and carry on with our working relationship. ●

It is important to use your dream insights to create a more whole or balanced attitude, rather than to merely exchange waking life feelings for dream feelings, which may be equally lopsided or exaggerated. Once you integrate your waking life and dream emotions, as the dreamer did in "The Lie", you can then act on them in a more responsible and constructive way.

Nightmares: Warning signals from the dreamworld. Even when we notice our dream emotions, we often reject the signals they may offer us. We have only to look at our usual reaction to nightmares to see how we do this. Our first impulse is to put the "bad dream" as far out of our minds as possible and forget about it. In doing so, we invite a reoccurrence of the same or similar dreams in nights to come; we also do ourselves the disservice of passing up an important opportunity for needed information or personal growth.

A healthier alternative is to view the unpleasant dream emotions as a signal of an especially important dream message. Nightmares are telling us in a dramatic and forceful way to pay attention to some part of ourselves or our environment that is frightening to us. This fear may arise from some rejected part of the personality, from a recent frightening experience in waking life, or from apprehension about some future event. Whatever the source, the first step to overcoming the fear is to face it and search for its source in waking life. In the following example, we see how one woman, who had been having nightmares about ghosts, trances, and other supernatural events, benefited by confronting the fears they represented.

CYCLOPS EYES

I am with a woman who asks me if I want to see ghosts. I tell her yes and am plunged immediately into a sea of presences. I am overwhelmed by my own terror. I want to scream and can't. I try again and again, and finally begin to come out of a trance as if surfacing from very deep water. Disembodied cyclops eyes whirl in the air around me. I still want to scream and a mumble finally escapes my lips. I wake up shaking.

I had this dream just before I planned to spend several days alone in the woods, reenacting rituals the American Indians used when seeking a guiding vision. Although I had been having nightmares for several nights, it wasn't until I had this dream that I acknowledged fearing as well as anticipating what the quest might bring. And a good thing, too, as I did experience a vivid, waking vision that might have been frightening rather than illuminating! Fortunately, the dream helped me confront and accept the idea that the atmosphere created by the rituals and the physical privations of the quest might break down the barriers between my waking and dreaming worlds. Once I confronted my fears through working with this dream, the nightmares went away. ●

THE MEDIUM IS THE MESSAGE

Your appreciation and understanding of your dreams need not depend solely on being able to interpret dream symbols or emotions in terms of waking life events. Sometimes the pictures in your dream landscapes offer information, support, or humor in a very direct way. In this sense, your dream *just as it is* is what's important: "The medium is the message." The following dream, for example, stands on its own without need for explanation.

THE PHEASANT'S MESSAGE
I find a bird cage and in it is the goofiest looking pheasant I have ever seen. I pick up the cage and the bird says to me, "Have a pheasant day!"

Keep in mind, then, as you begin your dream odyssey that there is no need to interpret every symbol to benefit from your dream and enjoy it. Remember not to make your dreams all work and no play!

part two

THE DREAM ODYSSEY: MODES OF TRAVEL

Introduction:
Finding Your Own Path

A dream is a personal document, a letter to oneself.

Calvin Hall[1]

Working with your dreams can be an exciting adventure which will take you places you never "dreamed" you could go. Whatever your present rapport with your dreams, you can enrich both your waking and sleeping worlds by learning more about your dreamworld. Part Two of this book will give you tools for doing just that—helping you enter into and broaden your dream horizons. If you are not in the habit of working with your dreams, it will probably take some practice and patience to begin to recognize your own particular style of dreaming and to find the most fruitful ways of gaining insights from your dreams. If you are still struggling to remember your dreams each morning, take heart. We will give you some tips for improving dream recall, too.

In the chapters ahead we will introduce you to a structured approach for tapping the valuable resources available in your dreamworld. The methods for exploring your dreams have been arranged here in an order you may find helpful to follow, particularly if your dreams are still relative strangers to you. However, following the exact order given is by no means a *necessity*. In fact, a strictly "mapped-out" approach to your dream journey may bring more disappointments than rewards. There are as many ways of relating to and understanding dreams as there are dreamers. We will offer a variety of approaches to working with your dreams, based on our own experiences and those of many friends and colleagues. We will suggest several directions here so that you may find your own path.

Some of the methods for dreamwork described here will appeal to you immediately, while others may not interest you at all. As your dreamlife grows and changes, you may be tempted to try some of the exercises you previously ignored. Go ahead and explore, at your own pace, in your own way. If you meet others along the way who want to share this adventure with you, so much the better. We have included many techniques for both individuals and groups, so that whatever your needs and interests, you should be able to find several approaches for exploring your unique dreamworld. Wherever you choose to start, you need to keep the following things in mind as you go along.

First, the feelings associated with your dreams are important keys to their messages. When these feelings arise, give yourself the time and space to sink into them and fully experience them. If the emotions you experience as you review a dream don't seem to fit your conscious assessment of the dream, stay with your dream feelings anyway. While you may not choose to *act* on the information provided by your dream feelings, it is still important to understand and accept them as a part of your inner world. Avoid the temptation to interpret the dream too soon, as this can be another way of ignoring your feelings about it. Also remember as you work through a dream to feel whatever is going on inside you—positive or negative. You may experience anger, jealousy, resentment, or fear about people and situations that seem to threaten your self-concept or comfortable situations in your life. These feelings themselves cannot hurt you; refusing to acknowledge them can.

Another important thing to remember as you work with your dreams is that they do not *have* to be interpreted at all to be appreciated. Some dreams, no matter what you do with them, will seem like completely impenetrable nonsense. Sometimes these same dreams become clear when set aside for a while and examined later, perhaps as part of a year's dream series; sometimes they remain a mystery. They are still *your* creations and carry your unique signature. They still have the power to amuse and move you if you let them. Here again, let your feelings be your guide.

Acquaint yourself with your dreamlife by inviting your dreams into your waking-life thoughts and activities. The meaning your dreams have for you will then become clearer gradually, and your dream memory will improve as you begin to look forward to the gifts the night will bring. You will find both your waking life and your dream life enriched by this process, for

> The dream universe, although qualitatively different from the waking life, is equally valid and equally real. . . . The person who focuses on the waking life to the exclusion of dream experience, or who focuses on dreams to the exclusion of waking life events, lives only half a life at best. . . . It is the integration of these two modes of consciousness that is . . . the truly real human life.[2]

chapter four
Own Your
Dreams

TAKE RESPONSIBILITY FOR YOUR DREAMS

You probably believe by now that your dreams have meaning. What you may not acknowledge, though, is that you are personally responsible for your dreams and the messages they carry. Accepting this responsibility is the first step in making your dreamlife work for you.

On the surface, your dreams may seem so silly and trivial that you are reluctant to admit that you would actually create anything so foolish. On the other hand, many of your dreams may be so deeply moving and awesome that you find it difficult to believe you could possibly create something so profound. The difficulty you may have in remembering your dreams may make them seem even more foreign.

You may also find it difficult to view your dreams as your own creations, because you may not feel *in control* during your dreams. Characters and objects behave unpredictably, and you may feel like a powerless victim of their actions. This feeling of powerlessness—which many women feel in *both* waking and dreaming life—lends itself to the belief that the dream is not really yours. Another reason why you may brush off dreams as something that "happens to you" is that the insights they offer are often right on target in pointing out things you may not want to face.

The fact is, every night each one of us writes, produces, directs, scores, and choreographs the "movies" that play in our heads. During the course of your lifetime, you will start up and shut down the projector thousands of times. In addition, you often star in your own movies and cast a carefully chosen line-up of characters to play the various supporting roles.

Thus, in learning to take responsibility for your dreams, it is important to view your dreamlife as an *active,* not a passive, process. A passive attitude toward dreaming is not only misleading; it can also be destructive, as it may work its way into your waking life. An active, creative approach to life's challenges can lead to personal growth and maturity. Viewing your dreams as part of this process is essential if you want to derive the most benefit from them.

It is also important to take responsibility for *every* element in your dreams—no matter how small or seemingly remote—as creations of your own making. Dreams often contain fragments of the day's events and may be influenced by bodily or external stimuli, but you must not be tempted to explain away a dream *solely* on the basis of "outside ingredients." When woven into your dreams, external elements always appear "by special permission" of your dreaming mind, and thus in some way represent your own unique *perceptions* of that outer reality. Dream elements have multi-level meanings, so that even an exact replica of a waking-life event or belief can offer useful insights when you view it as a picture of your inner reality. Thus, if you think of your dreams as reflections of *yourself,* and explore and appreciate them with that in mind, they will reward you with many opportunities for constructive and creative growth.

REMEMBER YOUR DREAMS

Some people seem to be natural-born dream recallers. They wake up each morning remembering a whole night's worth of dream adventures. Other people remember no dreams at all and believe that they never dream. Most of us probably fall somewhere in between these two extremes. We remember some dreams, especially the pleasant ones we treat ourselves to on mornings when we sleep in, and, of course, those terrifying nightmares from which we wake with our hearts pounding.

Whatever your level of dream recall, you can improve it if you are sufficiently motivated to do so. Learning to remember dreams, like learning most skills, requires patience, ample practice, and a positive attitude. Avoid the trap of becoming anxious or discouraged about not being able to remember your dreams. Changing lifetime habits and attitudes takes some time. Open yourself to the idea that your dreams have some things to say to you, and you'll soon find that they do.

An active appreciation of the gifts of your dreamworld will further enhance your recall ability. This can include sharing dreams with others, making objects from your dreams, acting on information or advice that comes from your dreams, and other activities we will explore in later chapters. Learn to deal with the dreams that frighten you—the danger dreams, the death dreams—for refusing to come to grips with them can inhibit your recall. Watch out for the tendency to dismiss any dream or dream fragment as trivial or incomplete. Even short fragments can offer valuable insights and may be more informative later when you examine your dreams in a series (see Chapter Eleven).

Choose carefully those to whom you tell your dreams. Telling your dreams to people who don't consider them important can be discouraging and may lull you back into ignoring or forgetting your dreams. Save your important dreams for those you think will genuinely appreciate them. This support from others can do wonders to increase your dream recall.

Now let's look at some specific techniques for improving dream recall. Some of these may seem strange to you at first, but if you apply them with a positive attitude, your dreaming mind will respond.

Before You Retire

There are several ways to prepare yourself and set the scene for vivid dreaming and dream recall before you go to sleep.

• Begin by having your recording equipment close by your bed so that you can get to it easily when you awaken. This might be a journal for writing down your dreams (discussed in Chapter Five) or a tape recorder. If you use a tape recorder, beware of something that happened to a professional comedian. Excited by the possibility of getting some new jokes from his dreams, he put a tape recorder by his pillow and waited for the material to come. That night he dreamed that a voice said, "Get ready—this is the world's best joke," and then told him the joke. He woke up and recorded the dream, but the following morning he turned on his tape recorder and found the joke was on him—the tape contained only sleepy grunts and mumbling! Be sure you wake up enough to give a clear report, and if you use a wind-up alarm clock, be sure to put it at a distance from your tape recorder to keep down the ticking noise.

• Visualize your recording equipment as a friend who is eager to hear from you, and picture yourself writing or narrating your dream in the morning.

• Give yourself a firm suggestion as you relax in bed: Repeat to yourself that you will dream tonight and that you will have dreams that are worth recalling. This can be a simple statement, such as "Tonight I will remember my dreams," or you might write a note to yourself and put it under your pillow, "tuning in" to the note just before falling asleep. If you have been using suggestion successfully for any other aspect of self-improvement, such as quitting smoking, falling asleep, or dealing with pain, try adapting your self-suggestion methods to dream recall.

• If you wake up to an alarm clock, try suggesting to yourself, while visualizing, the following: "When I hear the alarm in the morning, it is reminding me to remember my dreams." This can also be used to make early morning distractions, such as a crying baby, work for you as a cue for dream recall.

• Thumb through your dream journal or read from a book about dreams before going to sleep to help stimulate dream recall.

• Meditate on "dream power." Close your eyes and try to tune in to your "dreaming self." Whatever your concept of your dreaming self is, focus on it. Think back to the last time you remembered a dream; concentrate on the memory of it and allow yourself to savor this as fully as you can.

• Get a tape recorder and an appliance timer. Program the tape recorder to turn on quietly at a particular hour. You can use a recording of soft, instrumental music along with your own voice saying, "Wake up and tell me your dream." This will wake you up quietly and pleasantly while reminding you to focus on your dreams.

Sweet dreams!

"Good Morning"

• Wait! Keep your eyes closed! Don't move, and don't think about your nine a.m. staff meeting or milking the cow. Just lie very still and coax back as much of your dream as you can. Most of us have a tendency to think about all the things we have to do during the day, and it takes awhile to reorient our wakening attitudes and habits toward recalling dreams.

• Hang on to that fragment! If you capture only a tiny piece of the dream, stay with it. Other pieces of the puzzle may reappear and the dream sequences can then be put together.

• When you've got that much, turn over in bed to another position. This may stimulate still more dream recall. Try another position after that, until you have recalled all you can and have the dream firmly fixed in your mind.

• You may find it easier to remember the last part of the dream first, then work backwards, noting a key word from each segment to help you reconstruct the whole dream.

• If you are unable to remember the dream itself, but are in touch with the "feel" of the dream, try running through the various aspects of your life. You may hit upon something that brings back a dream fragment that can then be expanded into a whole dream.

• If you still remember nothing, meditate or just let your mind wander for a few minutes. Often you will spontaneously turn to thoughts closely connected with what you were dreaming about just before you woke up, and this can trigger your dream memory.

• Rehearse the dream once or twice to make sure you've got it. You might say the dream aloud in the present tense at this time. Even if no one is around to hear it, this can help to make the dream stick in your mind.

• Record the dream at this point, either in writing or on tape. You might think you will remember it anyway, but we often lose our dream memories shortly after getting up and into our daily routines.

• Be open during the day to remembering more of the dream or even other dreams of the same night. Often events during the day will trigger dream memories of the night before.

If You Are Still Not Able
To Remember Your Dreams

Learning to remember dreams takes time and practice. Don't be discouraged if, on your first or second try, you still don't recall any or catch only a few tiny dream fragments. If, however, you have devoted considerable effort to remembering your dreams over a period of time and still don't make any progress, you may need to take a closer look at your lifestyle, your attitudes toward your dreams, or even your feelings about self-exploration. It is helpful to remember that you have practiced ideas and attitudes for many years that may make dream recall seem awkward or difficult at first. Thus, you are not only learning new attitudes and practices as you explore your dreams, you are also *unlearning* old ones that may have caused your dreams to seem frightening or unaccessible to you for most of your life.

In the meantime, there are a few more tricks you can try in tracking down your dream memories. If you wake up to an alarm at the same time every morning, you may be waking up during non-dreaming sleep. Set your alarm for an earlier or later time than usual to help you wake up during a dreaming period; suggest to yourself as you fall asleep, "Tomorrow morning I will wake up at the *end* of a dream, and remember all of it."

If you sleep with someone, you might ask this person to suggest to you as you fall asleep that you will remember your dreams in the morning. Perhaps this person will agree to help you by watching for your eye movements in the morning and waking you gently, inquiring, "What are you dreaming now?"

All of these suggestions can be applied to improving, as well as initiating, dream recall. Don't push it, though. Whatever your current recall level, trying to *force* yourself to "be better at dream recall" can be counterproductive, often leading to no dream memories at all or to messages like this dreamer received in the following dream.

THE DREAM CONVENTION
I go to a dream convention led by a man named Dr. Ishtar. He tells us to turn in our dream journals, and I don't have mine. I tell him I can copy the dreams from my regular journal and give them to him later. This doesn't satisfy him, and he wants me to leave. I ask if

I can borrow his tape player to help transcribe my dreams. He tells me it's missing and accuses me of stealing it.

This dream came at a time when my dream recall was so high that I was seldom able to set aside the time necessary to write down my dreams right away. I felt bad every time I put it off or forgot some of them. The dream shows how I had begun to think of my dreaming mind as an adversary. The Dr. Ishtar part-of-me is nagging and making demands, but not helping me in my dreamwork. The exaggerated images in this dream helped me see that I was taking the whole thing *too* seriously, and I was able to adopt a more relaxed attitude toward remembering and recording my dreams.●

So relax, keep trying, and dream on! Your dreams will always be there waiting for you.

chapter five
Your Dream Travelog

KEEP A DREAM JOURNAL

Now that you are ready to embark on your dream journey, you will want some clues to put you on the right track and leave you with a good record or "travelog" of your trip. Keeping a dream journal is an important aid to your dream travels. It boosts your daily dream recall and gives you a permanent record of dreams you might otherwise soon forget. You will want to refer back to your dream journal in using some of the dreamwork techniques we discuss later. So—take a notebook along and enjoy your trip!

Suggested Materials

First, give some thought to the kind of book you will use as your dream journal, and make it special in some way. You may want to find a book that has a particularly appealing cover or color—or make your own book cover with original drawings, paintings, a collage, or batik.

FORMAT

Begin each new dream on a new page, and date each dream. Be sure to be consistent in using either the date on which you go to sleep or the date on which you awaken. You may also want to record the dream report in one column or on one page, leaving the opposite side or facing page free as workspace for comments, associations, drawings, and other related material.

Narrate Your Dream in the Present Tense

We cannot emphasize enough the importance of recording your dream in the present tense. If you fail to do this, you lose touch with the fact that the meaning and power of your dream are *present* realities. Telling your dream in the present tense also helps to recapture the dream and bring it to life.

Record Your Dream as Fully as You Can

No matter how trivial, fragmented, or embarrassing a dream may appear at the time, record it in as much detail as you can remember. The details may become very significant later as you work with the dream. If you are not sure exactly what happened, or in what order things came, note your uncertainty and the various possibilities. Describe the dream characters fully, as well as the action and setting. Note the ways in which the dream is like your waking life, and note what aspects of it seem bizarre and unreal. Describe vivid colors, sensations, sounds, and events. Record your dream feelings. Do you feel angry, afraid, astonished? Do you feel put on? Put off? Put down? These dream feelings may be the key to its meaning.

Title Your Dream

Titling your dream helps you find it again later. It also helps you single out the most important or unusual aspect of the dream. You may wish to title a dream in terms of a single dominant theme or an outstanding event, character, or emotion. If the dream clearly points to a personal course of action, you may want to use the dream message as a title.

Use Your Journal Workspace

There are several additional things you can record in your journal that will help you take your dreams beyond the realm of pure entertainment and put them to work as tools for introspection and self-knowledge. You will then have a handy reference for future dream travels. You might try some of the following practices, many of which are explained in greater detail in the chapters ahead.(See Chapters Five, Six, and Eleven.)

Comment on the dream. Writing out your comments can be helpful for both focusing your thoughts at the moment and examining your dreams later. Some of the things you may want to make note of include:

- Events and thoughts from the previous day. Your dreams are often related to these in some way.
- Any external or internal stimuli, such as physical sensations, that may have crept into your dreams.
- Whether you woke up naturally or were awakened by something such as an alarm clock, and whether you feel that your dream resolved itself or seems unfinished.
- How you felt upon waking. You may sometimes wake from an unpleasant dream feeling quite good or vice versa.

Write out your associations to the dream. Take each symbol and event in the dream and note the meaning it has for you. After doing this over a period of time, you will find you have created your own dream symbol glossary tailored to reflect the unique meanings your dream symbols hold for you. Be sure to record your associations even for those symbols you may not understand at the time. Such symbols often reappear in future dreams where their meaning is clear. If you single out these symbols as you dream about them, you can easily go back to them later.

Write out the dream, substituting meanings for symbols. You may wish to write out your dreams using dream language or substituting associations for your dream symbols where appropriate. These two approaches often yield many additional insights into the dream's meaning.

Summarize the dream message. In a brief paragraph, summarize what your dream is telling you. A key phrase from this may serve as the title for your dream.

State a resolution or action to be taken. Once you have come to understand the dream message, state what you will do with it. A course of action might mean re-examining an old attitude or taking some new action. You may also want to leave some workspace to record the results of your resolution at some later time.

Make a Reference Index

As you continue to work with your dreams, you will find it becomes more and more useful to your current dreamwork to be able to refer back to previous dreams. You may wish to keep a 3 X 5 card index of your dream symbols or themes, noting their significance (as you have in your journal workspace) and the dates of dreams in which they appear. Examining symbols in context as part of a dream series like this may help your understanding of a particular dream message.

Keep a Dream Yearbook

When you finish a notebook of recorded dreams, be sure to label it with the dates of the first and last dream, and put it on your shelf for reference. A spiral notebook usually holds anywhere from a month or two to a whole year's worth of dreams. A two-inch loose-leaf binder holds a year's dreams comfortably, at which point you can start a new notebook, using each one as a dream yearbook.

A SAMPLE JOURNAL ENTRY

DATE: Thursday, October 5, 1978

TITLE: "Hookworms"

There's something stuck in my throat. I reach in to pull it out, and it turns out to be a long white worm. It's pulling the other way and eventually it tears in half. I pull out one end but the other gets away. I force myself to throw up. Several of these long white worms come out of my mouth. They look like parasites or hookworms.

I decide to go to the doctor immediately. I get into the back seat of my car with three friends, one of whom is going to drive me to the doctor.

COMMENTS:

This is one of three dreams I remembered when I woke up just before the alarm went off in the morning. Yesterday I began work in a new job and also began to come down with a bad cold. I was feeling very frazzled and exhausted by the end of the day. I slept poorly and feel even worse today.

ASSOCIATIONS:

Something Stuck in My Throat: something I'm not expressing, possibly sadness, giving me a lump in my throat.

Worm: something I carry inside me; a parasite that saps my energy; something unconscious—I cannot grasp all of it, only a part.

Car: energy; means of moving forward; my physical self.

I Force Myself to Throw Up: I force myself to express something I can't "stomach" any longer.

Hookworms: something that is "hooking" me, getting to me.

I Decide to See a Doctor: It's time to take a look at what is going on here and heal myself.

Back Seat; Someone Else Driving: I am still not "in the driver's seat" where this situation is concerned, but am "being driven" by another part of me.

INDEX:

Worm: appeared in "Uprooting a Shrub in my Sole (Soul)" 2/1/78. Part of the past I carry with me, even though I have "pulled up roots" and moved on.

Throwing Up: appeared in "Throwing Up in the Custodian's Room" 1/14/78. I am swallowing feelings of mourning over separation and need to work at expressing them or I can make myself sick. Also in "The Indian Boy" 3/3/78. Here I was told by my dream helper that I had been ill for some time. One month after having this dream I had to be treated for anemia and an ovarian infection.

THEME:

Throwing up something

MESSAGE:

I have unexpressed, probably sad, feelings about a situation I am hooked by, possibly one in which I feel sorry for myself (pun on the song, "Nobody likes me, everybody hates me, I'm going to eat some worms"). This situation is sapping my strength, and I am making myself physically ill. I must force myself to examine my feelings and heal myself. I am not exercising control over the situation.

The message of my poor health is emphasized by other dreams of the same night, in which (1) a Mr. Bodily goes berserk, (2) I am warned that if I keep running I will get run down, and (3) I run out of gas (energy).

RESOLUTION:

I resolve to take a four-day weekend and spend most of the time in bed resting. I will also use this time to get in touch with the feelings of sadness and self-pity this dream gave clues to.

RESULTS:

At the time I had this dream I was working in a job I hated and was overqualified for. This dream message helped me redirect my energy from non-constructive frustration and depression into constructive steps to break into a career that would be more satisfying.

chapter six
A Phrase Book
for Dream Travelers

The words we use to describe things reflect and determine, to a large extent, how we see ourselves and the world around us. Thus, the language you use to describe and evaluate your dreams is very important in creating and maintaining the proper mind set for your dream journey. In any foreign country, you need to speak the native language to benefit most from your journey there. What we present for you here is a crash course in the native language of the dreamworld.

SAY YOUR DREAM ALOUD
IN THE PRESENT TENSE

The language of dreams is a present tense language. Using the present tense to tell your dream story recaptures the mood and vividness of the dream. It brings you back in touch with the meaning and power of your dream as a present reality. As you narrate your dream, you may find this important first step reminds you of a situation in your current life or even leads to a realization of the dream meaning itself.

Saying your dream aloud in the present tense, even if no one is there to listen, can give you a different perspective on your dream and provide some additional information. If you haven't already done so, you may want to tape your dream so that you can listen to your voice telling the dream story. What do your voice inflections tell you? What emotions does your voice suggest? Do you confuse or stumble over certain words? Perhaps some aspects of your dream are difficult to verbalize because they seem silly or offensive. If so, finish telling the dream, then focus on those parts with which you are uncomfortable and explore your beliefs about them. In dictating your dream narrative you may find many new things popping into your mind, such as images, voices, whole scenes, and details that you had forgotten.

THEN SAY YOUR DREAM ALOUD
IN DREAM LANGUAGE

In addition to using the present tense, there are other "translations" you will need to know to communicate in the language of the dreamworld. Learning this new "language" of dreams can heighten your sensitivity and expand your awareness in both your dreamlife and your waking life.

This *dream language* or "percept language," as its creator John Weir calls it,[1] emphasizes how you perceive yourself and how you relate to the world around you through your perceptions and impressions of it. You might say that the only reality each of us knows is what exists inside us in the form of sensations and images. For example, one person can look at half a glass of water and perceive it as being half empty, while another may see it as half full. Each one sees the same thing, yet thinks of it differently. We go through this process in forming perceptions of every object, every action, every exchange with other people and within ourselves. Each of us lives in a reality a little different from anyone else's because of our unique perceptions of the world. Since you know the world through your perceptions of it, everything you experience can be thought of as happening completely inside your own mind—continuously, here and now, from moment to moment.

In this context, dreams take on a new and powerful meaning: "My dreams are my own doing: I 'do' me when I 'dream me.' I can deny them or repress their content, but they still remain solely me doing me. Dreaming is my process."[2] Since they take place entirely inside your own head, dreams are the purest form of "me doing me."

Just as your dreams are your own creations, so, to a large extent, is your reality in waking life, which you construct through your perceptions and beliefs about the world. By learning to take responsibility for your dreamlife through the use of dream language, you get more in touch with your ability to direct and take responsibility for your waking life as well. Dream language helps you look at your dreams from this perspective by having you take responsibility for each aspect of the dream as you tell it. Let's take a look now at some of the rules of dream language.

RULE ONE: Dream language has no impersonal pronouns such as *it, that, this, what, one, you.* Instead, use *I, me, mine,* etc.

Ordinary Language	*Dream Language*
It doesn't matter.	I don't matter.
This is really nice.	I'm really nice.
You have to be careful.	I have to be careful.

RULE TWO: Ordinarily, you may speak of yourself as the passive object of something or someone—with things "happening *to* you." In dream language *you* are always responsible for your sensations and behavior, because you create them. To report your experience accurately, dream language changes all passive verbs into active ones.

Ordinary Language	*Dream Language*
I'm bored.	I bore me.
That hurts.	I hurt me.
I'm easily angered.	I anger me easily.

RULE THREE: We also often speak as though events, feelings, thoughts, and dreams are all visited upon us. Dream language uses the phrase "I have me . . ." at the beginning of every sentence or phrase to remind you that you do all these things to yourself.

Ordinary Language	*Dream Language*
I dream that . . .	I have me dream that . . .
That confuses me.	I have me be confused.
It's following me.	I have me be followed.

RULE FOUR: You are responsible for all the objects, images, and events in your dream, as well as the feelings you have about them. They do not exist except as you create them from your unconscious. Thus, in addition to representing real people, things, and events in your waking life, all these are also "parts of you." Even when you dream of someone or something that exists in waking life, you only know them through your perceptions of them, which are your own creations. Therefore, in dream language, you "own" each part of the dream by using the phrase "part-of-me" after every object, adjective, person, or pronoun (except *me*). Some words may be broken apart into their syllables, using the phrase "part-of-me" after each syllable. Turning some verbs and adverbs into nouns or adjectives and adding "part-of-me" may also reveal meanings that might otherwise be missed.

Ordinary Language	*Dream Language*
I fight with my mother.	I have me fight with the mother part-of-me.
I dance wildly.	I have me be the wild part-of-me dancing part-of-me.
I drive the motorcycle.	I have me be the driving part-of-me of the motor part-of-me cycle part-of-me.

Dream language will be awkward at first but will quickly become easier as you practice it. Say your dream first in the present tense in ordinary language. Then, without referring to your dream journal, say your dream aloud in dream language. You may want to use a tape recorder here. Notice any things you left out or said differently. These may be clues to the dream's meaning.

In using dream language there are only a few basic guidelines to remember: Stay in the present tense, take responsibility for your actions using only active verbs, and own each part of the dream by using personal pronouns and the phrase "part-of-me." Take your time and let the words sink in! An example here from one of the author's dreams shows what can happen to your understanding of a dream when you say it in dream language.

THE SILO

Present Tense:
I'm in a room shaped like a silo at a hotel with Paul. I'm trying, with much effort and fear, to find out what Paul is thinking and feeling. We make small talk first; then we're quiet. I wake up feeling anxious and angry.

Dream Language:
I have me in a room part-of-me shaped like a "sigh" part-of-me, "low" part-of-me at the hotel part-of-me with the Paul part-of-me. I have me try, with much effort part-of-me and fear part-of-me to find out what the Paul part-of-me is thinking and feeling. I have me and the Paul part-of-me make the small part-of-me talk part-of-me first; then I have me and the Paul part-of-me be the quiet part-of-me. I have me wake up feeling the anxious part-of-me and the angry part-of-me.

In telling this dream in dream language, I became aware of an important feeling which I had not been paying attention to—the sad, sighing part-of-me. It was only when I took a closer look in dream language at the word "silo," that I began to let myself feel and express the sadness ("low") in my frequent sighs. This sadness, I discovered, had been "stored up" in me for several weeks just as grain is stored in a silo. I had been afraid to let it out until I saw it and felt it as I repeated my dream in dream language. It was especially important for me to discuss these feelings with Paul, whom I had been making the "quiet," non-conversant part-of-me. When I saw it was all really "me doing me," I was able to talk with him about what had been troubling me rather than blaming him for my troubles.

Until I said this particular dream in dream language, I didn't really see the usefulness of this seemingly cumbersome language. I had tried using it with a few dreams before this one; but it was only with this dream that the potential power of dream language became real to me. Even though all the dreams I translate into dream language don't have as striking an impact for me as "The Silo," so many of them have that I find it well worth the time and effort to use it religiously in working with my dreams.

There are powerful consequences of becoming aware of your experiences, both awake and asleep, in terms of dream language. As John Weir discovered:

> I illuminate me when I consider me awake as if I were dreaming and when dreaming me, as if I were awake. Making this reversal and

living in it/me for a while has led me to an expanded self-awareness and convinced me of their/my interchangeability.[3]

LOOK FOR DREAM CLUES

Writing down your dream and saying it aloud in dream language may, in itself, lead to insights about the dream meaning. Just as often, however, your dream may still seem like a complete mystery. The next step is to look for clues in the dream that may shed some light on its meaning. In Chapter Three, you saw how your dreams usually talk to you in a picture language of symbols. Your associations to these symbols and your feelings about the dream are your main clues to the dream's message. The following are some clues that are especially helpful and easy to spot, yet are often overlooked.

Review the Previous Day's Events

Dreams usually deal with things that are currently on our minds, or with recently stirred up memories of past events. Thus, thinking over some of your thoughts and activities from the day previous to your dream should give you some important clues to the dream's meaning. Sometimes the connection between the events of the day and the dream is subtle or symbolically represented, so watch for related *themes.*

Check Your Dream for Literal Content

Usually the meaning of your dreams is hidden from you and has to be decoded from the dream symbols. Sometimes, however, a nagging concern lurking just below the surface of your conscious awareness will surface in your dreams in an undisguised way. For example, you may dream of loose teeth when you are overdue for a trip to the dentist. Check to see whether your dreams are directly telling you to pay attention to something neglected in your waking life.

Note Differences Between the Dream and Waking Life

Many people think of dreams as meaningless because they often seem bizarre or absurd. When the dream differs conspicuously from your waking life, however, these differences may point to the central concern of the dream. Your body may be changed; perhaps you discover that your hair is suddenly much longer or shorter than before, or you may find yourself dressed in an unusual way. People familiar to you may behave in ways that you would not expect of them in waking life; or some aspects of a familiar setting may be suddenly changed, as in the example following.

THE PIT

It is night and I am driving down one of the major boulevards near my old home. My street is coming up so I signal a left turn, but I am having trouble steering and the brakes aren't working. I pass my street. There is an intersection coming up where I can turn, but there is a lot of traffic there and I'm afraid of an accident. Now I come to a new street going back toward my old junior high school. I take it. I round a curve and I find an enormous pit in the ground. By this time my car has turned into a bicycle and I go over the edge. I am trying to steer along the sides so I won't go into some of the really deep holes in the middle. I am going over drops of several feet without losing control. ●

This dream came at a time when I was very depressed. (I often describe these depressions to myself as "falling into a black hole," depicted by the pit in this dream.) I realized that my old ways of coping were not effective (I am not in control and can't go home by the usual route), and that a crisis was imminent if I continued the way I was going (symbolized by the busy intersection ahead). The element of hope in the dream was the new street, one which does not actually exist in my waking life, but which leads toward a school and will permit the development of the surrounding area, representing the discovery of new possibilities for learning and further development. I realized then that I could look at my difficulties and my sad feelings as a necessary part of growth and change, and as an opportunity to learn. As the dream pointed out, I did not thereby escape my depression entirely, but this new outlook enabled me to feel more in control.

Check Your Dream for Double Meanings

One advantage to recording your dream is being able to stand back and look at the words you have used. Puns, put-together words, sound-alikes, cliches, and other words with double meanings all can be overlooked easily in an oral account of a dream. A way of focusing on just the words (without getting caught up in the dream story) is to read your report backwards (from the end of the dream to the beginning). You will be surprised at how often focusing on the words of your dream will point out double meanings that can give you some important dream clues, as the following dreamer discovered.

CHOW MEIN
I am wading around in an enormous bowl of chow mein, feeling very unhappy.

This dream made no sense to me until I looked at the chow mein as a visual pun meaning "Ciao, Maine." I had been in Maine at a two-week workshop and was getting ready to leave. I didn't realize how much I hated to go until I had this dream! •

Check for Related Themes in Other Dreams

Recent dreams, especially those of the same night, are often related. Refer back to other same-night dreams and to earlier dreams in which similar themes or symbols appear. When studied side by side, dreams may point to a new meaning or reveal patterns you wouldn't otherwise notice. Once a theme or symbol in one dream is understood, the same kernel of meaning may apply to other related dreams, expanding the amount you can learn.

"I STILL DON'T UNDERSTAND!"

Even with these clues and "translations," the language of your dreamworld may still seem foreign and confusing to you. For example, a dream may seem too bizarre, vague, or confusing. You may understand parts of your dream, such as puns, familiar symbols, or literal content, but be unable to see the central message. An association to a particular dream symbol may "fit" well enough that you feel you're on the right track, yet something about it may not seem quite right. The dream symbol or dream as a whole may feel especially important, but you may still not understand why.

Do not get discouraged when you get confused. In addition to this "phrase book" for your dream travels, there are many more approaches to understanding your dreams. These activities, described in the chapters ahead, will help you expand your awareness and offer unlimited creative outlets and entertainment. So dream on, and have a pleasant journey!

chapter seven
Travel Sketches and Souvenirs

So far, you have learned several approaches to exploring dreams verbally, using words both orally and in writing. There are also many useful nonverbal approaches to dreamwork. Women are generally more attuned to nonverbal sources of information than men are (see Chapter One), so using nonverbal dreamwork methods enables you to develop these valuable skills. Also, dreams do not always lend themselves to verbal translation, so nonverbal approaches may be crucial to tapping inner resources of expression and understanding of particular dreams or dream images.

DRAW YOUR DREAM

Making a dream drawing or painting can greatly enhance your appreciation and understanding of your dream universe.

> It's much easier to express your feelings and ideas through art . . . because it's not subject to the traditional type of censorship we exercise in verbal communications. All of us learn very early in life that words can be used to reveal, to conceal, and to manipulate. Precisely because it tends to be less subject to this kind of control and censor-

ship, art . . . is the direct release of very strong feelings—and, as such, it is a need, a basic necessity, and not a luxury or a privilege.[1]

Leave some space in your dream journal for drawings of dream characters, objects, and action. Your pictures do not have to be elaborate or "artistic." The exaggerated postures and facila expressions of stick figures can capture the important aspects of the dream and get you in touch with your feelings as effectively as a more complicated or time-consuming drawing. You might also try drawing a sequence of characters, objects, or events from the dream, perhaps in cartoon form.

If you share your dream in a group, a diagram may communicate the action more clearly to others than your narrative can. The sketch can also be a reference point in reconstructing the dream later. If your memory of the dream includes color, use it where it seems appropriate. If you tend to forget dream colors, using color in your drawings can stimulate your color recall, as well as add meaning to your dream objects and symbols.

As you examine your dream drawing, you may find forgotten dream fragments coming to mind. You may also grasp important meanings you missed earlier by asking yourself some questions about the drawing: What did I put into the drawing? What did I leave out? What figures are in the foreground, and what do I have as a background? How big are the figures in relation to one another? What kinds of facial expressions did I give the characters, and what emotions do they express? What colors did I use in drawing the dream? Did I omit any? Do the colors suggest a particular mood?

The following dream and drawing show dramatically how much insight can be gained with just a simple drawing. The dreamer was trying to conceive a child and had asked her dreams to point out any childbearing or childrearing issues that she may have overlooked.

MA BELL

There is a wide hole in the ground with a railing around it. We see a giant bell made of gold inside the hole. It rings with a perfectly beautiful tone. I turn to one of the people gathered there and say, "This is a great work of art!" He replies, "Undoubtedly a great deal of labor went into it." I think about "The Hunchback of Notre Dame" and wonder how much sorrow and blood went into its making and feel very sad. Next, a little child runs up and climbs on the rail. I tell him to get back, or he might fall in.

The theme of childrearing was obvious to me from the child and the clue words *dame* and *labor*. I drew the dream to discover the meaning of the bell. Halfway through drawing the bell, I stopped—what I had drawn was unmistakably a breast, and I was trying to keep the child away from it! I hadn't given any thought to the fact that my breasts would probably lose some of their "beautiful tone" in the process of breast-feeding. The dream compelled me to thoroughly re-examine my sense of physical attractiveness in regard to childrearing. ●

Figure 7-1. Ma Bell by Brooke Jones

You may want to post your dream drawing where you can see it, think about it, dream about it some more, and make it an intimate part of your life. Let it serve as a reminder and guide for future dreamlife and waking life changes. The following example shows how one woman used a dream drawing as a reminder to stop making judgments about people based on first impressions.

GET THE WEEDS OUT OF THE SEA (SEE)
An evil-looking mortician runs down to the beach, and I follow him. He takes a long piece of seaweed and goes up to a man lying on the beach and strangles him to death with it until his head falls off. Then he sews on the head of a doll, chuckling as he does so.

At the time of this dream, I had just begun an art class. The instructor seemed to have phony mannerisms, and I decided she wasn't anyone I would want to get to know. My dream made me look at the way I judge people on first impression and how this might be "strangling" the potential for meaningful interactions with them. I made this drawing and put it on my wall as a reminder to watch this in the future. I befriended the mortician to acknowledge symbolically in the drawing a part of myself I wanted to change. ●

In addition, you might want to draw a fantasy ending to an unfinished dream or use a drawing to help you in dream incubation. Dream drawing can also be incorporated into a "dream shield" (discussed later in this chapter). Finally, if you are an artist, dreams can provide you with a rich source of inspiration for working in many media. (See Chapter Fourteen.)

Figure 7-2. Get the Weeds Out of the Sea(See) by Brooke Jones

RECREATE OBJECTS FROM YOUR DREAMS

Recording and drawing dreams are both concrete ways of recreating a dream in waking life and affirming its importance and value. The Senoi tribe of Malaysia, described in Chapter Three, carry this idea of expressing the dream in concrete terms much further. One of the chief aims of their dreamlife is to obtain a "gift" or object of value from a dream character and share it with the community at large. Their waking activities are regularly filled with the re-creation of songs, stories, dances, functional, and ornamental objects revealed in dreams. Many American Indian tribes also owe important tribal customs to the influence of inspired dreamers. You do not actually have to make the objects from your dreams to benefit from bringing them into your life. You can purchase a similar item or have it made for you—but you profit most from these objects when they are of your own making, as they are in your dream.

Recreating an object from a dream can help you get in touch with the feelings and associations surrounding that symbol or remind you of what you gained from your dream. If this object then becomes part of your daily life—perhaps as an ornament or functional item—it helps you integrate your dreaming and waking lives in both a psychological and a tangible way. Indeed, your creations are not only useful items in their own right, but signify "trophies" of battles won and difficulties overcome through your dreamwork.

MAKE A DREAM SHIELD

One of the most powerful dream-inspired objects you can make is a "dream shield." The shield is a collection of symbols from your dreams, enclosed in the shape of a circle. Like a mandala,[2] the shield should be focused at the center of the circle, with a natural symmetry suggesting "a situation of opposed but balanced elements."[3]

You can start your dream shield by selecting a single central symbol and depicting its relationship to your waking life or to your other dream symbols. You can also create a potpourri by choosing symbols that reflect different aspects of your dreamlife or ones that depict a common theme. Henry Reed, the editor of the *Sundance Community Dream Journal,* explains the value of a dream shield as follows:

> . . . By collecting symbols from different dreams, you can rise above the vision of the single dream and begin to see the story of your symbolic life as a whole. Also, the visual nature of the dream shield provides a potent focus for contemplation and further opportunity for you to be moved by the consciousness-transforming energies of your dream symbols.[4]

The process of choosing the symbols for your dream shield or other creation is a good exercise in values clarification and self-discovery. Drawing a large circle on a sheet of paper and asking your dreams for guidance in choosing the symbols for your shield is a method of dream incubation. Dream objects such as masks, costumes, and other props may be used in a dramatic reenactment of a dream. (See Chapter Fourteen.)

Like the Senoi, you may want to share your dream-inspired creations with others. When you give a dream-inspired gift, you share a very special part of yourself. Dreams often portray symbolically what you wish to give to others and your perceptions of what they want from you. Bringing that symbolism into your relationships in this way is a simple and meaningful way of sharing yourself and using your dream awareness creatively.

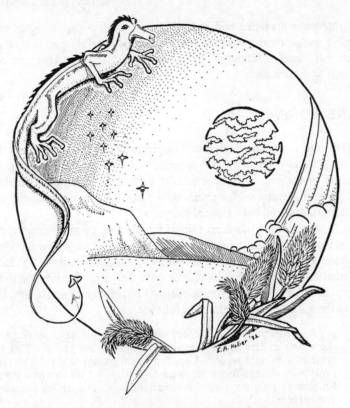

Figure 7-3. Dream Shield: The Beyond Within by E. Ann Hollier

CREATE A SPECIAL DREAMSPACE

Now that you know how to make dream objects, you may want to use them, as well as other symbols and rituals, to create a whole dream environment or special "dreamspace" for yourself. This is especially useful when you want to encourage dream recall, do some special problem solving, or conduct a dream experiment; following are some helpful tips:

- Meditate on a dream shield before you go to sleep.
- Wear a special piece of comfortable sleepwear. If a significant color appears frequently in your dreams, sleepwear of that color can be used. Embroider a dream symbol on a nightgown or favorite pair of pajamas.
- Wear a charm that represents some aspect of your dreaming self on a necklace while you are sleeping.

72

- Put a bulletin board near your bed to hold dream drawings and writings for special dreaming events.
- Make a "dream pillow." Mugwort, the "dream herb," or some other scented herbal mixture can be mixed with pillow stuffing and sewn into the pillow. The scent of the herb may then stimulate your dream recall.
- Bedding that is special in some way can also help induce dreams. A particular set of sheets or a "dream blanket" may serve to create a special dream atmosphere.
- You might even want to try sleeping in a different place on nights set aside for experimental dreaming purposes. A small tent, homemade tipi, or even a pyramid made of plywood (perhaps painted with bright colors of dream symbols and imagery) are some possibilities.

We often use rituals and symbols to mark important transitions in our lives, or to lend power to important undertakings. The potent psychological effect of symbolic rituals can work in dream exploration as well. Creating a pre-sleep dream ritual that you repeat on special occasions can help you focus on your dream quest and have a powerful effect on your dreamlife. These rituals can include things such as taking a bath with a specially scented bath oil, drinking a particular kind of herbal tea, burning your own brand of dream incense, or lighting a special dream candle before bedtime. One dreamer, at the tender age of seven, created such a ritual for herself to feel safe and prevent nightmares.

BEDTIME RITUAL

I would wait until I thought everyone else in the house had gone to sleep and then make my bed nice and smooth and neat. If I had just taken a bath and had clean sheets on the bed, so much the better. The flaps of the pillow case would have to be facing the outside of the bed. I would crawl down to the end of the bed where my window was and put my chin in my hands and look out. First I would try to locate the moon, and in the summertime, listen to the sound of the crickets. I would think deep thoughts about my life, about what had happened during the day. Then I would crawl very carefully under the covers and pull the corners of the blankets in toward me and turn my pillow over so it would be nice and cool (keeping the flaps to the outside of the bed of course!). I would then lie on my front with my left cheek against the pillow and my left leg up against my chest and go to sleep, confident that I would have safe and happy dreams.

chapter eight
Traveling
Companions

SOCIAL DREAMWORK

Working privately on your dreams can be an enjoyable way of spending special time alone, engaging in a kind of meditation, and getting in touch with your creativity. By going one step further and sharing your dreams with others, you can create even more opportunities to discover the value of your dreams and develop your own expressiveness. The support you experience through *social dreamwork,* telling your dreams to supportive friends or family members, can pave the way for further growth in both your waking and dreaming worlds.

The importance of support from others in dreamwork cannot be overemphasized. It is harder to benefit from what you learn from your dreams when those closest to you are unsupportive or unaware of changes in your feelings, needs, and actions. Often these changes require that others respond to you in a new way. Sharing your dreams with the important people in your life gives you a convenient way to communicate these changes and feelings on an ongoing basis.

You need not necessarily understand a dream in order to benefit from social dreamwork. Just the process of swapping dream stories leads to new friendships, new areas of mutual exploration, and often new areas of sharing and support in your current relationships. This is particularly important for us as women today, exploring new and more meaningful ways of being together. Sharing our dreams with each other provides an ongoing opportunity for us to discover and explore together our ideas and resources.

Social dreamwork may be especially well-suited, in fact, to women. Women are more willing than men to get close, make eye contact, and be touched by others,[1] all of which play an important role in exploring and making sense of the nonverbal and intuitive language of dreams in a group setting. Thus, social dreamwork brings together the intuitive and affiliative strengths of women as natural partners on our journey to self-discovery and self-expression. We are able to go beyond our usual, individual strengths and limitations via the contagion of feeling in the group and the support it provides. We can also pinpoint the cultural origins of our problems and see that for some of these problems, individual solutions alone are not sufficient. In this way, we can help ourselves and each other reach out toward lasting and fundamental change for all women—and, hence, for all humankind.

WORK WITH A FRIEND

Dream sharing can happen anytime or place—during meals, routine chores, while driving, jogging, or swimming. Sharing dreams with a partner before rising can be a wonderful way of starting the day, and sharing dream adventures over breakfast lets us tune into each other before going our separate ways for the day. One woman described sharing her dreams daily with a friend while they swam laps in a pool:

> We had a great time telling each other our dreams of the night before, laughing over the bizarre images and plots as we swam. Before we knew it, we had been swimming an hour and had also discovered new things about ourselves through our dream images. Now that my swim/dream partner has moved away, it's nice to have these fond memories of our special time together.

Social dreamwork has special significance when telling a dream to someone who appeared in it. Dreams often reflect your perceptions of and feelings toward those you share your personal life with—your "significant others"—more clearly and honestly than waking interactions with them do. Sharing dreams with significant others in your life will help them understand how you see them, both positively and negatively. It will also help *you* discover how you project your *own* qualities and feelings onto them. Too often we react to these *projections* rather than to the persons themselves. The following dream saved one woman from damaging her relationship with her roommate by helping her recognize such a projection.

THE QUARREL

I am having a huge argument with Sherry. We are screaming and shouting at each other at the top of our lungs and hitting each other. I wake up feeling extremely upset.

My roommate Sherry was 30 pounds overweight. Since I often kept her company on between-meal snacks, I was putting on weight myself. I was annoyed at this tendency of ours, and I suspected the dream was connected with it. I told her about my dream and we talked about it. From our discussion I realized I was blaming her for "tempting" me with food, instead of recognizing that I was using these opportunities as handy excuses to pig out; I was blaming *her* for my lack of self-control! Our dream sharing led me to take full responsibility for my own over-indulging, and enabled me to enjoy Sherry's company even more than I had before. ●

When you identify someone with a part of yourself, like the dreamer in "The Quarrel" did, it can be particularly useful to work out dream conflicts with that person. The Senoi tribe of Malaysia, in its practice of social dreamwork, requires that the dreamer apologize to another tribe member for an argument or fight that took place with that person in a dream. This practice helps to clear up conflicts not previously acknowledged by the dreamer, and can also help the dreamer deal with that part of herself represented by the dream friend or opponent. In this way, dream sharing can help us be more honest, open, and responsible with ourselves as well as with others.

An added bonus of dream sharing is gaining another person's perspective toward your dream. Often your dreamwork style will not pose the kinds of questions you need to understand a particular dream. We often dream of a specific issue precisely because we are denying it proper importance in waking life. The same lack of awareness that prompts the dream often makes it difficult to grasp the dream message on your own. Having others ask questions, contribute ideas from their own experiences, and point out similar themes from religion, mythology, or literature, can increase your understanding of the dream.

In sharing dreams regularly, you can also explore the possibility of mutual dreams and psychic events, discussed in Chapter Fifteen. It is always exciting to discover that you and a friend have had the "same" dream or dreams containing many similarities on a given night.

WORK WITH A DREAM GROUP

Unlike the regular morning activities of the Senoi, intensive dream sharing sessions are not part of the daily program at the average American breakfast table, nor in our schools or work environments. Although it is not uncommon to overhear someone mention a dream, most people would be taken aback to hear a statement like: "Okay, now you be the graveyard and I'll be the porpoise . . ." Meeting on a regular basis with other dream enthusiasts provides a way to bring your private dreamworld to life in an atmosphere where you know it will be welcomed and appreciated.

One of the most valuable things a dream group offers is simply that, like "two heads," several heads are better than one. Each of us has our blind spots, and sharing and working on our dreams with others who know us well makes up for the natural limitations of solo dreamwork. Over a period of time, the dream group can sharpen our dreamworking skills and make us more adept at asking the right questions to draw one another out. We become more attuned to the messages hidden in nonverbal cues such as facial expressions, tone of voice, and body posture. Dream group meetings can also be very entertaining. A dream group provides the opportunity for storytelling, theater, charades, artistic collaboration, information sharing, and meaningful social interaction.

There are several ways of becoming involved in a dream group. Check to see if an existing group has an opening, or you might start a group yourself. It isn't as difficult as it may seem. Contact friends or professionals who may be interested in dreams, post notices on college or community bulletin boards, notify your local women's center, or place an ad in the newspaper.

Several important considerations should be discussed at your first meeting:

- What does each person want from the group?
- What can each person offer? It is helpful if someone has experience in either working with dreams or groups, but this is not absolutely necessary.

- How many members will the group have? Four to six regular members seem to work best for a period of two to four hours per session.
- How often will you meet? Weekly sessions keep group interest and commitment high.
- Where will you meet? You might rotate hosting the sessions, or meet wherever space and privacy permit.
- Will men be included? If the group is to be mixed, try to get a balance of women and men. If you want to form an all-women's group, be sure that is understood and acceptable to everyone.
- What will the ground rules be? You need to make clear agreements regarding starting times, interruptions, absences, smoking or eating during sessions, and especially, confidentiality.

Exploring dreams together is not like discussing politics or movies. Laying the cards of your psyche out on the table for all to see involves some risk-taking. To make this process easier, it is essential that all group members be clear from the beginning about the extent to which information revealed to the group may be discussed with outsiders, and that they honor this agreement.

Don't be discouraged if things don't fall swiftly into place, or if some of the people at the first meetings decide the group is not for them. It may take some time to assemble a group of people who can work together comfortably and effectively, but it's well worth the effort. Keep trying!

Your Dream Group Session

Here is a suggested outline for dream group sessions. Use this model or create one to meet your own group's needs.

Sit in a circle.   A circular seating arrangement gives everyone eye contact with everyone else. The seating should be easily movable to provide a larger working space when necessary.

Check in with one another.   Start the session by going around the circle quickly. Have members talk about how they've been feeling in general, how they are feeling right now, what their dream lives have been like, and whether or not they have dreams to share. This gives the group time to settle and focus itself, and sets up an agenda for the session.

Share a dream. Have one person tell a dream in the present tense and then in dream language. It is best not to read your dreams from a written account, although you may want to have your journal handy to check for accuracy. The dreamer then offers comments related to the dream, such as associations to dream symbols, preceding day's associations, and similarities to previous dreams.

Amplify the dream. If the dreamer has made a dream drawing, now is the time to share it. Other members help explore the dream at this point, asking questions and offering comments. (See Chapters Nine and Ten for ideas your group can use.)

Time. Exploring a dream can take anywhere from ten minutes to the entire session. Agree on enough time for the dreamer to explore the dream to her own satisfaction. Avoid starting on an involved or emotionally powerful dream at the end of the session.

Follow-up. Bring the process to some kind of resolution before moving on to the next person, summing up what each person has gained from working with the dream. The dreamer may also make a resolution and then report the results of this new way of thinking or acting to the group at a later session.

Build trust. Everyone takes time to become secure in exposing their inner selves to other members in a group. To foster trust, you may want to spend some special social time together in addition to the regular sessions. Your group may visit a gallery to study art based on dreams, or plan an intensive overnight or weekend dream workshop, perhaps with an invited leader. You may find that the intensive sharing of a dream group leads to deep and long lasting friendships among group members, enriching the life of each person and strengthening the group as a whole.

WORK WITH A THERAPIST

While working on dreams with friends can be rewarding, you may want, or feel the need for, some professional guidance and support to complement your dreamwork. This may be the time to consider consulting a therapist who is experienced in working with dreams, to help you deal more effectively in waking life with the manifestations of your dream universe.

You need not feel totally distraught and disturbed in order to consult a therapist or counselor. You may have reached a plateau in working on your dreams alone or with your friends and want to experience new and different levels of awareness, or you may want to consult a professional when you find yourself stuck on a particular issue.

Therapy might also be helpful in dealing with those parts of yourself that are unpleasant or even frightening to confront as they emerge in your dreams. We often avoid recognizing or taking responsibility for these shadowy sides of ourselves, even when our dreams clearly urge us to do so. To fully express the positive parts of ourselves, we must also accept and integrate the negative ones. A good therapist can help you. The following dream and therapist's comments illustrate how one client was finally able to confront a frightening part of herself during a therapy session.

THE HEAD
I'm in a hospital. A man there is going mad, tearing things apart, with no expression on his face. I try to stop him. He stops, then his body disappears. His head is on a box with wheels and a little girl's dress. He chases me. I go outside where it is black and raining. I go home. No one there is talking. The head on the box is there. I pick it up and cry and apologize for leaving it.

The client, Martha, was a bright, young college student. I had her role play the head and have a dialogue with it. The "head" said: "I am useless, dangerous, childish, with no real goals. I'm her intuition, but she doesn't trust me. She judges too much; she can't open up to people." Martha reminisced about how much fun she had as a little girl when she felt free to use her intuition. However, her mother did not understand Martha's insights; she was frightened by her intuitive remarks and punished her for them. Martha closed off ("boxed in") this part of herself because she thought it was wrong.

Until she worked on this dream, Martha had made little progress in identifying the source of her conflict and had been reluctant to express her feelings openly. During this therapy session, Martha laughed and cried intensly for the first time in several months. The dreamwork she did in therapy helped Martha to acknowledge and accept her intuitive abilities and feelings—parts of herself that had been "alive" for her only in her dreamworld—so that she could integrate them into her waking life as well. ●

Whatever kind of social dreamwork experience you choose, sharing your dreams with others can provide valuable assistance in opening up new insights and experiences in both your waking and dreaming lives. You may need to shop around before you find the right partner, therapist, group, or routine for you. Once you find the right one, you can dream on to new heights of inner experience and self-understanding.

Here we will discuss dialogue, acting, movement, and dance as approaches to dreamwork that you can use either on your own or as part of a group. Now that you know about the benefits of social dreamwork, you may want to try some of the methods particularly well-suited to working in a group.

DIALOGUE WITH YOUR DREAM

You can re-experience your dream from new points of view and gain a fresh perspective on its meaning by *role playing* the characters or objects in the dream. Put yourself in the position of each dream figure and dialogue with it by allowing it to speak through you. In this way, you identify and take responsibility for your own feelings and behaviors as they are expressed through *all* of your dream characters. You may also discover some new or unappreciated parts of yourself by allowing yourself to "be" that character for awhile. Role playing is useful even when a familiar person, such as a family member or friend, appears in your dream. Even though they may behave as they do in waking life, you are representing *your* perceptions of them in your dream, which may be quite different from the way others see them.

There are several approaches to dialoguing that you can try in your dreamwork. You can dialogue with your dream characters in writing or as part of your dreamwork with a friend; or you may pick a spot, perhaps a pillow, to talk to out loud. Try to visualize your dream character sitting in that spot. Some people find this easier to do with their eyes closed. Tell your dream character what you think of it, how you feel about it, what things about it puzzle you. Ask it questions. How does it describe itself? What does it think of you? What is it doing in your dream? What does it want? What message does it have for you? Say whatever comes to you, and take whatever you get. Then, switch places. Become your dream character and speak from that perspective. You may want to switch back and forth, creating a continuous dialogue between yourself and the dream character or object, until you feel some sense of completion or understanding.

Do whatever is needed to reenact the dream and the emotions that go with it. Change your tone of voice with the change in characters; laugh, cry, shout, gesture, beat up your dream character (this is where a pillow comes in handy!) or make peace with it. It may take some practice to become comfortable with this technique; in the meantime, just let your feelings and words flow where they may, and see where they take you.

Here is a transcript from one of our dreamwork sessions in which the dreamer role plays several dream characters, including the sick part of herself and her infant son. It shows how such a dialogue can help you discover unknown parts of yourself, and apply these insights constructively in waking life.

THE BIRTHMARK

My husband has just given the baby a bath. He gives him to me and points out a large blue and red birthmark that goes all the way down the baby's back. I'm very upset.

Birthmark: I'm blue, and the red around me is the raw part of me. I'm like a rash. I attack babies, but I don't really hurt them. Anybody who looks at me thinks, "Yech! You're UGLY!" I don't think the baby is all that upset about me, but the mother is. I know she thinks that I'm hurting the baby. Right now I'm festering, but I will heal up.

Mother: Look, you crud! You leave me alone and you leave my baby alone. Get out of here! I'm sick of you! Just quit hanging

	around. You make me sick, and I don't want to be sick any more. Get out!
Birthmark:	Why should I? How are you going to make me?
Mother:	Okay, I'll make you. For one thing, I have this magic salve.
Salve:	I have medicinal cleansing qualities. I'm helpful. People don't make enough use of me. Doctors can't prescribe me. I'm just around and people have to recognize when I'm here. I'm really glad you have decided to use me: I'm part of you. I'm going to help you make yourself and the baby well.
Mother:	(Visualizing) So I take this salve and I put some on both hands. I lay my hands on the baby. I can see the scabs and rash shrinking and coming off his skin. I need help, so I say to my baby: I'm going to put this salve on my hands and put it on your back. When I put my hands on that spot, you concentrate healthful energy into it.
Baby:	Gee! I don't know if I can do that. I'm just a baby.
Mother:	You can do it. Even babies have energy. I want you to start putting your energy there now, okay?
Baby:	Okay, I'll do it.
Mother:	(Visualizing) So I take the salve and put it on his back. The rash is fading fast. I take it off and throw it away. I see it explode like firecrackers into a million pieces and disappear. Then I put some more of this salve on my hands and rub it on my face ... my eyes ... my nose ... my mouth ... my throat ... my chest ... my neck ... my shoulders ... my back. I take all of the sick parts and I throw them out, and there's a HUGE explosion. It lights up the sky, and then it's gone. I close up the salve and put it in my drawer, so I'll always know where it is.

My son and I both had bad colds at the time of this dream. After the dialogue with the sick part-of-me (the birthmark), I made a resolution to use my "healing cream" three times a day until I felt well again. The sudden improvement in my health that began while I was working on this dream was remarkable.

The dialogue with the son part-of-me was also very significant as it helped me see my six-month-old son in a new way. I no longer feel total responsibility for everything that happens to him; I no longer blame myself every time he cries or gets sick. Rather, I am able to see how he, too, as young as he is, has some responsibility for his own experience. •

A dialogue between dream characters is especially helpful if the dream depicts a conflict or intensely emotional situation. If you are successful in choosing the two characters that represent opposite sides of a

conflict or impasse, they will start out fighting each other,[1] just as the
mother and the birthmark did above. Through the dialogue, you can find
out what each one wants, and what they represent, enabling you to make
lasting changes in your waking life.

If you are working with a friend or a group, you can role play a
dream character and have the others guide you or conduct an "interview"
with you. This method is used to explore a baffling dream image related to
fear of intimacy in the following example.

THE HAIRPIECE

I am trying to put on a hairpiece. It has a comb on it that is supposed to hold it on, but it isn't staying in place very well. Now the
hairpiece falls off and I find that all my hair has fallen out underneath it, leaving a big bald spot. I am very upset.

Hairpiece:	I'm just sitting here. I used to be the hair on some-one's head, but now I'm made up into a wig.
Group Member #1:	What do you do?
Hairpiece:	Hang around. I guess usually Dianne uses me to look better, or to look different than she usually does.
Group Member #2:	Do you do your job well?
Hairpiece:	No. I keep falling off. I don't think I would look very good anyway because I look kind of artificial. She *has* to use me right now though because everyone will see that she's bald underneath if she doesn't.
Group Member #1:	Would you be the bald spot?
Bald Spot:	Well, I don't have any hair on me, and I don't like it. I would rather be covered up. I'm not used to being exposed like this and . . . um . . .
Group Member #1:	What's happening right now?
Dianne:	I just realized that this dream is about having a hard time acting naturally around my boyfriend. I'm afraid that if he gets to know me too well, he might not like me the way I am underneath—the way I really am. I *know* I'm acting artificial, like the hair-piece, but I can't seem to stop—I feel so naked and vulnerable underneath.

You can also dialogue with your dream or dreams as a whole. Tell your
dreams what you think of them: "I'm frustrated with you for hiding from
me," "I am afraid of you because you tell me things I don't want to
know." Then play the role of the dreaming part-of-you and answer back.
You might find yourself saying such things as, "I have plenty to say to you

but you're usually too busy to listen," "Even though I show you parts of yourself you don't like, I also show you the positive things to be found there," or "The more you believe in my power to amuse and entertain you, the more fantastic I will become." This exercise is especially helpful if you are new at working with your dreams. You may discover that you are holding yourself back by secret fears of what your dreamlife holds for you, or find that your dreams urge you on with promises of delight. In any case, this is one way to explore the interplay between your waking and dreaming selves and identify ways to strengthen a cooperative working relationship between the two.

Feedback from other people after your dialogue can give you another perspective on your dream. It can also provide you with valuable objective information on things you may not have noticed at the time, such as your use of gestures, tone of voice, and choice of words.

ACT OUT YOUR DREAM

Just as your dream contains hidden verbal messages such as puns and word associations, it also contains a wealth of nonverbal information. Everyone is familiar with the meaning of such nonverbal messages as smiles, frowns, a nod or a shake of the head. Yet, we use our bodies to express our emotions in many other ways as well: through tensing certain muscles, through our posture, the way we move and use the space around us, eye and body contact with others or the lack of it. When you physically reenact the actions of your dream characters, you gain insights into the dream which dialogue alone may not offer. Although you may not yet understand the connection between emotions and certain gestures or postures, you can learn to recognize them.

Acting out your dream using both dialogue and physical movements integrates your verbal and nonverbal experiences in a drama that vividly brings your dreams to life—and you can do all this on a low budget and without a heavy rehearsal schedule! Since you create your dreams, you have all you need within you, like the woman in the following dream, to produce your own dream theater right *now*. So don't wait to get your ticket—curtain's going up!

THE GIGOLO

I see a used car, and I think I might buy it. A man comes up to me and starts making advances. He is Italian, and a gigolo. He swaggers, tells me *he* can get me a car, and speaks in an exaggerated way.

When I acted out the gigolo part-of-me, swaggering around and talking in an exaggerated, "suave" way, I began laughing. I kept doing it, and suddenly I felt in touch with that part of myself that sells me, that tries to act like a BIG part-of-me MAN part-of-me. The exaggerated motions and swaggering walk were a physical magnification of these parts of me. I felt a release of tension acting out these parts of myself that I dislike, both in myself and others.●

If you are working on your dream in a group, you can have the group members act out your dream characters. You can then direct your own dream play by setting up the scene, giving instructions on character interpretations, and interpreting or changing the script. Feedback on how each group member felt while playing the various characters can give you new perspectives on yourself and your dream, as in the following example.

SHOVELING LEAVES

I am shoveling autumn leaves into a grave. I keep shoveling but can't fill up the grave . . . I see a devilish female figure in the grave. She's ugly—with horns, big eyebrows, and wrinkles. She tries to climb out, and I keep shoveling faster and faster. Eventually I cover her up and the leaves fill up the grave so that it is indistinguishable from the ground. I feel a sense of disappointment.

We acted out this dream and Ned was me shoveling, Len was the leaves, and Kathy was the devilish female. Ned said he felt more secure when the grave was covered, and Kathy said she felt powerful for a while and then destroyed. Len said he felt like he actually controlled everything. This made me realize that I have a choice about how much I want to "cover up" about myself—to get involved in things that are painful or troublesome to me, or to "bury" the problems for now and present a calm exterior. Either choice has its positive and negative points: Going down deep will be hard work and will cause some pain, but may eventually help me; the other way, "covering things over," brings security (as Ned pointed out), at least for awhile. I finally realized I can take one direction for awhile, and if the going gets too hard, I can go in the other direction.●

Acting out a dream can be a learning experience not only for the dreamer but for the actors as well. Taking the time for feedback or some kind of "debriefing" gives them a chance to express and learn from feelings that may have been stirred up by the characters they portrayed. In the following example, the comments following the dream show how playing a part in one woman's dream helped another person realize that he needed to be more assertive.

THE TRAIN RIDE

I am at a subway train station. I go to get a coke. Suddenly the whistle blows, all the passengers get on, and the train leaves. I go running after it and just miss grabbing it. This same scene happens over and over as the train goes along in the tunnel. Finally, it comes to a stopping place and I am able to get on. I am in front when the train comes out into the sunlight.

As we acted out Anna's dream, I was the train. I enjoyed mightily being the center of attention, chugging around the room. At first I thought of it as simply a game. But then I noticed Anna's intense involvement in the dream play and the various characters. This prompted me to think about the issues raised in the dream to see if there wasn't something in it, after all. I began to think about Anna's feeling that she was ignored by her friends, that she wasn't truly important to them, that they would do fine if she missed the train. Having had the same feeling many times myself, I was curious to see how she worked them out. Her solution in the dream play *was* new to me. The idea of taking control of the situation, of being the engineer of the train, was something I had not been audacious enough to consider. I could then understand why the dream was so satisfying to Anna, and how thinking about it could be useful to me as well.●

Another way to involve other people in your dream play is to perform it in front of an audience. This can be done informally before a group of your friends or fellow dreamworkers or you may want to use your dreams as the basis for a more formal production. One woman theater professor has her students use their dreams to create dramatic characters that reflect the personal parts of themselves.[2]

EXPERIMENT WITH MOVEMENT AND DANCE

You can intensely experience the power of physical expression in your dreamwork when you allow it to emerge from your feelings and dream images without using any words, such as through movement and dance. We start out in the world as infants, interacting with the environment through our bodies, and this continues to be an important way to communicate, especially for women, as we discussed earlier. Thus, a great deal of valuable knowledge of which we are often unaware, is stored in our nonverbal physical experience. The physical mode of communication tapped through movement and dance, in conjunction with our dreams, offers us a means of getting in touch with this unconscious information.

To use these nonverbal resources, it is not necessary that you be skilled in physical or dance techniques. All the methods suggested here can be performed by women of any age, shape, or form. Take one of the characters or objects from your dream, meditate on it or dialogue with it, and then allow yourself to begin moving in response to your feelings about this part of yourself. Gradually, exaggerate your movements and move yourself across the room. You may want to add some music or sound to your "dance" to enhance the mood. What is important is that you let yourself get into the movement and the feelings associated with it, suspending judgments or analysis until you feel finished with the movement. Your body and physical sensations will "tell you" what you need to know if you will just listen to them. When you feel a sense of completion about your movement, then you may want to describe your experience using written or verbal language. Do not distract yourself during your movement or dance, thinking ahead to what you will say or write. The insights will be there and meaningful if you allow them to emerge from your primary, physical experience of them.

The dreamer in the following example was feeling blocked in both her waking and dreaming lives. She was having difficulty making sense of her dream until she worked on it using movement, with some dramatic results.

RUNNING FOR BUS # 30

I dream that I am running to catch a bus—#30. I stop one bus in the middle of the street as it is leaving the bus stop. The bus driver is annoyed. He says that it is not #30 and drives off. I keep running for Bus #30, but there is no bus there. A man comes by in his car and offers to give me a ride. I get in the car. He acts very friendly, moves closer to me, and asks me to stay with him. I say "No!" very strongly. I am getting very upset.

In working on this dream, I decided to try running as I imagined I was in the dream. I went into the back yard and discovered that, after running a short distance, I began to run in place as if on a treadmill. I wanted to move ahead but found myself exerting tremendous effort and going nowhere. I kept at this for several minutes until I felt a burst of energy and ran all the way across the yard. When I got there I "found" Bus #30—a bright red bus with "30" painted on the front in big yellow numbers.

I had a dialogue with the "#30" part-of-me. I recalled that five years ago at the age of 30, got divorced, became unstuck from old patterns, and was feeling secure enough to reach out and embark on new challenges. The #30 part-of-me reminded me that I could *move on now*, get control of my energy and take some new risks in my life.

I am struck by how easy it is for me to forget about the strong, secure parts of me and my life even though I know they're always there. However, *knowing* it and *feeling* it are two different things. The movement dreamwork helped me to get in touch with these feelings in ways that verbal discussion alone could not. ●

If you have a dream with a clear physical interaction in it, you can have other people act out that movement with you. No words should be used; just focus on the sensations and feelings associated with the physical movement. The dreamer in the following example did this with a partner to explore her difficulties in asserting herself and setting limits on her interactions with men.

THE PASS
I'm at a conference with several graduate students. Professor Dan Night comes in. He seems drunk. He puts his foot on mine and rubs against me. He gets behind me and rubs against me again. I kind of struggle and laugh. I feel awkward when he does this. I don't respond much. I'm not sure what to do.

While working on this dream with a friend, she suggested we try acting out the physical interactions. At first, when she rubbed against me, I tried to get away, but she kept coming after me. Then I turned and faced her, and we pushed against each other with our hands. During this pushing movement, I got in touch with a tremendous amount of anger that I must have been blocking because I was totally unaware of it in either the dream or my waking life interactions with this man, nor had I gotten in touch with it through dialoguing with the dream character. After pushing, I noticed that I felt stronger, freer, and more energetic.

When a number of people are working together on dreams, it is possible to choreograph some beautiful and interesting group "dances" from dream material. As with other modes of dreamwork, the goals of using movement and dance as a group are twofold. One goal is to use moving together as a means to an end, that is, to gain more understanding of both our physical and dream selves and hence our total beings. The second goal is to derive pleasure from the process itself, that is, moving and dancing as a group in the direction of discovering and enjoying our dream selves. We have already seen that women often have strong nonverbal and social strengths and needs. Thus, acting out your dreams with others in movement brings together the affiliative nature as well as the nonverbal qualities in women. These are our natural partners in the joy and struggle of our mutual journey to self-discovery and creative self-expression. The following example from a women's dream workshop that the authors conducted illustrates how this can be done by using the dream of a group member as the focus.

THE WHITE ARMADILLO

There are three cedars, growing in a triangle. On the bare ground inside the triangle, Indians dance in a circle. They are shadowy figures, without faces, and they dance their rhythmic, flowing dance in absolute silence as if in a trance. In the center of the circle, and obviously the focus of the ceremonial dance, is a white armadillo. It seems indifferent to the Indians and just sits there placidly, twitching its ears.

During the workshop, I asked some members of the group to help me re-create the dance in the dream. I chose one woman to act out the armadillo and several others volunteered to be the Indians. I had one "Indian" be the leader and described the sweeping movements of the dance to her. The others were to imitate her movements as they danced, circling around the armadillo. After the dance, one woman said she felt awkward and anonymous following the leader, while another said she felt cut off from the armadillo. The "armadillo" said she felt drawn into herself—not cognizant of people around her, not allowing their actions to have an impact on her. I then asked them to dance again, this time creating their own individual dances as they circled. This they did with much enthusiasm.

Acting out this dream was the culmination of what the dream was trying to express—bringing us together, putting us in touch with a very expressive and serene part of ourselves and one another. The other women were glowing when they finished the dance—and so was I. For this dream, the movement *was* the message. ●

As with other forms of group dreamwork, there is as much potential value for the participants in a dream movement as there is for the dreamer. The following remarks from one of the women participating in "The White Armadillo" dance shows how much can be gained individually and as a group when we "move" together.

When asked to participate in the movement aspect of the dream analysis, I was skeptical and hesitant about looking foolish at first. But as the dreamer arranged us and told us how she wanted us to move, I felt less awkward. The role we were asked to play was easy to assume—shadowy figures moving gracefully in a circle. As we went around, I felt more and more at one with the others. It was as though any motion I made was a part of the whole group's will. During the dance, I felt the urge to reach towards the center and touch the "White Armadillo"—a movement not directed by the dreamer. This was picked up by the other dancers and repeated until we were all touching the "armadillo" like the spokes of a wheel. This contact seemed to be important to everyone involved—as though it was needed for the dream to be complete. Everyone sensed this, I think, because we all stopped in accord, without saying a word.

My feelings after participating were quite different from those at the start. I felt that we had helped the dreamer see something in her dream that she hadn't thought about before. I also felt a change in myself. It was a new experience for me to act out an idea through movement. It was exciting, and I think part of the excitement stemmed from realizing a new potential in myself.

chapter ten
Alternate Routes

UNFINISHED DREAMS

Often you may find your dreaming interrupted (sometimes at a crisis point) by things outside of your dreamworld—alarm clocks, crying babies, and other disturbances. These interruptions can be as frustrating as having to leave a movie during the chase scene. Often, unfinished dream themes are resolved spontaneously in dreams over the next few nights. However, you may want to give such dreams a more immediate ending, especially if you feel that the interruption prevents you from benefiting fully from the dream.

Another kind of dream that may need to be resolved is one that leaves you feeling anxious, for example, a "falling" dream, where you wake yourself up before reaching the bottom. You may have unconsciously awakened yourself just before the most revealing moment, afraid of discovering something "at the bottom" of yourself that you might not be ready to examine; or you may have forgotten or repressed the ending of a dream if its message seemed too painful or frightening to accept.

Finishing your dreams gives you an opportunity to learn from these problem areas. One way to do this is to use dream incubation as discussed later in this chapter. Before going to sleep the following night tell yourself, "I will complete this dream, and I will remember it in vivid detail." Then review the unfinished dream in your mind as you fall asleep, and repeat the process on consecutive nights if the dream still seems unfinished. A clear resolution to the unfinished dream may appear in a different form, rather than resuming where the first one left off. Pay special attention to the dreams you have during this time, and work with each one until the original one seems resolved.

Another way to finish your dreams is in waking fantasy. Your conscious mind plays an active role in this, so the outcome of the dream may be different than if your dreaming mind were in charge. Yet this technique can give you valuable insights because you are the director of your dream, and your unconscious mind and imagination are constantly involved in your dreamwork, whether you are awake or asleep. Here are some methods to help you get back into the dream, resolve it, and experience new insights.

FINISH YOUR DREAM IN FANTASY

Take several minutes to relax your body and let yourself unwind. You may want to close your eyes. If you just woke up, sit up in bed so you do not fall asleep again. When you are in a relaxed and meditative state, replay the dream in your mind. Visualize it as distinctly as possible, examining every detail and recreating the dream feelings. If reporting your dream aloud to a friend or dream group, be sure to tell it in the present tense. Do everything possible to bring the dream alive again as something you are *now experiencing.* When you reach the point where you woke up, just continue imagining the dream and let it go where it seems to flow naturally. Keep going until you feel finished with your dream fantasy.

With some practice, your visualized endings will become almost as vivid as the dreams themselves. Work with them just as you do your dreams. In the following example, a mother was able to make some helpful changes in her new role by finishing an important dream in fantasy.

THE TWO-STORY HOUSE
I'm in a big two-story house with my husband and son, Bobby, and some other people. It becomes clear that some kind of attack or invasion is about to take place. I'm told to take Bobby and go to

another room with the women. I'm told that's the way it's all set up. I'm confused and scared.

(Fantasy ending):
I go into a women's meeting with Bobby. A young woman is explaining that we are here to plan new approaches to parenting and family life. Our primary belief is that of shared responsibilities between a couple. The plan is to present this as a political platform in the next election. We are in the midst of a revolution, she says, and things are going to change for the better! The men are developing a similar platform from their own point of view. We will get together with them soon, and they will take their turn looking after the children. I feel encouraged and excited by the meeting and plan to become more involved in the political end of it.

Finishing this dream in fantasy helped me see myself actively involved in reorganizing my homelife after my baby was born. Instead of feeling depressed, confused, and scared, as I was in the dream, I could imagine another way (a "second story"): taking control and making constructive changes in my life. It seemed like "a revolution" and I could get excited about using my power to make a difference in parenting practices for myself and others. In fact, since completing this dream, I have confronted my husband more directly, spoken out with my friends, and even appeared on a TV show on the subject. I'm definitely over my post-partum depression now! ●

CHANGE YOUR DREAM

There is no such thing as a "bad dream." All dreams are potentially positive and beneficial because they offer valuable information. However, some dreams may express parts of you that seem disturbing or negative, things you may want to change. The Senoi, discussed in Chapter Three, refer to these negative images as the "evil spirits of the dream universe." They believe that, if ignored, these hostile spirits will join forces with one another and forever hold power over the dreamer in both the dream universe and in waking life.

The Senoi, as well as others,[1] have ways to confront and change the "evil spirits" that emerge in dreams. Once overcome, a hostile spirit can be reworked or "reborn" into a "dream helper." This dream ally can then help conquer other evil spirits and provide the dreamer with messages and gifts for use in waking life. In this way, the Senoi use their dreams to get in touch with negative or frightening parts of themselves and transform them into positive and creative energy. By changing your dream images in similar ways, you can achieve growth and maturity in your dream universe that is reflected in your waking life.

Many women find that gaining more control over their dream universe helps them take charge and shape their waking lives more effectively. You may want to change dreams where you are a victim or in some way out of control.[2] For example, if there is a car (often a symbol of energy) in your dream, you should be in the driver's seat, guiding it where you need to go; if someone else is driving, change the dream in fantasy, rewrite or role play it. Put *yourself* behind the wheel in control of your energy.

If some other figure or object is in control in your dream, discover and confront it through dialogue. If the figure disappears or refuses to answer, "chase" it and bring it back; call on other dream characters for help if necessary. Ask it questions: Who are you? What do you want from me? How may I help you? What is the source of your power? What gift or message do you have for me? Now be that figure and answer the questions. It is important to stay in contact with the character or symbol, using whatever methods are necessary, until you find out what it represents and what message it has for you. Then change the dream figure or dream story so that you are in control of the direction and outcome of your dream. The following example shows how one woman changed a dream and used it to feel more effective in her work.

THE PSYCHOLOGY EXAM

I am taking an exam for psychologists. A woman is giving the test. I get a score of 275. That's not very good. I am angry and question her about it—especially after she tells me how well another person (a man) did on the exam. He got a score of 675. She says it has something to do with my lack of sensitivity to the client. I don't really understand or agree. I argue with her.

I confronted the examiner part-of-me and questioned her about the score she gave me on the exam. The message she had for me was to pay more attention to the client part-of-me, the part that needed support and caring. This was very important for me at the time, as I had been pushing myself very hard in my work. Once I understood this, I stood up to this examiner and said I deserved a better score, certainly as good as the one the man received. This helped me acknowledge that I was as good as the men in my profession. I changed the dream in role playing to have the examiner raise my score to 675. It was important for me to assert myself and judge my own worth as a professional, helping me feel much more confident and powerful in my work. ●

Another way to change your dreams is to modify or destroy the harmful images appearing in your dreams and replace them with helpers or allies. Try burning, exploding, incinerating, killing, melting, eliminating, or defecating out the negative images in your dreams. Totally destroy or transform the harmful images so that no negative parts of yourself remain to clutter up and sabotage your dreamworld and waking life. In doing this, you are *changing a part of you that is no longer useful,* so that you can bring it back in a more useful form. Keeping this in mind may make it easier to dispense with unneeded parts of yourself without feeling guilty or regretful about it.

If you still feel reluctant to destroy a negative or unhelpful dream figure, make sure there isn't something more it has to give or say to you. After receiving that final gift or message, then it's time to let it go, as this dreamer did in destroying a dream figure that represented a part of herself which kept her from achieving warmth and intimacy in her relationships.

THE BLUE VELVET DRESS

I see Joe sitting with Mary at a table. Mary has on a long, midnight blue velvet dress. I try to sit with them; it is for some reason impossible. I feel excluded. I strangle Mary—I see that I am killing her. I'm glad. All the people in the room come toward me in a threatening way and seem to collapse in on me. I wake up screaming.

In working on this dream, I discovered that Mary represented a cold, frigid part-of-me that stood between me and Joe. I decided I wanted to get rid of that part of me, but when I recreated the dream in fantasy, I didn't feel comfortable killing Mary. I felt there was a part of her I wanted to keep. A friend suggested I have Mary give me a gift, representing something from her that I needed and wanted to keep as part of myself. I went back into the fantasy and had Mary give me the dress she was wearing. The part of her I wanted to keep was her calmness, her self-possession, her attractiveness, her thinness—and the dress embodies those qualities for me. Then I strangled Mary, in my fantasy, without a qualm. ●

Once you have received all its messages and destroyed it, the dream figure can be safely brought back or "reborn" in fantasy as a helper or ally, making its positive energy available to you in waking life. The following example shows how one dreamer reworked her negative dream images, helping her adjust to her recent divorce.

FIDDLER ON THE ROOF

I'm going through the musical score of "Fiddler On the Roof" with a number of other people. I go out for a break. When I return, a woman is singing a solo, "Sunrise, Sunset." There is one solo left. I'm upset that I got left out of the solos. Then the director tells me to sing the next one. I nervously try to find the song in the score. The pages aren't there. Someone nearby hands me another score. I sing the solo but I'm drowned out by the chorus. I'm nervous and upset. I say, "It's not fair."

In working on this dream, I realized that the "Fiddler" score was connected with my wedding and my ex-husband, whom I had just recently divorced. Since I no longer needed that part of me, I followed a suggestion made by the dream group leader to burn both scores in fantasy, having everyone in the dream join in on the bonfire! Then I wrote my own script and sang my own song from my own score—loud and clear! This was an important step for me emotionally in acknowledging my divorce and asserting myself in a confident way—without being paralyzed by fear or guilt.●

You can also change your dreams by strengthening the positive images and characters that appear in them, making them more supportive, serviceable, warm, or whatever you may need from a particular dream figure. When you transform your dream images to make them more helpful and positive, you increase your ability to tap the constructive inner resources and positive attitudes they represent. In the following example, the dreamer used waking fantasy to change a negative dream character and enhance a positive one, thereby strengthening her physical and sexual self-image.

NUDE SCENE

I'm walking down a hall—nude, my hair uncombed, carrying my purse. Jane passes by; she glances at me, frowning, and walks on. I feel embarrassed. I go into a ladies room and sit on the toilet wondering what to do. Next, I'm lying down next to my husband, his penis inside of me—flaccid. I awake feeling calm and tender—but feeling a bit disturbed by the nude scene.

Jane, an elderly professor and friend, was clearly a mother figure for me in the dream. Instead of her disapproving frown, I went back in fantasy and had her approve of my nudity. My husband represented the loving, sexual part-of-me; I wanted to strengthen him, making him a more virile and complete figure in my dream. I did this in fantasy by expanding and finishing the love-making scene in a more satisfying and complete way. I felt more comfortable with my body and my sexuality after confronting the ambivalence expressed in this dream, working it through, and replacing it with imagery that expressed a more positive physical and sexual self-image.●

INCUBATE YOUR DREAM

You don't always have to wait for your dreams or fantasies to come to you. You can seek them out in your dreamworld. Through dream incubation, you can program your dreaming mind to give you any kind of dream you want. Just as a brooding hen incubates her eggs by sitting on them, protecting and warming them until they hatch, you can incubate your dreams to help you "hatch" ideas, insights, and solutions to problems in waking life.

Dream incubation is a practice with a long and distinguished history. For many centuries, dreamers slept in temples and other special dream environments. There, they meditated and performed rituals to summon dream helpers who told them how to heal their illnesses or gave them direction for the future. For example, in the *vision quest,* a practice of many American Indian tribes, youths were required as a rite of passage into adulthood to go alone into the wilderness where they spent many days fasting and meditating. In this way, each youth incubated a guiding dream or vision, which often determined that person's future name, occupation, and status in the tribe.

Incubation can be used successfully for problem solving of many kinds. Special rituals, such as purification rites, meditation, or sleeping in a special or sacred place,[3] create an atmosphere that can help you focus on an important issue or problem at hand. When you prepare yourself properly, a dream incubation ritual will help you find the dream you need; if the issue is especially emotional or important, and your focus through incubation rituals is especially strong, you may even have a vision-like experience similar to those experienced by Native Americans and by the dreamer in the example following.

This dreamer conducted her own "vision quest" at a crossroads in her life, in search of direction and guidance in making decisions for her future. She chose a special place deep in the woods. She used Native American customs—sweat baths, fasting, chanting, meditation and other purification rituals, trusting she would receive, through dreams or waking meditation, the insight she needed and wanted. She did not expect what actually happened:

> ### THE GUIDING EYE (I)
>
> Above me near the ceiling of the tent is an "eye" of bright white light, not unlike those which have frightened me in nightmares before. Despite the fact that this is no dream I am utterly unafraid, as if finally able to accept the power and awareness it represents.
>
> "I am Silverwing," it says to me. "I am here to guide you. You are in this place to be reborn. You are ready to move to a higher plane."
>
> "Will you show me the way?" I ask her.
>
> "You know the way. You have only to look," Silverwing replies, and the light begins to waver, slowly fading out.

This was a waking experience that I had on the final night of my stay in the woods. I came away feeling refreshed, elated, and peaceful. I felt I had contacted a source of inner wisdom and strength that I often lost touch with in my busy workaday life. I was later able to use the imagery from this vision to incubate dreams for solutions to specific problems and plans of action. ●

While potentially very rewarding, you don't have to use such elaborate preparations to incubate a dream. In fact, you have probably incubated dreams in the past without even realizing it. Whenever you concentrate intensively on a single issue or problem just before going to bed, you are likely to set the dream incubation process in motion and continue to work on the issue in your dreams that night. You can make this natural tendency work for you by consciously focusing on the thing you want to dream about as you fall asleep. When you go to bed, summarize in a sentence or two what you hope a dream will make clear to you. Then use this summary as a meditation, repeating it to yourself over and over as you fall asleep. The more completely you can lose yourself in this meditation, shutting out all other thoughts, the more likely you are to have the dream you want. In addition to seeking guidance and answers to practical problems, dream incubation can be used for such purposes as repeating a pleasurable dream, changing a dream from a destructive to a constructive resolution, or exploring a puzzling dream symbol. You can also use dream incubation to conduct lucid or psychic dream experiments, as well as to generate ideas for creative work of all kinds, areas that will be explored more fully in later chapters.

chapter eleven
More Dream Travels

EXAMINE YOUR DREAMS IN A SERIES

After you have kept your dream journal for some time, you will find that
certain themes and symbols recur. Usually, these have the same, or a similar, meaning for the various dreams in which they appear. Dreams that
seem nonsensical or baffling may make perfect sense later when the same
theme or symbol appears again in a dream where its meaning is clear. In
the series of dreams following, you can see how recurring themes concerning sexuality and relationships with men are depicted slightly differently
in successive dreams.

> THE MAN WITH AN AXE
> I "wake up" to find a man standing over my bed with an axe in one
> hand.

I was literally paralyzed with fear as a young adolescent each time I had
this recurring nightmare. Years later, I realized that the issues I was examining in my current dreamwork—my feelings about men as sexual

102

partners—echoed the adolescent conflicts that produced my nightmares. Some months after this insight I had a very positive, powerful dream:

> THE BURIED HATCHET
>
> I am digging for buried treasure and notice something shiny atop the mounds of upturned dirt. I think this is the metal head to a hatchet . . . I later shovel this dirt aside and find the treasure I seek.

In working on this dream, I realized that in order to discover my inner "buried treasures" I must also dig up and make peace with some unpleasant and even fearful parts of myself, represented by the buried head of the hatchet. I resolved to incubate a dream where I would meet my nightmare man again. Then I dreamed the following:

> THE FOSSILIZED MAN
>
> I'm camping on the beach with friends. Two men start chipping away at a huge boulder to free a third man inside a rock. It is strongly reminiscent of unearthing a fossil. Suddenly the man is sitting on a park bench. He is old and stout, with white hair and an accent. He's basking in the sun, babbling to himself. We pay no attention.

The old man is my nightmare character, an old fossil unearthed. He does not carry the same power he used to, this half-senile man sunning on a park bench. The dream seemed to say he is no longer cause for fear. This was confirmed five months later, when I dreamed:

> THE EXECUTION
>
> I am in a formal garden. A man attacks me, wielding a heavy, double-edged broadsword. I find a rusty scythe blade, and we battle, our weapons so ponderous we can hardly lift them. It seems to be a matter of who can outlast the other. Then someone hands me an axe. I quickly knock the sword from my opponent's hand. He stands before me submissively. I ask him, "Will you die a fitting death? I shall be merciful." Silently he walks to a low stone platform, kneels before it and puts his head on it. I stand above him, and taking great care, behead him.

Just as your attitudes and behavior in relation to a particular issue may change over time, so a dream series will reflect and parallel the patterns of your waking life. For this reason, some dreamers celebrate their birthday or the new year by reading over the last year's dream entries in their journals. The dream series is thus a portrait of experiences and feelings that can offer you a unique perspective on your past.●

PLAY WITH YOUR DREAMS

In addition to analyzing or doing structured activities with your dreams, you might also try taking a more playful attitude toward them. You might act out pleasurable dream sequences, or celebrate a dream symbol or event, or do something really special and fun while in the dream state. You can incubate a specific dream activity, or perhaps suggest to yourself, "Tonight I will have a wonderful time in my dreams." Playing with dreams involves many of the approaches to dreamwork already discussed, as you can see from the following examples.

GIANT BURRITO
I'm in the kitchen with some friends, standing around talking. I open the refrigerator and see a mysterious item wrapped in aluminum foil. We unwrap it and discover a giant burrito! We get plates and forks and divide it up and everyone has some. It is very tasty and we enjoy eating it.

This dream gave me the idea for a Giant Burrito party. I invited my friends who celebrate dreams and like Mexican food, asking each to bring an ingredient: beans, onions, cheese, peppers, sauce, and so on. We put it together, baked it, and had a great time eating it. ⬤

Dream play, while it may seem frivolous at times, can also be used in "serious" ways, leading to significant outcomes in both the dreamworld and waking reality, as the following dreamer discovered.

After working in a dream workshop on "The Silo" dream (described on page 63), I decided to change my name for a few days to "Silo."[1] Having people call me this made me more aware of when I sighed and what I was sighing about. This helped me acknowledge my feelings and work on them more openly and directly. It also gave me a lighter, more "playful" perspective on the issues involved.

Sometimes playing with a dream can lead to a whole series of pleasurable and meaningful experiences that no amount of *working* on a dream can produce. Such was the discovery of a dreamer who had a series of puzzling dreams about turtles. After having little success understanding them in dreamwork, she decided to stop trying to analyze these dreams and play with them instead, with the following results.

SEA TORTOISE
I'm a huge tortoise swimming in the ocean. I'm very ancient, having survived because I'm not vulnerable to other sea creatures. I do not eat food like other turtles. I draw my sustenance by constantly sharpen-

ing my sensitivity to all things around me—color, texture, mass, depth, speed, motion, direction, movement, special relationships. I find great pleasure in exploring the floor and watching the sea flora and fauna, and the interplay between the living and the inorganic.

I bought a turquoise and silver turtle ring which has become my most cherished possession. I also bought a small straw box with a turtle on top, filled with scented herbs. I discovered I could induce very potent "turtle dreams" by smelling the herbs before going to sleep. This led me to experiment with dream incubation, with which I'd had little success before. Another experiment came to me while swimming in a pool. Bored with counting laps, I pretended to be a turtle and created the fantasy. I found this fantasy to be extremely energizing and much more fun than counting laps! I use variations on this fantasy now, transforming the bottom of the pool into a huge aquatic wonderland. ●

As you can see, dream play can be applied to a broad range of activities. How will you know which dreams can or should be acted upon playfully? *If a dream symbol or event leaves you feeling really good, find a way to bring it into your waking life.* Remember that not all experiences can be put into words. Celebrate your dreams and dream symbols like the dreamers above—paint, dance, share, smell, fantasize, wear, or eat them! Whatever you do, you will get in touch with the dream at its source—that intuitive and creative wellspring that knows the meaning of the dreams it sends you. Like other avenues of dream exploration, trusting your dreams to reveal new ways of enjoying yourself can result in better dream recall and a richer, more varied dreamlife.

So many of the issues in women's lives today—rape, abortion, equal rights—are serious and weighty and require hard work and concentrated effort. Give yourself a break and balance your perspective by *playing* with your dreams once in a while!

MAKE RESOLUTIONS

Often a distinct message emerges from a dream, urging you to change old habits, cultivate new attitudes, or let go of the past and create a new vision of yourself and others. This aspect of dream exploration requires that you make resolutions based on your dream awareness, and then act on them. Following through on your dream awareness brings your waking and dreaming selves together in a strong and lively partnership that will continue to work for you. In making and acting upon resolutions from your dreams, critical evaluation is essential for getting the most from them. Dreams often show only a particular aspect of an issue and may suggest solutions that, without conscious evaluation, could be impractical or even risky. Dreaming and waking thought present two different perspectives that must be used together to gain a balanced assessment of a situation.

Making resolutions based on your dreams may mean paying more attention to your feelings in waking life, or it may call for more drastic action, perhaps a radical change in a situation or relationship that has become destructive. The following example shows how a dream gave one young woman the resolve she needed to mend and improve a strained relationship with her mother.

HOLDING MY MOTHER

It is night and I'm trying to find a place to sleep. I go outside. My mother is there, and I sit just in back of her, putting my arms around her and resting my head on the back of her neck. There is something very beautiful and strong about her. I sleep with a feeling of peace and security.

I had this dream many years after leaving home, just before going back to visit my parents. Communication with my mother had been difficult and strained for a long time, something I felt sad about, but too intimidated by her anger to try to change. I was so moved by this dream that I resolved to make a special effort while at home to let her know how much I love and admire her, despite our disagreements. I followed through on this and our relationship has improved steadily ever since.●

You can learn from your dreams through their messages. Like all learning, these messages serve you best when you carry them forward in your life through actions that reflect your new wisdom. Whatever the message, it will be of little help to you unless you believe in it, and this is not always easy to do. Like the familiar New Year's resolutions, your dream resolutions will sometimes seem easier to make than to keep. Patience and persistence are essential, for even the most earnest intentions for change must be renewed time and time again.

Realize, too, that all of your problems will not be solved simply because you worked on them in a dreamwork session. Certain problem areas will arise again and again in both your waking and dreaming lives. Your dreams can help you cope with them better, but dreamwork, like personal growth, is an ongoing process that takes place a step at a time. Each problem and message can be seen as more information to help you continue your journeys and discoveries through your waking and dreaming worlds.

As you proceed on your dream travels, you will get lost, confused, and frustrated at times. This is a perfectly normal and necessary part of the process of growth and change. Without some period of confusion, there could be no change—your life would remain predictable, totally understandable, and probably very boring! Your confusion is a sign of a forthcoming insight or enlightenment, the "aha!" experience; so just accept where you are at the moment, and allow yourself to experience whatever arises when you examine your dreams.

PROCEED WITH CAUTION

When you interpret your dream symbols or messages, leave your interpretations open to all the gifts your dreamworld has to offer. If you close off the exploration of alternate or multiple meanings, you risk losing some valuable information, or worse, embarking on a precipitous course of action that may be inappropriate. Be open to unexpected discoveries and insights that may come at any time, whether you are awake or asleep. Very often, when working on a particular symbol or goal, insight into others will appear unexpectedly. Discoveries like these help you accept and integrate the limitations and frustrations you sometimes experience in working on your dreams.

Similarly, beware of approaching your dreamwork through only one method. Sometimes focusing on one method is useful, such as in dream incubation where repeated efforts may be necessary to get results. Yet, locking yourself into one particular style of relating to your dreams can be limiting. Explore your dreamworld from different vantage points to enjoy your dream journey more, and take advantage of the wide spectrum of dream experiences available to you along the way.

Your dreams use an intuitive language of symbols, metaphor, and feeling. If you can trust what you learn from this intuitive way of thinking in your dreamwork as well, you may reach a kind of understanding that you cannot achieve by merely categorizing, labeling, or analyzing.

You will find that, like other skills, evaluating your dream messages becomes easier with practice. In the meantime, it may be reassuring to know that when a dream is misunderstood or its message misapplied, other dreams usually follow to remedy the situation. Such dreams may point out the error, restating the original message or reemphasizing it. How we act on our dreams is a challenge each of us must meet in a different way, one we meet anew many times in the process of self-discovery.

THROUGH THE DREAM DOOR

Free from the demands of waking life, your dreamworld can function as your own private laboratory where you can discover and experiment with

Figure 11-1. Through the Dream Door: "Colasberos" by E. Ann Hollier

new dimensions of yourself. Your dreams hold the power to teach you something new each day. Each dream door you open can lead to greater personal awareness.

In Part Three, we will look at how some of these dream doors can be used to open whole new areas of experience to you, areas of inner experience and awareness you may have completely ignored until now.

part three
JOURNEYS
INTO
INNER SPACE

Introduction:
New Frontiers

And spirits of Truth were the birds that sang,
And spirits of Love were the stars that glowed,
And spirits of Peace were the streams that flowed
In that magical wood in the land of sleep

Sarojini Naidu[1]

Dreams are sometimes called an "altered state of consciousness." This term may have been applied to dreams in order to set them apart from our ordinary waking experiences. Yet, it can be misleading. It suggests that, because they are "altered," dream experiences are false realities, less valid than what you experience in waking life, and that if you pay too much attention to them they may lead you astray. Dreams *do* alter consciousness, but, in doing so, they lead you into yourself, making you aware of new perspectives and viewpoints, new frontiers to be explored. As with any new frontier, you will make many unusual discoveries and cover much strange territory. In Part Three we will take a closer look at some of these untamed frontiers that you may encounter on your dream odyssey, and show you the value therein.

By now you understand that your dreams, while different from your waking life, are as real and revealing in their own way, and as deserving of your attention. Now we want to take this idea a step further. Here we will show you how closely your dream reality is related to fantasy, creativity, extrasensory perception, and other expanded states of consciousness. Even if you feel that you have no imagination or creative ability, and have never had an ESP experience in your life, these realities lie sleeping within you. You can explore these worlds, if you want to, through your dreams and by building on some of the dreamwork techniques you have already learned. As you explore and reclaim these parts of yourself, you will find that your dreamworld becomes richer and more varied as well.

chapter twelve
Guided
Fantasy

You have already seen how waking fantasy can play an important role in changing and finishing dreams, and in integrating your waking and dreaming realities. Your potential for self-knowledge can also be explored through the related means of *guided fantasy*. Both dreams and guided fantasy are useful shortcuts to unconscious, intuitive knowledge that is usually unavailable or ignored. Because your dreams and your imagination are so closely tied, using a guided fantasy, even one not directly related to your dreams, can enrich and explain them.

Guided fantasy is just what it sounds like: One person, the "guide," narrates a fantasy while others actively visualize and embellish it. Afterwards, a great deal can be learned by sharing the various descriptions and impressions of the fantasy experience, as you look at the similarities and differences between the symbols of your inner world and those evident in the dreams of others. While fantasy is a more conscious experience than dreaming, you can gain insight into how you interpret, and at times distort, waking life events. By looking at what your imagination does with the objective information provided by the guide, you can become aware of the biases or "mind sets" that you bring to different situations, both in your waking life and in your dreams.

Fantasy offers some advantages over dreams as a basis for inner exploration. Unlike your dreamworld, your fantasy world is always accessible to you. Even when you are unable to remember any dreams at all, you can use your imagination to explore similar kinds of thoughts and images, stimulating your dream recall for the future.

Fantasy is also worthy of exploration in its own right. As with many sources of knowledge and insight, we too readily dismiss "daydreaming" as a waste of time. On the contrary, fantasy exercises your creative imagination and enables you to be in touch with the intuitive sources of information that are so vital to us as women.

In using guided fantasy, it is important to relax first, removing all sources of distraction. Total relaxation allows you to create a more vivid experience. Following is a "deepening exercise" to relax your body and clear your mind before beginning your fantasy. It may be read by one person, the "guide," to another person or to a group of people. You can also tape it for your own use in preparation for a guided fantasy, meditation, a dream incubation, finishing or changing your dreams, or just as an antidote for insomnia.

In the exercises and fantasies that follow, ellipses indicate a pause; the more dots the longer the break. You may want to practice at first with another person to get feedback on just how to modulate your voice, how fast to talk, and how long to pause between images. You might also have someone guide you through a fantasy yourself so that you have a better feel for the nature and timing of the experience.

DEEPENING EXERCISE[1]

Make yourself comfortable. Close your eyes and relax. (Wait until everyone settles down.)

See or sense yourself holding a notebook with lined paper in one hand and a pencil or pen in the other hand.... Now, on the upper left-hand side of the first page, write your name or whatever you call yourself. ... Now, over to the right on that same line, write the word "relax." ... Now, on the second line, just beneath your name, again write your name. ... Now over to the right beneath where you wrote "relax," again write "relax." ... Every time you write your name and the word "relax" you become more focused. Continue writing your name and the word "relax" on as many lines for as many pages as you need to, to make it real for yourself. As you write you'll feel yourself becoming completely relaxed, more and more focused, more and more receptive and relaxed and peaceful. When you feel you are as fully relaxed as you want to be, stop writing and just wait until you hear my voice again. Until you reach that state, continue writing your name on the left and the word "relax" on the right. (Wait *at least* one minute.)

And now, however focused and relaxed you feel you've become, continue to write, but this time over at the left, under the last place where you wrote your name, write the word "deeper,". . . and over to the right beneath where you last wrote the word "relax," again write the word "deeper.". . . Over at the left, write "deeper,". . . and over at the right, write "deeper." . . . And as you write "deeper" on the left and "deeper" on the right you'll go deeper and deeper, and you will feel yourself going deeper and deeper. The writing will carry you deeper and deeper, and you'll just be aware of the writing and of the voice that's speaking to you and of going deeper and deeper, becoming more and more relaxed, more and more peaceful, more and more focused, more and more receptive, going deeper and deeper into this state of relaxation as you continue writing.

You may return to your usual consciousness at any time, if someone calls your name, or by counting from one to five, or by saying the word "out" and opening your eyes—telling yourself that you're wide awake and full of energy. Until that time, continue to write "deeper" on the left side of the page and "deeper" on the right side of the page, allowing this voice to guide you. . . . . . .

After a while, you may feel that you've gone just as deeply as you can go, and when you feel that you're just as deep as you can go, then you'll put down your pen and close your notebook, and you'll just sit waiting, as if in a kind of bubble outside of time and space, a kind of comfortable little eternity that you'll wait in, very restfully, for a little while. But until you reach that state, continue writing "deeper" on the left and "deeper" on the right, as you now go deeper and deeper, completely relaxing, completely letting go. (If going on to another activity, wait at least one minute.)

When the participants are completely relaxed, you are ready to begin the guided fantasy. As the guide, you may use a fantasy that has already been written or tested, such as those that follow, or use the instructions given later to make up your own, based on your most vivid and powerful dreams, or a story you know, or whatever comes out of your own imagination.

Allow enough time after finishing the narrative for some stretching and refocusing of attention to the outside world. If someone you are guiding does not open her eyes on her own, call her softly by name. It is not at all unusual, especially at first, for some people to fall soundly asleep during a guided fantasy. Do not be distressed by this! Often they are unaccustomed to relaxing so deeply *without* falling asleep and will have to learn gradually how to do so. They may have a dream or some hypnagogic imagery to report, and this frequently turns out to have been influenced by the narrative that went on while they were sound asleep.

TREE FANTASY[2]

It is a beautiful spring day. The sun is shining brightly and the breeze is blowing softly through the trees. You can hear the sounds of birds in the distance and smell the fragrance of flowers in the air.

And now, you realize that you are the seed of a tree being blown by the wind through the forest and across the fields. . . . You can feel yourself gently tossed through the air, preparing to find a place to settle into the earth. . . . Look around you, and see where you are being carried. . . . . . Now, the wind dies down and you notice where you have landed. . . . . . . Gradually, you begin to feel yourself breaking out of your tight covering . . . sending down roots . . . now feel yourself pushing up, pushing up hard . . . harder . . . until finally you feel yourself breaking through the ground and rising up into the sunlight. . . . Now feel your first leaves unfolding . . . feel yourself stretching and growing, making new leaves, and twigs, and branches, growing strong and tall . . . growing and growing . . . and growing. (Wait one to three minutes) And now I'm going to count to three, and when I get to three, you will open your eyes and feel wide awake, remembering everything you have experienced, knowing you can use this information, now and in the future. One . . . start to come back . . . two . . . almost back . . . and three . . . open your eyes.

The following comments, using dream language, show how one of the authors experienced this fantasy during a group exercise at a personal growth workshop.

> . . . I plant me and grow me on the lawn in front of the big group house. I feel my roots spread out and anchor me firmly in the soft, dark, rich earth. I feel my shoot break through, reaching up toward the sun. I feel myself round me out and add layers of strength—soft layers on the outside of me. I have people come by and admire me, saying, "This is going to be a fine tree." I have

me branch out and bloom me with thick, green leaves. I have flowers grow up around me and birds flying above me. I reach me up toward the sun, spreading out my branches, and stretching me up to my full height. I have me cry with tears of joy.

Figure 12-1. La Xtabay by Eliezer Canul, reproduced from *Sundance Community Dream Journal, 3,* no. 2 (Summer, 1979), 149.

A year later at a workshop, I completed this same fantasy in a different way, imagining myself as a young pine tree in the yard of my own home, "growing me" on my own turf, separate and differentiated from the group. The following year at another workshop, I repeated this exercise a third time and saw myself as a full-grown apple tree in my back yard, sheltering and nurturing other trees, flowers, and birds around me. In retrospect, it seems that the images in this series of tree fantasies depict my psychological growth towards independence at various stages of my life.

By exploring your changing imagery in one fantasy, you will see that such images are metaphors expressing corresponding changes in thought or action in your everyday life. The previous comments show how for one of the authors, the process of maturing, represented by the imagery of the tree, came to be associated over time with establishing her independence and developing her capacity for love and nurturance toward others.

In creating new options for ourselves and other women, it is important that we acknowledge and understand the feelings associated with our past experiences. The following is a fantasy designed to put you in touch with the part of your past as a little girl, which may continue to influence your feelings or behavior in the present and future. You can use fantasies such as this one to integrate your past and present in a way that gives you more conscious control over the choices you make in your waking life.

THE LITTLE GIRL[3]

Take yourself back to a time when you were a little girl . . . when you were needing something. Go back through the years, until you can see yourself as this little girl who needs you. . . . Notice what she looks like . . . how old she is . . . what she's wearing . . . how her hair is fixed . . . what's around her. Hear the sounds. Notice the odors. *Be* there now. Pay attention to how you feel as this little girl. . . . Notice how it feels to be needing something. . . . . And now see yourself, as an adult, with all the strengths and resources that you have, off in the distance moving toward this little girl part-of-you. See yourself coming closer to her. And as you get closer, reach out your arms toward her, and take her hands in yours. Let her know that you're here to listen to her and help her, that you know that she has done her best and made the best choices that she could to take care of herself up to this time. Now you would like a message from her so you may know what else there is that you can do to help her get what she needs. Let her know that you are ready to listen to her, and have her give you her message now. .... Even if it doesn't make sense—you will be able to use this message to meet both of your needs more effectively now and in the future. Tell her, using your resources, what would help her now. See yourself giving her this information. .... And now as you prepare to depart, ask the little girl part-of-you to think of a gift for you, something tangible that you can take with you to symbolize your helping relationship, to remind you how you can help each other. Ask her to give you this gift, and have her give it to you now. Take whatever you get. .... Once you've received her gift, thank her for it, and for communicating with you. Let her know that you will use all she's given you, now and in the future, to better take care of her and yourself. ... And now draw her closer to you, hold her, and say goodbye in some way. .... When you have said your goodbyes, look into her eyes, and begin to walk away, bringing with you everything that you have received from her. Travel forward through the years ... back into the present ... back into this room. ...

And now I'm going to count to three, and when I get to three, you will open your eyes and feel wide awake, remembering everything you have experienced, knowing you can use it now and in the future to better take care of yourself, and that you can remind yourself of how to do this by recalling the images of the little girl and her gifts that you have received just now. One ... start to come back ... two ... almost back ... and three ... open your eyes.

The following comments show how one woman used this fantasy to explore her earliest memory of separation and loss.

I go back to a time when I am about four or five. My grandmother has died and my mother has left for several days to go to the funeral. It is late afternoon, and I am in bed in my room. My father and uncle are here taking care of me and my brothers and sisters while my mother is away. They make me go to bed early for a nap and won't let me get up. I don't understand why my mother is gone or why everyone seems so gloomy. No one will answer my questions and I'm afraid—I know something is wrong.

The adult me appears and sits down on the bed, hugging the child part-of-me and holding her close, letting her know that everything is okay and her mother will be back in a few days. The adult also tells the child not to be afraid to ask for affection, attention, or comforting when she needs it. Even if she isn't always given what she needs, she will feel better about herself if she tries, instead of feeling helpless and ignored as she did then. In return, the child gives the adult a small white plastic horse named Scheherazade. (This horse was my favorite plaything, and she was always personified as a leader—strong, serene, sensitive, and wise.)

I knew before this fantasy that this early experience colors my gut reactions to loss—whether it involves death, separation, or rejection. This was the first time, though, that I had ever gone back and explored what it had been like in any detail. It enabled me to realize what a truly frightening experience that was for me as a young child—and put me in touch with all the resources I have now for coping with and understanding separation or loss in a way that wasn't possible for me then. This was definitely an illuminating experience for me, as it helped me to sort out and understand my child and adult reactions and recognize them both as valid.●

This is a fantasy which you may find useful in many circumstances—particularly when you are feeling needy, hopeless, or alone. You can also use it simply as a way of exploring and appreciating once again what it was like to be a child, reviewing memories which many of us have allowed to grow dim. As with other fantasies, you may also apply many of the dreamwork techniques discussed earlier in exploring the various images you find.

Often we dream about our bodies and our feelings about physical and sexual issues. These issues are often disguised in our dreams, and are difficult to deal with, making us feel embarrassed or anxious. The fantasy which follows is designed to help you get more in touch with your feelings about your body and your sexuality.

THE BODY JOURNEY

Prepare to take a journey. Just relax—I will be your guide. This journey is very close to home; you will be taking a journey through your own body. Begin now by paying attention to the sensation of your body resting against the chair (the cushions, the rug, the floor). . . . Notice any parts of your body that you feel yourself tensing or deadening. Pay attention to those parts of your body now. . . . . . And now, let my voice guide you as you journey through all the parts of your body, exploring as you go the sensations you feel, and noticing any memories which come back to you as you journey through each part. . . . Pay attention now to your head. Notice the sensations in your scalp . . . your forehead . . . your eyes . . . your ears . . . your nose . . . your cheeks . . . your mouth . . . your chin . . . pay attention to any memories that come back to you as you explore these parts of your head and face. . . . . . Journeying on now, pay attention to the sensations in your neck . . . your throat . . . your shoulders . . . your arms . . . your wrists . . . your palms . . . your fingers . . . What memories come back to you as you explore these parts of your body? . . . . . . Traveling back up your arms now, pay attention to the sensations in your shoulder blades . . . your chest . . . your ribs . . . your breasts . . . Notice the memories which each of these parts holds for you. . . . . . . Now journey lower, and pay attention to what you experience as you travel into your waist . . . your stomach . . . your hips . . . your pelvis . . . your genitals. . . . Notice the memories that come back to you as you journey through each part. . . . . . . Traveling to your back, pay attention to the sensations in your lower back . . . your buttocks . . . your anus. . . . Notice the memories these parts of your body carry with them. . . . . . . Now travel into your thighs . . . your knees . . . your calves . . . your ankles . . . your feet . . . your toes . . . Pay attention to the sensations and the memories you discover in these parts of your body. . . . . . . Now that you have traveled through your whole body, notice any part of your body that may still feel tense or deadened. . . . Go to that part of your body now. . . . And now, have that part give you a message. Take whatever you get. . . . . . . Now check to see if there is any *other* part of your body which feels tense or deadened. . . . Go to that part of your body now, and have it give you its message. Take whatever you get. . . . . . . And now take a deep breath, and as you inhale, feel yourself breathing energy into those parts of your body that feel deadened. Take another deep breath, and as you exhale, feel yourself releasing tension from those parts of your body that feel tense. Continue breathing deeply in this way, filling yourself with energy as you inhale, releasing and emptying yourself of tension as you exhale. . . . . And now go back and thank the parts of you that have communicated with you and let them know that you will make use of their messages, even if they don't make sense now, to take better care of yourself now and in the future. . . . . . . Now I'm going to count to three, and when I get to three, you will open your eyes and feel wide awake, remembering everything you have experienced, knowing you can use this information, now and in the future. One ... start to come back ... two ... almost back ... and three ... open your eyes.

The important thing about this fantasy is for you to explore new ways of regarding your body, which may lead to more constructive behavior patterns and images of yourself as a woman in your everyday life. As you achieve new patterns and attitudes, you come to choose a particular fashion because it pleases you, not only others; you choose to give birth to your children naturally and consciously; you acknowledge your sexuality when, how, and with whom you please. As long as you operate out of this core of integrity for your body and your creative imagination, your lifestyle can be fulfilling and enriching, no matter what it may be like.

This fantasy can help you find this core within yourself by making you more comfortable with your body and more aware of *all* of your bodily sensations and memories. Releasing tensions stored up and ignored for so long also releases energy that you can then put to use in positive ways. The comments that follow show how this fantasy helped one of the authors become aware of how some difficult physical traumas from the past were affecting her functioning in the present.

> As I focus on the various parts of my body, I recall the motorcycle accident I had eight years ago. The memories that come back to me are surprising, as I have almost forgotten some of the places I have been injured (hands, legs, etc.) and the feelings associated with them. Remembering and feeling them gives me a sense of finally finishing with the pain I experienced then.
>
> The second incident I recall is of hemorrhaging after a tonsillectomy I had when I was four years old. The "message" I receive from my throat related to that almost-fatal experience is, "You survived that trauma then, so you can certainly do it again." I feel anxious regarding a long trip I am taking the next day. I have been worried for several days that something bad might happen on the flight or while I am away. After going through this part of the fantasy, I feel more relaxed and excited (rather than nervous) about the trip. I also have some sensual feelings in my thighs at the end of the body journey.

As these comments indicate, a guided fantasy can be very useful in dealing with specific issues or feelings that may be troubling you in your waking life. When working with your dreams does not seem to give you what you need at the moment, you can direct yourself more consciously through a guided fantasy. The "Body Journey" may be particularly helpful if you often have physical reactions to stressful experiences. Any fantasy you choose will do, however, as long as you trust your feelings to take you where you need to go.

CREATE YOUR OWN GUIDED FANTASY

Another way to learn more about yourself is to use your own dreams or fantasies as the raw materials for a guided fantasy to share with others. In doing so, you may gain insights from other people's comments that will help you understand more fully what your dream means for you, and what it can mean to others. You are telling a story when you guide a fantasy, so you may want to adjust your dream to make it more vivid and easier to follow for those who will be listening to it. Here are some things you may want to think about:

- Include cues to involve more of your listeners' senses. In addition to the rich visual imagery of your dreams, your fantasy can be made even more vivid if you include sounds, smells, tastes, movements, and other sensations. Keep these details fairly open to allow the listeners to embellish the fantasy in their own ways.

- Make the transition smoother and more logical between scenes. A change in scenes that is too abrupt can be difficult for others to follow.

- Decide whether to include dream elements that do not seem central to the theme or mood you are trying to create. They can be distracting.

- Give the fantasy a neutral or positive ending. You may want to change an ending if it is upsetting to you (and hence may be to those you guide); or you may guide the listeners up to the conflict and give them some time at the end of the fantasy to create their own ending.

Here is one of the authors' own dreams, followed by the guided fantasy designed from it.

THE TEACHER
I come to a woman's house to ask about art lessons. She is quite accomplished as a musician and artist and also is quite obviously

a witch. She asks me if I've come to learn music and I reply, "No, I've come to learn your art." We talk a while about painting. She has many occult paintings in very wide, ornate wood frames. One painting is of a wizard, his face lit by candle- or firelight, voluminous black robes billowing out around him in some invisible wind. There are glowing globes of various hues, floating in the air around him. The painting looks so real that only the wide wooden frame serves to tell me it is only a painting after all.

THE TEACHER FANTASY

You are knocking at the door of a strange house. You are very eager to meet the woman who lives here, someone you have heard a great deal about, a very wise and gifted person, a great teacher. You have come here to learn something very important that she alone can teach you. You want to be her pupil. Now you hear footsteps in the house. They come closer and closer, nearer and nearer. At last the door opens, and you see the person you have been longing to meet.

You go into the house now, following her without saying a word. It is very dark inside. You follow her as she takes you down a long, dark corridor until at last, at the end of the corridor, you come to a room with no windows. You can hear the rustle of heavy, dark curtains, which she pulls across the doorway, and you smell the heavy scent of incense in the air. She gives you a mug from which you sip slowly, savoring the flavor of the warm potion she has given you. Now you begin to feel that warmth spreading throughout your body; the warmer and more relaxed your body becomes, the sharper each of your senses becomes, and you sink into a deeply relaxed, yet alert state. The potion vividly prepares you to experience and remember what your teacher is about to show you.........

Now, as you look around the room, you see for the first time many paintings hanging on the walls, paintings your teacher has made. Each has a story or message, and she will use them to teach you what you have come here to learn. You light a candle and go to the first picture, holding the candle high so that you can see it clearly.

In this picture you see a wizard, his black robes rustling and billowing in an invisible wind. He is standing before a fire, making glowing globes of colored light which float all around him, each one a different color, each one more lovely and more fantastic than the last, growing, changing. As you watch you can begin to feel the wind that blows against his robes plucking at your own clothing. You begin to hear the fire crackling and feel its heat against your face, to smell the wood burning. The wizard looks up from his work and nods to you in greeting. As you watch him, you learn something from him. He gives you a gift, perhaps an object, an idea, or a word of advice, something of great value to you. You take this with you back to the dark room where your teacher is waiting. . . . .

She smiles and tells you that she is pleased with your lesson. She says to you that gradually, as you come to visit her over and over again, you will learn more and more about her many paintings, and about how she makes them, until after a while you too will be able to make paintings like these, each one with its own story to tell. But now it is time to leave. You walk back down the long dark corridor and finally out of the house. . . . . .

Now I'm going to count to three, and when I get to three, you will open your eyes and feel wide awake, remembering everything you have experienced, knowing you can use this information, now and in the future. One . . . start to come back . . . two . . . almost back . . . and three . . . open your eyes. Get up now and stretch. . . . . It is time to share the stories told to you by your teacher's paintings.

Afterwards, in going over a group fantasy, you will find that each person has had quite a different experience. Some elements, however, may be unexpectedly similar, which can lead to some interesting discussions and insights about how we process the world—both consciously and unconsciously—in relation to other people.

When three people were led through "The Teacher" fantasy together, one visualized an old white clapboard house, one saw a nineteenth century house with turrets, big bay windows, and "gingerbread" trim, while the third envisioned the house of a friend she had not seen or thought of since her childhood. All three, however, imagined a similar teacher—an old woman with long gray hair. The correspondence in her appearance for these three people led to a discussion of "teacher aspects" of old women who have appeared in their dreams and in real life. Each one felt that the house they had chosen was "right" for them, and they discussed why they might each have had such a different representation for such a place of mystery and knowledge. The discussion produced greater insight into their own dream images and waking life experiences.

Many of the images appearing in your imagination and in fairy tales are similar to those that appear in your dreams. In fact, some people who use fantasy regularly find that a kind of dialogue develops between their dreams and their fantasies, with images that originated in one reappearing in a different or more elaborate form in the other. By reawakening your imagination, you reopen and exercise a channel of communication with your unconscious mind that may have been closed to you since early childhood. As you discover the meanings these fantasy images hold for you, you can come to understand and appreciate more fully the symbols that appear in your dreams as well.

chapter thirteen
Cultivating Your Dream Garden

YOUR CREATIVE IMAGINATION

The creative process involves a special way of thinking. It is different from solving a mathematical problem, where you narrow down possibilities step by methodical step until you arrive at the one right answer. Instead, creative thinking involves an ability to generate many possible solutions, to be open to the unexpected, to see similarities where none seem to be, to make intuitive leaps. Such a freewheeling openness to possibilities is vital to creativity.

The dream odyssey is, above all, a journey into the creative self. Your dreams can open you up to your creativity because dream thought works in a way similar to the creative process. It often explores an issue or idea from many perspectives, some seemingly absurd, and some more practical. In your dreams you see the relationships between things through associations and through symbols. Your usual ideas of what *ought* to make sense are temporarily suspended in dreams. This is a necessary part of creative discovery because it allows you to consider new viewpoints and to discover meaning at a deeper level.

In addition to a period of intense concentration, creative work also requires a period of digestion or incubation, during which all the information about a problem can be sorted out and considered. Dreams free you from distractions and daily routine and allow this incubation process to occur. You may have noticed that when you have worked on something very hard or been preoccupied with some problem just before going to sleep at night, it is especially likely to show up in your dreams. You will often wake up in the morning, after having "slept on it," with a solution or at least a new direction to follow. This is your creative mind at work.

A HISTORY OF DREAM CREATIVITY

Women may be able to draw from their dreams for creative work even more readily than most men, since they seem to be more in touch with and more willing to trust their intuitive insights. However, we do not know very much about the role dreams may have played in the creative lives of women, since history has largely ignored their contributions to civilization until recently. If the pages of history would tell us more about women's lives, we would surely find evidence for the influence of dreams in their creative work, as we do with the accomplishments of great men in the arts and sciences.

Two areas in which dream ideas are often used are literature and art. Dream images are so vivid and the plots often so fantastic and bizarre that it is little wonder they have long been a source of inspiration for writers and painters. For example, *The Strange Case of Dr. Jekyll and Mr. Hyde* by Robert Louis Stevenson was inspired by a dream. Stevenson regularly turned to the "little people," or "Brownies" as he called them, of his dreams to give him exciting and entertaining stories for his books. He says of *Dr. Jekyll:*

> I had long been trying to write a story on this subject, to find a body, a vehicle, for that strong sense of man's double being, which must at times come in upon and overwhelm the mind of every thinking creature . . . For two days I went about racking my brains for a plot of any sort; and on the second night I dreamed the scene at the window, and a scene afterwards split in two, in which Hyde, pursued for some crime, took the powder and underwent the change in the presence of his pursuers.[1]

Some of our great artists also owe their inspiration to their dreams. The bizarre images and contrasts of Paul Klee[2] and Marc Chagall, for example, have the power to move or excite us because they are so jarringly at variance with reality; this power comes directly from the fact that they are made of the stuff of dreams. They speak to us at the same intuitive and emotional level as the dream does.

Figure 13-1. With Dreams Upon My Bed by William Blake. Courtesy of the National Art Gallery, Rosenwald Collection, Washington, D.C.

Musicians, too, have received inspiration from their dreams. Wagner, Mozart, Beethoven, Schumann, and Saint-Saens[3] all report hearing some of their music in their dreams, and transcribing it as faithfully as possible upon awakening. One of the most dramatic examples of the creative power of dreams comes from the life of composer Giuseppe Tartini. In a dream, he heard the devil playing on the violin a sonata

> . . . of such exquisite beauty as surpassed the boldest flights of my imagination. I felt enraptured, transported, enchanted; my breath was taken away, and I awoke. Seizing my violin I tried to retain the sounds I had heard. But it was in vain. The piece I then composed, the "Devil's Sonata," was the best I ever wrote, but how far below the one I had heard in my dream![4]

Despite the fact that it is devilishly difficult to play, the "Devil's Sonata" is still performed by virtuoso violinists today, while other Tartini pieces are seldom heard.

It is not surprising to find dream material appearing in the arts, since the work of the artist is to show us the obvious in the unexpected, the beauty in the mundane, the simplicity in the complexities of life, and the complexity in what we thought simple. Since dreams deal with such paradoxes and surprises, they are a natural source of ideas and images for the arts. It may be more startling for you to discover that dreams have made their mark in the sciences as well.

Dreams were directly responsible for Kekul's solution to the riddle of the structure of the benzene molecule and Herschel's discovery of the planet Uranus. It was in a dream that Otto Loewi first devised an experiment to prove that nerve impulses are transmitted chemically, a discovery for which he won a Nobel Prize.[5]

A well-known tale of the work of dreams in science is the story of Elias Howe, inventor of the sewing machine. He had worked for years to perfect the machine without success, as he was unable to design a workable needle for it. Then he dreamed that he was captured by savages and taken before their king:

THE EYE OF THE NEEDLE

"Elias Howe," roared the monarch, "I command you on pain of death to finish this machine at once."

Cold sweat poured down his brow, his hands shook with fear, his knees quaked. Try as he would, the inventor could not get the missing figure in the problem over which he had worked so long. All this was so real to him that he cried aloud. In the vision he saw himself surrounded by dark-skinned and painted warriors, who formed a hollow square about him and led him to the place of execution. Suddenly he noticed that near the heads of the spears which his guards carried, there were eye-shaped holes! He had solved the secret! What he needed was a needle with an eye near the point![6]

The dream helped Howe to consider possible solutions to the problem that might have seemed absurd in waking life, for a needle "always" has its point at one end and the eye at the other. Also, the dream gave him a specific solution, as is often the case in creative dreams, in the imagery of the spears.

Dreams have been used throughout history, then, as a source of inspiration for many forms of creative art and scientific discovery. You do not have to be a creative genius, however, to tap your own creative ability through dreams. If you are already paying attention to your dreams, you know what unexpected gifts they can bring. Now you can learn to mine them for the raw materials you can use to bring creative inspiration and beauty into your waking life.

DREAM IT UP!

Creative inspiration doesn't come automatically, awake or asleep. In fact, if you are not used to thinking of yourself as having creative ability, you may have to work at *unlearning* blocks you have unconsciously created, barriers that interfere with creative thought. Even the most talented people have this problem from time to time, when the creative ideas just won't flow. Your dreams can point to blocks in your creative process, and sometimes they even suggest how you may overcome them, as in the following example.

OVER THE RAINBOW

I am taking my piano lesson. The teacher sits in the chair and tells me to sing "Over the Rainbow" all the way through *a capella*. I say I don't sing very well, but she insists. I clear my throat and nothing comes out. She sits there waiting and looking over her glasses at me. Finally I manage to sing a few bars, and then I sing the whole song all the way through. It gets easier, and although I don't like my voice, my piano teacher doesn't judge me.

I had this dream shortly after I began song writing. After writing several songs, I worked out the harmonies on guitar and taped them. My singing voice is not very good, and after hearing those songs on tape, I suffered a "dry spell"—inspiration for more songs just wouldn't come. When I had this dream, I realized that my attitude toward my poor singing voice was getting in the way. I secretly feared giving the tapes to performers to listen to, because I was embarrassed by my singing voice. Singing before a music teacher in my dream helped me loosen up about my singing voice, and just sing! After this, I was able to start writing songs again and feel easier about presenting them to performers.●

Once you have opened yourself to the idea of using your dreams in creative work, you will find that they are a ready source of the fresh perspectives and illuminating realizations that are so essential to the creative process. In the following example, one dreamer relates how a dream gave her the new angle she needed for writing a song she had been thinking about for some time.

ODE TO GRANDFATHER
I am sitting and talking with my grandmother. I notice that her face looks questioning and nosy. She seems displeased.

My grandfather had died several years ago, and I had thought about writing a song about him, but it wasn't until I had this dream that I found the direction I needed. My grandmother never really appreciated my grandfather, and this dream made me see that I wanted to write a song for her about the way I wished he could have been seen; I glorified him to show my grandmother how neat he really was. This was a very different song than the one I had originally planned.●

In addition to giving you new perspectives to work from, your dreams can give you specific ideas to include in your work as well. Even the most "ordinary" dreams can provide seed ideas that can be used in creative work. In the following example, one of the authors describes how she used her dreams in developing the plot and characters in a novel she was working on. The plot revolves around a number of people, unknown to each other at first, who each choose to leave the U.S. and settle on a small Pacific island as part of an experiment. She decided to rely on a minimum of conscious ideas and let her dreams map out most of the story. For example, after introducing a minor character, she asked her dreams to give her a clue as to what was needed next, and here is the dream she had:

THERE WAS A CROOKED HOUSE
I visit some friends who live in a huge old Victorian house. I go inside, but have trouble walking up the steps, because the steps are

crooked. I notice that the railing is also crooked, and so are the walls and floors. In fact, everything in the house is crooked.

So crookedness was what the story needed! My characters thus far had plenty of conflicts, but they were all nice, decent folks. I wrote "Give me a crook" on a piece of paper and put it under my mattress to help me incubate a dream. A few nights later, I had the following dream:

THE MAN WHO DONE IT

I'm in a cafeteria. A man enters and looks around nervously. There is sweat on his forehead and apprehension and fear are oozing from every pore of his body. He dashes into line and grabs a tray. His hands are trembling so much that, as he reaches for food, the dishes rattle against each other. A woman appears at the door with a pistol in her hand. There are other women standing behind her. Now I understand: this man raped a woman, but because he had a good lawyer and is well respected in the community, he was never convicted. This gang of women is going to take justice into their own hands.

So there was my crooked character, complete with a motive for going to the island! In this way, my dreams continually provided themes, characters, and events for my story, along with guidance when I needed it. I found that because I had actually witnessed the experiences and emotions of my characters in my dreams, I was able to write about them with authority, and this was a great asset to me in crafting a story that was both vivid and entertaining. ●

Even if you rely mostly on waking thoughts and inspirations in your creative work, you can combine elements from your dreams with the material you have consciously developed. In the following example, a woman playwright tells how she used symbolism from her dreams in an original dramatic production that combines music, dance, and dialogue.

ROSES

I am with my true love. Words don't mean anything. We communicate through our thoughts, by using ESP. Coiled ribbons of roses stream out in a double-helix. This makes me think of the double-helix structure of DNA, the basic matrix of life, the language in which the blueprints for all living things are coded.

The main prop for this production is a large dummy, a rag doll that has other props inside of it and which becomes various characters during the play. Many of these props come from my "Roses" dream, and I put them inside of the doll to show that what comes out of people is not always orderly or rational.

Inspired by this dream, I put ribbons and roses inside the doll. When they come streaming out, it is like the streaming out of another language, something nonverbal, intuitive, and symbolic. I love ribbons and laces and delicate things—aspects of my aristocratic life. In the play, I have the ribbons start strangling me. I want to show symbolically that a search for *only* beauty and the ethereal can drag you down, that I need a plainer life. Using dreams in my work in this way enables me to tell what's closest to the truth about myself and the character I portray, while making it collectively understandable to an audience.[7] ●

Because the language of dreams is nonverbal and symbolic, it lends itself easily to guiding work in the nonverbal as well as the verbal arts. Dreams can provide impressions and specific images that can be used in dance, mime, painting, and instrumental music. In the following example, one of the authors relates how she used her dreams to guide her work.

I was asked to design a logo for an arts and crafts fair. I wanted to do something showing an artist at work, something that captured the spirit of artistic work, the process of creating something from nothing. As the deadline drew near, I was still unsatisfied with the preliminary work I had done. I went to bed one night thinking about this and asked my dreams to help me.

THE LOGO
I am working on my sketches for the fair. I discard several preliminary sketches and begin work on a new idea. I draw two hands carving a rabbit out of wood. The rabbit is still unfinished, still just a suggestion outlined in the smooth curves of the wood. To emphasize the impression of the rabbit as something only beginning to come into being, I draw the artist's hands in great detail to contrast them with the broad lines and unfinished surfaces of the rabbit.

This sketch from my dream struck exactly the note I had in mind. I was so excited when I woke up that I started drawing right away, to capture what I had seen in my dream as exactly as possible. When I submitted the logo it was well received. ●

As you can see, there are many possibilities for tapping the creative abilities that lie sleeping within you. Furthermore, when you record the stories, poetry, music, images, or other works of art suggested by your dreams, you encourage additional dream gifts in the future. Use your dreams to draw upon the fertile source of inspiration that great women and men have turned to through the centuries.

Figure 13-2. Greenwood Arts and Crafts Fair Logo by E. Ann Hollier

chapter fourteen
Exploring the Horizons of Consciousness

As you pay more attention to your dreams and remember them more often, you will find your dreamlife is much richer and more varied than you once thought: you may very well find things happening in your dreams that you never thought were possible. In this chapter we will travel to the world of dreams on the horizons of consciousness, so that you can recognize and use the special opportunities these kinds of dreams offer for expanding your own horizons.

HIGH DREAMS

In a high dream you experience an "expansion of self," or a feeling of merging with the universe. Dreamers who have high dreams often report feeling euphoric or having a mystical sense of unusual calm and centeredness; others describe landscapes in high dreams as unusually vivid, as in the following dream.

THE CHOIR OF RED HIBISCUS

A low voice tells me I must go to Western Samoa. Suddenly I'm there, standing near a beautiful waterfall with hundreds of beautiful large red hibiscus flowers around me. Choral music is coming from the flowers. It melds with the color of the flowers and begins to flow through my veins until my whole body is pulsating in ecstasy. I become the flowers, the music, the jungle, and the waterfall, and they become me.

You can cultivate high dreams in your own dreamlife by using the dream incubation techniques described in Chapter Ten. You may want to use your high dreams as raw material for a guided fantasy, for creative art or writing, or as a focal point for relaxation and meditation.

LUCID DREAMS

Unlike most dreams, in a lucid dream you are *aware* that you are dreaming. Almost everyone has a lucid dream at one time or another. For most people, lucidity commonly occurs during a nightmare, when they suddenly realize that their frightening experiences are taking place in a dream rather than in waking life. Sometimes this thought alone is enough to relieve the fear, and the dream continues. However, most dreamers wake up, or try to, at this point, as in the following dream.

THE SPRAY OF SALT

I see that the curtains are open and a man is staring at me through the window. I scream and run into the other room to call the police. I pick up the phone with trembling hands and dial the operator. As I wait for an answer, I notice a spray of salt coming out of the telephone. I think to myself, "Salt doesn't come out of telephones. This must be a dream!" The operator answers, and I say, "Operator, I've changed my mind. This is a dream and a scary one at that, so I've decided to wake up." She says "Okay." I hang up the phone and wake up.

Although frightening dreams are the most common experience of lucid awareness in dreams, it is possible to have a more pleasant kind of lucid dream. In these dreams, you can act as a "dream director," consciously changing dream characters or influencing events as they develop, fully aware of your role as their creator. Lucid dreams like these can be very pleasurable and fascinating experiences, as the following example illustrates.

FUN WITH LUCIDITY

I'm visiting Martin one night at his apartment in Chicago. I wonder what I am doing there when I should be at work. How did I get here? Perhaps I'm dreaming. On the wall in front of me is an abstract painting. If I am dreaming, I can command that abstract picture to turn into a picture of a flower. I wave my hand and the painting instantly changes into a flower painting. I become very excited. I wander into the next room and look into a long mirror. I wave my hand and there appears in the mirror a reflection of a young man next to mine. I wonder if this is how I would appear if I had been born male. Now his reflection makes a gesture and *my* reflection disappears! I make another gesture and *his* reflection disappears, then a second gesture makes my reflection reappear.

Many dreamers find it hard to stay lucid once they realize they are dreaming, often slipping back into their usual dream state or waking themselves up from excitement. Holding onto the lucid state is a skill that can be practiced and gets easier with experience, however. Lucidity can even begin spontaneously when you have been paying attention to and thinking about your dreams in waking life for awhile. It may also help, at least at first, to use dream incubation before you go to sleep, to "program" yourself to carry out a particular, predetermined action once you realize you are dreaming. You may plan to use your lucidity to focus on a particularly pleasurable experience, such as flying, making love, or getting a gift from a dream character, or to learn more about a particularly puzzling or frightening symbol from a previous dream. Planning ahead for lucidity in this way may help you stay lucid until you become used to this extraordinary dream state.

You will know that you are getting close to lucidity in your dreams when you begin examining your dream environment more critically—for example, when you recognize characters or objects from previous dreams, when you begin thinking about your dream symbols and what they mean while you are dreaming, or when you begin to look for signs that what you are experiencing is a dream. This can lead to some humorous situations, as it did for the following dreamer.

THE HORSE WITH THE RED RUBBER SHOES

I'm buying a horse from a woman. The horse is wearing "shoes" made of hard, bright red rubber, like galoshes, that cover his hooves. I've never seen horseshoes like these, but I think perhaps they are something new. Then I get another idea: maybe this is a dream. So I start looking for signs of a dream. The horse puts his hind foot up on his rear. I think, now this has *got* to be a dream, but the way he has his foot positioned on his rump somehow looks plausible. I think to myself, there is no way of knowing if this is a dream unless I wake up. I laugh as I look at the horse's rump and think, either way, I'm a horse's ass to believe all this!

PSI DREAMS

There is an impressive body of evidence documenting the occurrence of psychic phenomena, both spontaneously and in laboratory studies. Yet, although psychic events often take place in dreams, we still know very little about how psychic (or PSI) dreams work or what causes them. The fact that science cannot explain PSI phenomena in dreams through the usual kinds of explanations does not mean, however, that they do not exist or cannot be useful. PSI dreams (precognitive, telepathic, and clairvoyant dreams) are one of the many unsolved mysteries in both our inner and outer universes that can be used to our advantage even though we do not yet understand them completely. This is especially true for women, who report PSI dreams more often than men do.

One way to think of PSI dreaming phenomena is to think of the human mind as a radio. We may tune our dial to a particular station at a given broadcasting frequency, yet other channels are broadcasting as well, even though we only hear the station to which we are tuned. PSI dreaming might be viewed in the same way, as the presence of additional "dream channels" existing in our unconscious. Our sensory systems appear to be biased toward certain channels or types of information and against others. In PSI dreaming, it is as if waking life distractions get "turned off," sleeping brain activity and the imagination get "turned on," and your consciousness enjoys a much higher degree of freedom and flexibility in the type of information it "tunes in" to.

Precognition

A precognitive dream (sometimes called a prophetic or premonitory dream) is one in which you dream of an event that later actually happens, as in the following example.

McPHERSON'S DEATH
I'm in Mr. McPherson's house. There are people standing about, and he is talking about getting all his papers in order. He mentions the

registration papers on his car. Suddenly he begins to cough and clutch his chest. He says he wants to be taken to the hospital. There is an oxygen tank in his room. The people there say it is too late to save him, and he dies.

Mr. McPherson was a long-time friend of the family, although I hadn't seen him or heard anything about him for several years. One month after my dream my mother called to tell me he had just died of lung cancer. The details of his death were very much like my dream: he called his friends and relatives to his room to tell them to get his papers in order. A discussion ensued over whether or not he could be moved to the hospital in his car. His doctor ordered an oxygen tank sent to his home, but by the time it arrived, he had expired. ●

Clairvoyance

The word *clairvoyance* comes from the French language, meaning *clear view*. In a clairvoyant dream, the dreamer "sees" an event or object from waking life directly, without being influenced by communication from another person. Following is an example of a clairvoyant dream.

MOTEL ROOM COLORS
I open the door to a motel room and look at the decor. The walls are painted yellow. The bedspread and furniture coverings are bright blue, and the curtains are of a blue, yellow, and white floral print. The furniture is dark wood, and the carpet is beige. Above the high dresser is a small painting of a lighthouse. The window looks out onto a charming little garden.

I had this dream and recorded it before booking my accommodations at a small motel in a foreign country. I had never been to that country before, and had never seen any pictures of the motel. The room I later stayed in looked *exactly* like the one in my dream in every detail.

Telepathy

A telepathic dream involves direct communication between two or more persons, as in the following example.

WARNING
I run into David. He is glad to see me. I have a caftan on, and he sticks his arm down one sleeve and puts the tip of his finger into my vagina. "It's been a long time," he murmurs, and I answer,

"Yes, it has been." I tell him I want to talk to him, but I will have to come back later.

David and I had broken off our relationship, and I'd seen little of him for several months. I was still physically attracted and emotionally involved with him, but didn't think the relationship was very good for me. "What would I do if a situation like this came up?" I thought as I woke up from the dream. I'd hardly had time to pose the question to myself when the doorbell rang. It was David, come to talk about a reconciliation; I had the dream while he was on his way over to see me! I wisely took my dream's advice and told him I wanted to talk to him, but needed some time to think things over first. ●

Mutual Dreams

A mutual dream is a telepathic experience in which two or more persons have the same or similar dream. Note the similarities and differences in the following dreams, shared the morning after an overnight dream workshop.

GERMAN SHEPHERD

Dream #1: I'm in a room with some other people. A black and brown German Shepherd runs up excitedly and jumps on me, licking my face. I think to myself that the dog should be sent to obedience school.

Dream #2: I'm in a room with Brenda (Dreamer #1). A black and brown German Shepherd runs up to me and jumps on me. It is wagging its tail and licking my face. I turn to Brenda and say, "There's nothing wrong with this dog, he just needs to go to obedience school to learn where to lick!"

Dream #3: ...A gray German Shepherd runs in and jumps on me...

Dream #4: ...A gray lamb runs into the room and jumps up on me.

While mutual dreams usually occur on the same night, they do not necessarily happen at exactly the same time. (The four dreams just cited were recorded at various times throughout the same night of the workshop.) Sharing mutual dreams can lead us to examine important issues that affect ourselves and others. This was the case in the dream workshop mentioned. All of the participants were women, and in addition to the "German Shepherd," over half of the women had another mutual dream in which the entire group was being held captive by a mob of men who were plotting to rape and kill them. In discussing this dream, the group members shared their most intimate feelings about their own sexuality and about male violence toward women. All agreed that this dream-sharing session had been a valuable experience, allowing them to share their feelings with other women in a safe and supportive atmosphere.

Mutual dreams are probably more common, and certainly are more often detected, between people who share a close emotional bond, such as partners, or parents and children. Exploring these dreams together can make an important contribution to a better understanding of your loved ones and your relationship with them.

RECOGNIZING A PSI DREAM

In developing PSI dreaming ability, it is important to be able to tell a genuine psychic dream from one that is not. Dreams that appear at face value to be PSI dreams can have other plausible explanations. The following dream example is one that *may* not be a true PSI dream.

> THE OLD MAN AND THE SPEEDING TRAIN
> I see an old man reaching his head and arm out from a speeding train. The dream is abruptly cut off at this point.

I had this dream several times when I was young. I knew very little about my great-grandfather except that he worked on the railroad. I just recently learned how he died: In those days a railroadman picked up the mail by reaching out of the moving train and grabbing the mailbag as the train passed the station; my great-grandfather was killed when he reached out of the train for the mailbag and hit a post. ●

It is difficult to be certain that "The Old Man and the Speeding Train" is a genuine PSI dream. The dreamer may have overheard a discussion of her great-grandfather's death when she was young and forgotten about it. To definitely qualify as a PSI dream, even the *possibility* of such known but previously unnoticed or forgotten information must be ruled out completely.

Dreams about events that are likely to occur in the future must also be ruled out when distinguishing PSI dreams, as must shared experiences or knowledge. For example, two women reported having mutual dreams of sailing across the ocean on a luxury oceanliner. These two women were actually preparing to leave on such a cruise together, and both began dreaming about the upcoming event with great frequency as the day of the voyage grew near. Because the event was on their minds, their dreams were not conclusively "mutual."

An additional problem in distinguishing PSI dreams from others is the possibility of sheer coincidence. However, while you might write off one such dream as a chance occurrence, this is an implausible explanation for the regular appearance of PSI information in your dreams. In addition, some dreamers report that their PSI dreams are different from other dreams. One dreamer comments, "All my PSI dreams have an 'old time movie' feel about them. They are always in black and white, with a grainy texture." Another dreamer says, "I always know when I've had a PSI dream, because the colors become more intense and the dream seems more vivid."

EXPERIMENTING WITH PSI DREAMS

PSI dreams may occur spontaneously for you, but, like lucid dreams, they can also be consciously cultivated and applied to your waking life.

A Telepathy Experiment

You can try the following telepathy experiment with your family, a friend, or any gathering, such as a campout, where a group of people sleep in close proximity. You need six pictures about the size of a standard sheet of 8½ X 11-inch paper. The pictures should portray simple themes and be as dissimilar from one another as possible.

One person agrees to be the *sender* and chooses a picture as the *target picture* to transmit to the others while they sleep. She should try to visualize the picture several times during the night, perhaps superimposed over the face of each sleeping person; or she might visualize a network of fine "psychic threads" connecting her to her friends with the mental image of the target picture moving out in all directions on these threads. The *receivers* try to "tune in" to the picture before going to sleep and give themselves a strong suggestion to incubate a psychic dream, such as, "Tonight I will dream about the picture that is being sent my way."

The following morning, the receivers record their dreams privately. The sender then displays *all six* pictures to the dreamers, together with any associations she herself may have to the pictures. The dreamers each jot down their private guesses of the target picture, based on their dreams. Then everyone shares her dreams and discusses why she chose the picture she did. The sender can then reveal which picture was her target picture. The probability of choosing the correct picture by chance alone is one in six, but you may find that you choose correctly much more often as you exercise your PSI dreaming abilities.

A Clairvoyance Experiment

You can also try a clairvoyance experiment. You should perform this one alone, to avoid any possibility of telepathy. You will need 20 or 30 color pictures cut out from magazines, simple in theme and content and dissimilar from one another. Insert the pictures into separate, identical large manila envelopes (one for each picture), and give them a thorough shuffling.

Pick out one and place a small "x" on the underside of the envelope with a light pencil mark. Without looking at the picture, put the envelope under your pillow or mattress. Before going to sleep, tell yourself that you will dream about the picture and that you will wake in the morning and remember your dream. In the morning, record your dreams, retrieve the envelope from under your mattress and gather up five envelopes from the larger pool. Shuffle these thoroughly. Now lay the six envelopes out in front of you, face up, so that the "x" on the marked envelope doesn't show. Remove each picture, placing it on its corresponding envelope and try to guess which one was the target picture. Then turn the envelopes over and check them to see if you chose the correct one.

Serendipity

Like a shortwave radio, psychically projected thoughts may travel on unpredictable "airwaves," leading you to pick up information you might not have expected. For example, in one telepathy experiment, the sender had experienced a lot of stress that week, including having had three flat tires, and had difficulty relaxing and focusing before "sending" the target picture of an Indian weaving. The receiver did not know about these tire problems, yet every dream she had that night was about tires! She might never have known that her dreams contained PSI information had the sender not seen the relationship and told her about it. For this reason, it is important to have the sender discuss her associations to the target pictures and relate recent emotionally charged events in her life, for sometimes this is the information reflected in the receiver's dreams, rather than the target picture itself.

HEALING DREAMS

Every day we unconsciously make note of many forms of peripheral information such as conversations overheard, physical states, signs and advertisements, and other details we barely notice in passing. These *subliminal perceptions* often appear later in our dreams, giving information about our physical well-being. Thus, we can look to our dreams to give us health advice in healing.

Physical Healing

You need not be sick or injured in order to have a spontaneous healing dream. Though you may be in good health, your dreams may point the way to *better* health, perhaps by indicating a need for more exercise or a change in diet, as the following dream example illustrates.

THE IRON C
I'm looking at my naked body from outside of myself, as I would if I were someone else. A zipper appears in my belly and unzips itself. An object comes out that is shaped like the letter C and it is made of iron. It disappears back inside my body, then the zipper closes itself and disappears.

This dream seemed to be pointing out my need for more iron and Vitamin C in my diet, as those are two nutrients I never seem to get enough of. ●

It is also possible to have a dream about someone else's health condition, since just caring for someone can often be enough to stimulate PSI dreams about them. Such was the case for the mother in the following dream about her son.

THE WHISPERING TREES
Everything is dark around me and I can't see a thing. I'm not afraid, though, as the dark is comforting and I feel safe and secure. I hear the rustle of leaves in the wind and then feel the presence of a very old and wise tree. I can faintly hear the wind in the trees whispering,

"Jamie has a pea in his ear, Jamie has a pea in his ear." The voice continues to say this until I wake up in the middle of the night.

I woke up from this dream worried about my son, Jamie. I got up and went to his room, but he was sleeping soundly. The next morning he came down to breakfast hitting the side of his head with his hand and complaining that he had lost his hearing. We took him to a specialist that day, who removed a ball of wax the size of a pea from Jamie's ear. ●

You don't have to wait for your dreams to offer you health advice spontaneously. You can educate them to provide this advice when you need it, through dream incubation. If you wish to help a friend by incubating a telepathic dream of her condition, it may help to get a personal item, such as a scarf or piece of jewelry, to help you focus on her. You can then take this item to bed with you and suggest to yourself that you are going to dream for your friend's benefit.

Psychological Healing

PSI dreams can also bring about what we might call "psychological healing." An unexpected experience at a dream group involving two of the authors illustrates the emotional healing value of PSI dreaming.

THE RING OF POWER
I am given a ring with a plain, narrow silver band and a dark red stone in it. It is an heirloom that has been passed down from one female relative to another in my family and now has come to me. The ring has great magical powers and the ability to protect the wearer from harm.
Now I'm in a house with two men and a woman. I look out the window and see a tornado heading straight for the house. We panic and start screaming and running around. Suddenly I remember the ring. I hold it up and summon up its protective powers. The tornado dissipates before it reaches us and we are all safe.

Author #1: When I woke up, I wondered what kind of stone the ring had. I wanted to believe it was a ruby because of the great value attached to that kind of gem, but I decided it most likely had been a garnet, since the color was a very deep, wine red. I had this dream on the morning of July thirtieth and shared it a few days later at a dream group session.
Author #2: On the night of July twenty-ninth, I was thinking about a ring my grandmother had given me that I had lost a few years ago. The ring was a very simple one, having a narrow silver band with four prongs

setting the stone. When I first saw it, I wondered whether the stone was a ruby or a garnet. I wanted it to be a ruby, since that is my birthstone, but since the color was a very deep red, I guessed it was a garnet.

I felt a very deep sorrow that night over having lost the ring, and the more I thought about it, the worse I felt. Imagine my surprise at the dream group meeting when my co-author reported a dream that seemed to be picking up on my thoughts and feelings of the night before! No consoling or supportive words like "Don't be so hard on yourself" would have done the trick, but I felt much better after hearing that my friend had "found" the ring and used it so well. ●

Consciousness has broader horizons than we often realize. PSI dreams can teach us to open these new channels and explore the realm beyond our five senses, challenging our fixed concepts of space, time, and sources of knowledge. Working receptively with PSI dreams can lead to a new awareness of the world around us, one that allows for the unexpected. Adopting this flexible attitude toward our inner and outer worlds allows us to change as we learn, growing beyond the former horizons that bounded our understanding of ourselves and the world around us.

part four
CROSSROADS

Introduction: Exploring Transitions Through Dreams— Changes Along The Way

Whatever you can do, or dream you can, begin it.
Boldness has genius, power and magic in it.

Goethe[1]

"Mommy ate half my cookie and took away my teddy bear!" cried a 2½-year-old boy as he awakened in the middle of the night. This little boy's mother was six months pregnant at the time he had this dream. As they talked about the dream, the mother became aware of her young son's feelings of sibling rivalry and anxiety, apparently triggered by the approaching birth of the second child in the family. Discussing these feelings gave both mother and child the opportunity to deal with them satisfactorily.

Your dreams and those of your loved ones can give you many such opportunities to take a closer look at the changes and transitions in your life. By examining the messages and hints that your dreams give you about these transitions, you can anticipate and prepare for the shock and strain of the inevitable adjustments to come in your life. You may even be able to make changes and choices along the way that can minimize the conflict and stress which often accompany these major transitions.

In the chapters that follow, we will explore some of the major crossroads and transitions in the lives of women today: changing roles, intimate relationships, family life, children, and landmarks of the aging process. We will focus on how women have used their own dreams and dreamwork with loved ones and associates to cope with major issues in their lives. Even if you are not now experiencing these issues in your own life, you may still identify with the dreams they relate, since their experiences represent some parts of us all as women in transition.

chapter fifteen
You Are
What You Dream

We are living in the midst of a transition in values and expectations for women, forcing us to choose constantly between traditional and nontraditional roles. It is easy to rely on black-and-white thinking in making our choices, accepting or rejecting new options simply because we have labeled ourselves as basically traditional or nontraditional in our outlook. When we do this, we cut ourselves off from making choices that are best for us as *individuals*, regardless of whether they fit in with the stereotype of the "traditional" or "liberated" woman. It is time to move beyond this split and recognize that all kinds of choices are valid, for ourselves and for other women, and that in each area of our lives there are many options available.

In this chapter, we will explore some of the areas in which our changing self-image is most keenly felt as our roles and choices change. Women are learning a new vocabulary of competence and power as we move into positions of prominence and leadership in the world outside the home. At the same time, we struggle to maintain our former roles as nurturers, caretakers, and homemakers. This forces us to come to grips with balancing our own needs with those of others, and to confront our human limitations in accomplishing our goals, in and out of the home.

Along with our changing social image, our biological self-image is changing, too. Women are taking a new look at notions about childbearing and motherhood; we are reexamining our attitudes about appearance and physical attractiveness, as well as our sexuality.

All of these issues are explored here as they are mirrored in our dreams. Options for dealing with these issues are presented through examples of women working on their dreams to change their lives. Through dreamwork, you too can find new solutions that are uniquely your own, for *you are what you dream.* ●

COMPETENCE AND CONFIDENCE

THE HAIRCUT
Kara is sitting across from me. I tell her I like the way her hair has been cut. Laura "confesses" that she cut it. I tell her what a good job she's done and she replies, 'Well, I hope I didn't mess it up too badly.' I walk away feeling very annoyed with her, but then realize that I too make it difficult for people to give me compliments.

Compliments have always embarrassed me, and I have never learned to accept them gracefully. When I played the role of Laura in my dreamwork, I discovered how I often undermine my confidence by playing down my special skills and abilities to myself as well as to others. This dream made me think about the fine line between being modest without putting myself down on the one hand, and acknowledging my abilities without being vain on the other. I still have trouble with this, but I am better at it since I worked on this dream.

If you were asked to explain the reason for some successful endeavor in your life, would you take credit for it unashamedly? Probably not! Like the dreamer in the previous example, most women don't take credit for themselves where credit is due. Women are most likely to attribute their success to the help or efforts of some other person or to luck, that is, to circumstances *outside* themselves. Men, on the other hand, will more often attribute their successes to their own personal efforts. While we encounter many realistic obstacles in the outside world, we also create our own obstacles through inner conflicts and past training, which often cause us to fear and ignore our strengths in the present.

Your dreams can help you discover and confront your own barriers to feeling competent and successful; they can guide you in developing a more confident and assertive approach to life, as in the following example.

TAKING CHARGE

I'm in a psychology class. I take over and lead it. I ask for ten minutes alone to get my thoughts together. I go to a room where I see a typewriter with some notes in it that Joe has made. They are obtuse and detailed, and I decide not to use them. I make a few brief notes about major topics ("Perception," "Responsibility"). I go back into the room and start taking charge with authority, telling people to find places in the room and start focusing in on themselves.

This dream helped me realize how much I had always looked to Joe, my ex-husband, and before that to my father, for direction in what I did. Now finally, as in the dream, I was beginning to acknowledge my own capabilities—which I could use more effectively than anything I could get from others.●

Many women today can remember growing up in a time when there was only one model of success for every female: Success meant *having* certain things—a nice home, a successful husband, and lovely children, and *being* certain things—a pretty woman, a good wife, housekeeper, and mother. Many of us as girls believed wholeheartedly in these messages and trusted them throughout our growing years. However, as we have seen, dreams can lead us to our own truths. The following dream example illustrates how one young girl, through a dream, glimpsed her own truth about success despite strong family messages to the contrary.

THE CARPENTER

I'm walking along a cold and lonely beach. I see a wood frame house going up ahead and only one person building it. This seems strange because my grandfather and other carpenters all work together building a house. I step inside the frame and look up at the carpenter hammering above. It is a woman! She smiles and winks at me. I feel very proud that we share a special secret between us.

When I was eight years old I told my grandfather, a successful carpenter, that I might want to be a carpenter when I grew up. My whole family laughed at this. My mother said that women's arms aren't strong enough. My father said a woman could never be a *successful* carpenter, because the job requires logic and common sense, and women were weak in this area. My grandfather put an end to it by saying, "If women could be carpenters, why don't you see them working at building sites?" I thought this over and decided disappointedly he must be right. That night I had this dream.

I never shared this dream with anyone, but the image of the woman working above me stayed with me for a long time and was a source of inspiration for me throughout my high school and college years. •

Some women have traded the female success model for the male definition of success. That is, "Earn a lot of money, be a good provider, play to win, climb the corporate ladder," and so forth. While some women who "make it" on these terms feel they have achieved genuine success, others, like the dreamer following, feel disappointed or unfulfilled.

THE PUNCHING BAG
Two of the fellows from Public Relations are in the gym, hitting a punching bag. They ask me if I want to join them. I say sure and walk over. Then I notice the punching bag is a globe turned upside down. I start to punch it, but don't enjoy it. I turn and punch at the two men.

So this was what I had studied and worked so hard for, to be like men, aggressively taking punches at the world! I had pursued a career in a field dominated by men, and I was becoming like them; but my dream said something inside me was wanting to change. I did some deep soul-searching during this time and eventually changed careers to work with the more human side of life. •

Even the most confident and capable woman may feel like she needs to prove herself constantly to *others* around her who may secretly (or not so secretly!) believe she should be home taking care of her husband and children. Thus, a woman must be on guard for demands placed on her— often demands she puts on *herself*—to "measure up." The woman in the following dream found she was able to relax much more when she looked at what her dreams were telling her about the pressures and demands she felt.

RIDE HOME
I'm at work when I look at my watch and notice I have worked past quitting time and probably have missed my ride home. I panic and try to call various friends to explain my situation to them. Either they aren't at home or they don't understand what I'm saying. I'm

upset, as I have no other way to get home. I become very angry at myself and start to throw things in a fit of anger, when Glenda walks in and says, "It's 5:00 and I've come to take you home."

Being involved in a number of work projects, I often feel inadequate at managing my own life. I forget things and become worried about whether or not I can juggle everything. Sometimes these doubts get completely out of hand, and I get upset or depressed. The message this dream had for me was: "RELAX! Everything is all right, and you are perfectly capable of managing your life despite small setbacks now and then!" ●

Working on your dreams can help you to keep a realistic perspective, and to forgive yourself for your failures and shortcomings. You can then respect and accept yourself as you are now—regardless of others' opinions—even while you continue to work toward your potential and the goals you set for yourself. This involves learning the lesson of *autonomy:* separate out your vision of yourself from others' expectations of you, and take responsibility for fulfilling that vision for yourself rather than depending on others to do it for you. Because most women are brought up to try to please others and to find their sense of identity and self-worth in providing for others, this is often a difficult—but necessary—step. The following woman came to understand this lesson through the message conveyed in a dream.

THE BALLOON

I'm in a chorus line. Our leader tells me to take over for her. I don't know what she expects me to do, but I know it's supposed to be clear to me, and that if I do the wrong thing something terrible will happen. The leader blows up a balloon that has my childhood names and nicknames written all over it. The balloon floats down to me, and with effort I break it. The dread is past. I did what I was supposed to do. "I think it is time to end rehearsal," I say to the leader.

I had this dream just as I was striking out on my own in the world. I was scared and confused. When I worked on this dream, I found that part of the confusion stemmed from trying to continue to live according to the expectations of others—parents, teachers, old friends, lovers. These expectations were represented by the names on the balloon—"old selves" that had to be destroyed before I could become my true self. ●

Like this dreamer, you must dare to burst the bubble of others' expectations in order to discover your own resources and rely on your own strengths. This is both the burden and the joy of the many new choices available to us as women today.

LEADERSHIP AND POWER

"Castrating bitch!" If used against us, this term is often enough to deter us from being straightforward and assertive. What we may fail to see is that these words reflect merely a male fear of female power. As women begin to move out of traditional, often subservient roles, we will certainly be seen as a threat by the dominant male system that, by and large, wants to keep us there.

Rather than give in to the pressure to be submissive, look at your own fear of taking power and assuming leadership. Your immediate reaction to asserting yourself in a power struggle, especially if it is with a man, may well be a fear of being rejected or attacked. The temptation in such situations is often to retreat or take only that power which men will *allow* you to have, according to their rules. Such a compromise only diverts your energies from the full realization of the use of your creativity and power.

We need to face our fears, take risks, and acknowledge and use our power where we can make the most impact. Working on our dreams can help us move from submissiveness and passivity to initiative and assertiveness more easily. One woman was able to do this and confront the hostile reaction of men to her position of power with the help of the following dream.

THE FEMINIST PRODUCTION
I'm directing a large political (feminist) musical production. A man in a motorcycle helmet and jacket comes up to me and threatens to kill me. I stand up to him, and he leaves. Another man comes over threateningly and I get rid of him, too. I am worried about getting the show off on time. I'm half an hour late for the rehearsal because I was trying to get some things for the show that I thought were important. I'm uneasy about being late but no one complains. I'm surprised.

At the time of this dream, I was working in an agency directed by two very chauvinistic men. I had just designed and implemented several new programs ("productions") at the agency. This dream helped me see that these two men (like the two men in the dream) were threatened by what I was doing—asserting myself and doing some "directing" on my own (which included supporting women's rights at the agency). I was concerned about being attacked by them and having my programs "killed." At the same time, I was unsure of my own ability to have the show "come off," that is, to be effective and supported in my work. I found that the staff did, in fact, learn from me and stand behind me. Working on this dream helped me decide to keep pushing for my programs and stand up for my ideas to the bitter end. I finally quit this job and went out on my own—but not out of fear. Rather, this decision grew out of the power of my convictions and a desire to carry out my ideas in a more receptive setting.●

Because of negative reactions from men, or fears of such reactions, many of us may believe that asserting ourselves effectively is wrong or even destructive. We may then feel guilty and back off, putting ourselves down to build men up—perhaps out of a fear that they may not otherwise be there for us to depend on. We may also worry about depriving or hurting others—men, women, or children—if we move out of our familiar and expected passive, dependent, and nurturant roles. Such is the case in the following dream as this woman begins to try out using her power.

BOWS AND ARROWS

I'm in a room with several other people, mostly women. I'm teaching them how to shoot bows and arrows. As I distribute the arrows, I realize how sharp they are and that they may be dangerous.

When I had this dream I was teaching graduate students (mostly women) about organizational power and tactics. I was encouraging them to get clear about their feelings and voice their opinions assertively. This dream revealed my fears of getting them and myself into trouble with our male superiors if we spoke out too "sharply" or "to the point." It was tempting to back off and protect them from hurting themselves or others. This dream helped me keep on going by making me more aware of my power, and giving me more understanding of my fear of it. In turn, I was better able to guide my students in confronting these issues for themselves.●

We need to face our fears of getting hurt or hurting others if we as women are ever to establish our influence in the public world. This means fighting it out, if necessary, for spheres of influence and leadership among ourselves as well as with men. We don't always need to agree with each other in order to work together. Only by risking confrontation can we organize to use our power and strength effectively in the public arena.

Once you decide actively to pursue and use your leadership and power, you need to be careful of going overboard and suddenly realizing that all your time is filled up. This can be a dangerous situation, because when your energy becomes too scattered, you lose your effectiveness and "burn out." Assigning priorities may be difficult, however, especially if you feel pulled in a number of different directions at once. The following example illustrates how a dream helped a political activist in Hawaii to reach an important decision about where to channel her political efforts.

MUUMUUS AND MOUSTACHES

I'm in a room with some women, and all of them have their backs to me. They are all wearing dresses and muumuus, and they are telling me I should be wearing a dress. Some of them are angry and say, "Why do you wear jeans and army pants? Don't you want to look like a lady?" I get mad and start to argue back, when suddenly they all turn around in unison and face me. Each woman is sporting a thick, dark moustache.

I had this dream after being asked to appear on a talk show dealing with homosexuality and lesbianism. The director told me they wanted a lesbian to appear on the show but wanted me to dress up, so as not to "encourage the public's stereotypic image of a lesbian." I asked him what he meant, and he said, "Well, you know, wear something pretty, like a muumuu." This dream made me realize that there was no way I was going to dress up to please men—not even a gay man. I called the director and told him I would not appear on the show. The dream also helped me decide to give up this kind of outreach work and do what I really enjoyed most, working with other women at the women's resource center. ●

THE SUPERWOMAN SYNDROME

Women today often feel they need to do it *all:* They must be physically fit, mentally brilliant, great lovers, super parents, and champion bread-winners. In addition, they feel they must be able to juggle all of these activities and commitments with grace and ease. Advertising's new image of the ideal woman is the beautiful, well-groomed, efficient executive who comes home smiling to take care of her children and husband and dogs and then cooks a gourmet dinner—still smiling, of course!

What is left out of this picture is the frustration, tension, and needs of this "superwoman" as she tries to balance the pressures of both her job and her homelife. Working women today are "doubly burdened" as Betty Friedan points out in her book *The Second Stage,* when equality in jobs is not matched by domestic equality in the family and home.[1] Evidence of this can be seen in the many cases of women entering therapy, either to find out why they can't live up to this ideal of success, or to get help in coping with all the pressures this self-imposed success model presents. Such ambitious and self-sacrificing women contribute to the myth of the superwoman by not taking care of themselves better. Whatever our life-style—working in the home and/or outside of it, children or not—we need to take responsibility for recognizing our basic human (*not* superhuman!) needs for nurturance and support. If *we* don't do it, it's unlikely that anyone will.

By looking into your dreams, you can find clues to the frustrations and needs you may not take the time to notice in your waking life, or which you may not even feel justified in having at a conscious level. These kinds of messages were conveyed in the following dream to a pregnant woman who had just started teaching along with keeping her business going.

THERAPY

I'm at my therapy appointment with Dr. Day. A student comes in and starts telling a dream to Dr. Day. Others come in and a group discussion starts. I'm angry and I break in yelling, "I paid for this session and I want to tell my dream!" People start leaving. I see my husband. He tells me I should tell Dr. Day what I want. I tell her how upset I am and go to lie down. Dr. Day lies down next to me. I start to fall asleep, but then I say "I need to get up." Dr. Day says, "You need your rest now that you're pregnant and teaching." It feels good to hear her say that, but I get up to go meet a friend for lunch. I'm 20 minutes late and my friend has already eaten. I'm hungry!

This dream helped me see how I was depriving myself of meeting my most basic physical and emotional needs—good food, rest, warmth, intimacy. Having this dream gave me the courage I needed to tell my therapist, Dr. Day, after nearly two years in therapy, what I needed from her and others. It led to a dramatic breakthrough in my therapy and an increased feeling of closeness to her as a person. From there I went on to be more direct with my family and friends about what I needed from them as well. I still have a long way to go on this, but since this dream, at least I'm aware of it and working on it. ●

MOTHERHOOD AND CHILDBIRTH

As the public image and expectations for women have been changing, the more personal aspects of our lives have also been in transition. Until recently, the crucial issues of motherhood—"how, when, and even where women should conceive, bear, nourish and indoctrinate their children"[2] — have been dictated by men. We have allowed primarily male doctors, lawyers, and policy-makers, as well as our own fathers, lovers, and husbands, to define and direct our experience of motherhood. It is time that we trust our own attitudes about mothering so that we can fulfill our maternal needs honestly and completely. Our dreams can help by guiding us to the source of our knowledge, feelings, and intuitions about mothering in our unconscious. There, we can find new answers and give new direction to our experience of motherhood.

The first issue that we may confront is the choice of whether to be or not to be a mother at all—a choice that has only recently been made readily available to women. This choice is vital to women's control over their bodies and lives. It is a very difficult choice for many of us and one worth examining very carefully, as one woman did through the following dream.

> BABE IN ARMS
>
> Rob and I have just arrived at our destination. We are in a very old, but very well preserved car; he is driving. He gets out and comes around to my side to open my door. I am a little surprised by the formality, but when he opens the door, I find I am holding our newborn baby in my arms and really do need the assistance.

I had this dream at a time when I had just learned I had a medical condition that might soon prevent me from having children. Rob, whom I had recently started living with, told me that he was willing to go ahead and have a child now. I was startled and avoided discussing it. This dream made me confront the issue squarely: Did I want a child? Did I want one *now?* Did I want to have one with Rob? Did I want to get married? (In the dream I represent marriage as an old but serviceable vehicle, which gave me pause for thought since I had always rejected the idea.) My dream made me realize the questions I needed to be asking myself about marriage and children. I finally concluded that I really did want children, but didn't want a child in my life then, even if it meant I might have to adopt one later.●

Once the decision to conceive a child is made, you may be confronted with several other issues during the process of conception and pregnancy. Many women find themselves having to deal with an inability to conceive or with having a miscarriage or abortion. Dreams and dreamwork can be invaluable in such situations for facing and working through the inevitable feelings of inadequacy and loss accompanying such traumatic experiences. These feelings must be dealt with, not only at the time of the loss, but whenever the woman is confronted again with the possible or actual conception of a child. It is important to work through these feelings when they arise, as the woman in the following example does through her dreamwork.

THE BROTHEL BABY

I go to a brothel where I've heard I can get a baby. I push my way into one small room jammed with women. These women—prostitutes—are conceiving and having babies at an incredible rate, without labor or afterbirth. Doll-babies are all over the place—some with black hair and some with blond hair. I go to an even tinier room. Three women are there handling the surplus of babies. I'm aware they are doing something illegal. I hear loud music coming from behind a tiny partition, where a teenage mother lives. She comes out and says she's going to feed the baby now. I feel sorry for the baby and ask one of the women if I can have it. She says no and we argue. The three women are now strangling the doll-babies to death and disposing of the bodies. I get angry but they carry out their deed with a sense of purpose and spiritual clarity. I respect them and walk out. Outside is a police car. I walk home, feeling very sad, thinking about the baby holed up in that horrible place.

Because I was considering having a baby at the time I had this dream, it seemed like a very bad omen. Then I decided to change the dream in fantasy. I went back to the brothel and told the teenager I wanted to love her baby and give it a good home. When she resisted, I strangled her and took the baby away with me. I felt very good about my fantasy, despite the violence, and suddenly understood the dream. I had an illegal (symbolized by the police car) abortion some years ago. I was not ready to be a mother then and took a very matter-of-fact attitude toward it. Back then, at age 21, I saw things in black and white (like the doll-babies' hair) and didn't allow myself to feel any sadness over the abortion. Like the prostitutes in my dream, I didn't "labor" over the issue or have any afterthoughts (afterbirth). The dream was telling me to deal with those "partitioned off" feelings about the abortion now that I was trying to get pregnant. Through changing my dream in waking fantasy, I was able to confront and work through those unresolved feelings. ●

Doubts about being a competent parent also arise during and after pregnancy. This dream by a woman one week before delivery of her first child shows how our dreams can prepare us for the uncertainties of mothering by reminding us of the strengths we may not notice in waking life.

THE JUDGE

Sandra and Aaron are at a court hearing to find out whether they will be awarded custody of their child. The judge (who I think is me) is very knowledgeable in childrearing and will decide who gets the child. She decides that Sandra and Aaron should get custody. They are very pleased but also scared and concerned about the responsibility involved.

At one level I identified in this dream with Sandra (my ex-husband's new wife) and her anxieties about her adequacy as a parent. The presence of

Figure 15-1. Pregnancy Dream by Pat Gerhardstein, reproduced from *Sundance Community Dream Journal, 3* no. 2 (Summer 1979), 157.

the judge also made me aware of the abilities and strengths I had as a potential parent. I could then, as the judge, act as a dreamhelper for the anxious parent part-of-me by judging the parents competent to take on the responsibility of childrearing. •

Concerns about mothering will continue to come up in your dreams and in your waking life, of course, well after the child's birth. Having dealt with them previously through dreamwork, however, will help you to handle your anxiety as it occurs. Similarly, women who have confronted their fears about childbirth and hospitals in their dreams during pregnancy have been shown to have significantly shorter labors.[3] Paying attention to our dreams during this critical transition can thus be of immense value in coping with the stresses of both childbirth and mothering.

BODY CONSCIOUSNESS AND SEXUALITY

From the time we are born, we relate to the world through our bodies. As infants, without the benefit of reasoning, we depend upon our senses for everything we know about the world. As we grow older, we continue to do this far more than most of us realize. There is also evidence that women tend to use even more physical cues and nonverbal communication in their daily lives than men do. Perhaps this is partly because we experience more physical changes than do men.

By the time we reach adolescence, women are acutely aware of their bodies and sexuality. We are constantly reminded of the physical cycles and sensations that are intensifying and changing in us so rapidly. As we enter adulthood, this sensitivity is magnified by the potential or actual physical experience of childbirth. Yet, while such physical experiences as menstruation and childbirth have a tremendous physical and psychological impact on us, they are often devalued by both men and women in our culture. Menstruation is referred to as "the curse," many women are embarrassed about their physical appearance during pregnancy or breast-feeding, and so forth.

It is no wonder that we as women tend to be self-conscious about our bodies in a culture where a "woman's world is the universe of appearance,"[4] where worth and power are determined by what a man *does* and how a woman *looks,* and where the standards by which our bodies and appearances are judged are set by men—in fashion, medicine, politics, and law. Fortunately, women today are exercising more control over what happens to their bodies, making conscious choices and taking stands about their physical functions, appearance, and development, rather than deferring these decisions to men. One woman's struggle to come to terms with her physical self-definition is clearly portrayed in the following dream about leg hair.

CLOSE SHAVE
I am a slave working in a medieval tavern. My "owner," a big, burly, coarse man, is trying to make me shave my legs. I have a coat of silky fur all over my legs and up my back as far as my waist, like a satyr. I refuse to part with it. He gets furious, grabs me bodily and begins to shave the hair away with a razor. I struggle against him, kicking, crying, pleading with him, saying that I will die without it.

I had this dream just after a confrontation with an employer over my unshaven legs. I have always felt that the practice of shaving body hair was silly and unnecessary, and I disliked the stubble that women's legs are covered with most of the time. Still, I have never been entirely comfortable with the way my legs look, since I do have more and darker leg hair than most women. This dream enabled me to be more in touch with my self-image and more comfortable with my decision concerning my appearance. I could be less concerned about other's expectations of me and concentrate more on what pleases *me*.

Our ambivalence about whether our appearance is attractive or proper can be especially keen for pregnant women and nursing mothers. Not only do we have to deal with the conflict about body image that follows any major change in physical appearance, but we also have to deal with our culture's ambivalence about this public display of our sexuality. In the following example, one woman comes to grips with these negative attitudes.

TWO QUESTIONABLE THINGS
I'm at a dance when I notice my pantyhose have a run in them. I go outside in the parking lot to take them off. Two policemen come along and start questioning me and three other women who are there with me. The police say the other women are okay, but I have two questionable things in my record. I go behind a car and try to take off my pantyhose before the policemen see me. Then I notice that the top of my dress has slipped down, and my breasts are showing. I feel uneasy and pull up my dress.

I had this dream shortly after I gave birth to my first child—a clear public indication that I did, in fact, engage in sex! As long as I can remember, I have at times felt a little anxious, self-conscious, and guilty about my body and my sexuality. In working on this dream I came to see the policemen as symbolizing my parents who, especially during my adolescence, were constantly judging and watching over my sexual activity. They were particularly judgmental and punishing just before I became engaged when I had two boyfriends at once—two questionable things in my record.

My mother was very much against my not wearing a bra and always "having my breasts showing." Now that I was nursing my baby (often in public) my breasts ("two more questionable things!") were, in fact, showing—something of which my mother did not approve, as she had just informed me. Working on this dream helped me feel more comfortable about nursing in public, and about my body and sexuality in general. ●

In recent years, many of us have come to recognize our bodies as *sexual* and not just *sexy*. As we give up our need to have our bodies look alluring solely to attract men, we can begin to recognize them as sources of personal and physical pleasure; and we can begin to enjoy our sexuality without self-consciousness and guilt. Women have long been made to feel that any intense sexual desire they might have is deviant, promiscuous, and even sinful. The woman in the following dream is able to confront the intensity of her sexuality and become more comfortable with it.

THE DEMON
I am making love with Paul. There are parts of a poem that I see as we make love, each part describing a different part of lovemaking. We get to the last section of the poem and I realize that if we make love in that way, I will be a demon. I think Paul is a demon—smiling, sexual, and inviting with his long dark hair. He wants me to do this part of the poem/lovemaking; I think he wants me to be a demon. I get very scared and scream—I wake up, crying out.

During my dreamwork, I role played the powerful demon part-of-me: I am a force that gets inside my body, takes over, isn't human; I am sexuality, sexual pleasure. Then I play the rational part-of-me who is scared of the demon part, afraid of losing thought, rationality, control. We have a dialogue. The dialogue between the two parts was helpful because I experienced *both* as parts of me. I then gave myself the message that the demon was human—not inhuman—passion. This demon/human passion part-of-me was the source of the great pleasure I had the night before in lovemaking—and this part did *not* wipe out all the other parts of me. ●

There are other aspects of our sexuality that may be so repressed due to cultural taboos that we may become aware of them for the first time only in our dreams. These include sexual feelings toward family members and toward other women. Our dreams can help us see that feeling such attractions are natural parts of us all. Working on dreams of incestuous or lesbian lovemaking can help us to come to terms with these aspects of our sexuality, regardless of our decisions about sexual partners in waking life, as the following dreamer discovered.

THE HERMAPHRODITE AND THE KEY
I am making love with someone tall and dark, a hermaphrodite. S/he has a beautiful woman's body, and both a penis and a vagina. First, s/he makes love with me as a man would, penetrating me until I climax. Then I make love to her, kissing her and caressing her, penetrating her with my fingers. I take out a large key and use it and my fingers to bring her to orgasm over and over again.

I had this dream at a time when I had both a male and (for the first time) a female lover. I was still not completely at ease about my lesbian relationship or my bisexuality. Role playing the hermaphrodite and having a dialogue with it put me more in touch with my feelings about having sex with both men and women. I also became aware of her/him as a part of myself—that the capacity for loving both men and women was a "key" part of my sexuality and not something to be ashamed of. ●

Another important (often overlooked) area in which sexual feelings or fantasies may arise is the mother-daughter relationship. The psychological literature is filled with references to sexual feelings arising between fathers and sons as well as between mothers and sons (the famous Oedipal triangle, for example), but there is very little written about female homosexual fantasies, perhaps because it has been men who have done most of the writing about these phenomena. There is clearly a strong bond, however, between mothers and daughters that is quite different from the mother-son relationship and that may be experienced as intensely sensual or even sexual in nature. After observing several hundred families, the therapists Norman and Betty Paul theorize that this may be because, for the mother, "there's a thrust to have the kid become a carbon copy of herself. And with a boy it's already different by virtue of gender."[5] As daughters, we may handle this close identification by either trying to be just like our mothers or by rejecting their views entirely. As many of us may know, it is possible to distract ourselves from the intensity of the mother-daughter attraction by fighting with each other.

Acknowledging the powerful sensual and emotional connection with our own mothers and daughters can go a long way toward improving our relationships with them, by freeing us to explore and celebrate *both* our similarities and our differences. Our dreams can help us do this by providing us with the unconscious information we may be unable to confront in any other way. Once we have faced these sexual feelings for our daughters and mothers, we can then deal with the feelings through dreamwork, for, as the Pauls point out, ". . . there is no harm in imagining anything, as long as you know it does not have to be actualized."[6]

One woman discovered the intensity of her affection for her teenage daughter through a dream she had while on a camping trip with her.

THE SAME BODY

I woke up in our tent knowing I had had an erotic dream about myself and another woman. There was no sense of anything taboo in it. I looked over at my daughter and suddenly realized how intimate our relationship is—in a different way from my son. The same body coming out of the same body. I feel one with her.

Another woman dreamer made a similar discovery about her feelings for her mother through the following dream.

INCEST

I am in the master bedroom of my childhood home. An older man (my father?) comes in. He begins to make love to me. I am very ill at ease. I lie on the bed, unresisting but unresponsive. He leaves and an older woman (my mother?) comes in and makes love to me. Outwardly I don't respond, but I am aroused by her and have an orgasm.

As a teenager my relationship with my mother was filled with conflict over my sexual activity. I had this dream later when I was again living temporarily in my parents' home. This dream expressed my uneasiness about my "unacceptable" sex life, and in fact I was so disturbed about the idea of having sexual feelings for my parents, even in a dream, that it was years later before I saw what I might have learned from it: Before my parents, particularly my mother, and I could accept our differences in values about sexuality, we first had to recognize and accept one another *as sexual beings.* This included accepting the hidden sensuality in our own relationship—the physical affection my mother and I expressed toward one another, and the vicarious pleasure we each got from knowing that men found the other attractive (because secretly we consider each other sexy as well). The constant strife in my teenage years prevented us at that time from confronting and accepting the changes that were inevitable in our relationship as it changed from mother-child to include a mutual recognition and appreciation of our womanhood, which includes our sexual feelings. ●

As you can see, your dreams can help you to understand and accept your sexual feelings and sort out your feelings about your sexuality and other aspects of your life. Dreams may sometimes exaggerate or distort, and they always require some examination and thought in waking life before acting upon them; but as you use your dreams to gain a different perspective on the various arenas of your life, you will see yourself in all these dream selves, and be reminded again and again that you truly *are* what you dream.

chapter sixteen
The Alchemy of Relationships

What do women today want from intimate love relationships? Not long ago this question might have received a pat answer: A successful marriage and children should be the ultimate fulfillment for any woman. Familial relationships were expected to be the focus of her energies, providing most or all of her emotional and social needs. Once married, she had little power to change her situation if her choice proved unsatisfying. Today, more women demand partnerships that are emotionally supportive, intellectually stimulating, and sexually satisfying. Many women today are forming committed love relationships with both men and women outside of marriage. Others are openly exploring relationships with lovers different from their own age group, racial, or ethnic background; still others are questioning altogether the traditional institutions of monogamy and parenthood. This is surely a far cry from the options our grand-mothers—even our own mothers—considered open to them!

As Adrienne Rich says, "The possibilities that exist between two people, or among a group of people, are a kind of alchemy. They are the most interesting thing in life."[1] As exciting as this new realm of possi-bilities appears, exploring it can be difficult. Many of us cannot look to our own parents as models for the kinds of relationships we want today.

Having no ready guidelines for negotiating the inevitable changes and conflicts in our close, ongoing relationships makes it harder to confront the new situations and complex feelings they produce. The further away we venture from established social norms about relationships, the more we must deal with our own uncertainties and the negativity or outright hostility we may encounter from our families, social, and work environments.

Our dreams can give us the strength of conviction we need to explore new models for our relationships by reflecting and revealing our deepest psychological and spiritual needs. The following example illustrates how a mid-life dream reflected one woman's intuitive understanding of what she came to want most from a relationship.

THE TWINS
It is night and I see two huge white horses running swiftly amid the stars. The moonlight casts a yellow glow on the twin creatures, who have broad backs and strong legs.

After many years of being married and raising a family I began to question what I was doing with my life and how I wanted to live out the rest of it. For the first time I began to acknowledge my sexual feelings for other women. I divorced my husband and began to explore my sexuality with women, dating a lot of women from various backgrounds. Gradually, I became dissatisfied with just dating, and this dream started to occur when I realized what I wanted most now—to meet and settle down with a woman who was just like me in as many ways as possible. This future relationship became my most important goal, and the dream of the twin horses recurred many times. The dream portrayed the strength and beauty I felt was possible in such a relationship. When I met Joanna, the woman I'm now married to, the dream stopped. ●

Our dreams can help us deal with our love relationships by revealing how we view them, helping to pinpoint problem areas, offering clues for ways to enhance our relationships, and reflecting our progress as we grow. Since any kind of relationship or behavior is acceptable in the dreamworld, there is no limit to the possible choices or solutions available there. The only censor in your dreams is you. Thus, dreamwork offers a wide range of perspectives and options for exploring the relationships in your life.

The life cycle of intimate love relationships can be divided into three basic parts: *coming together, intimacy,* and *being apart.* These same issues underlie close friendships and other close relationships as well; the focus here, however, is on these issues as they emerge in the romantic attachments of women today. You will see how attending to their dream messages enabled a number of women to gain more insight into, and control over, these issues in their intimate love relationships.

COMING TOGETHER

Establishing Trust

Trust is a basic issue in coming together with another person. To establish trust, both partners must be sure of their importance to the other person. Only then can they share the vulnerabilities and fears that can lead to increased trust and intimacy as the relationship grows. Each of us has a personal history regarding issues of trust and mistrust that goes back to our first relationships with our parents and caretakers. These past experiences strongly influence how comfortable we now feel about disclosing or exposing ourselves to others.

By revealing our unconscious fears and desires, our dreams help us understand our needs and make decisions regarding crucial issues of trust, as one woman discovered through a dream she used to establish trust in a new relationship.

> THE GLASS BUBBLE
> I see Rob and go to greet him, but just before I reach him I run into a barrier. He is inside a big glass bubble. He seems to take it for granted. I pick up a rock, intending to throw it against the bubble and shatter the glass. Rob panics and signals that I must not do this. Now we are both extremely upset and frightened.

Rob was a long-time friend, but our sexual relationship was relatively new. I had incubated a dream to help me understand why he seemed to want contact and yet made himself so unapproachable. This dream followed and helped me see that he might not be conscious of the barriers he put between us—and that I was just as afraid of breaking them down and becoming vulnerable as he was. I told him about the dream, and this dreamsharing marked the beginning of genuine trust and intimacy in our relationship.●

Confronting Romantic Myths

Most of us grew up with the romantic myth of the knight in shining armor who will bring us total bliss and eternal harmony. (Such romantic myths are not held exclusively by heterosexual women either: Many lesbians seek to be "rescued" by a handsome Amazon on a white horse!) We need to be more realistic about what relationships can offer and what we must put into them before we can trust our relationships to meet our needs. Our dreams can help us see the unexamined, distorted assumptions we may have about relationships which, if ignored, can lead to deep resentments and disappointments. This frees us to see our partners as they really are, as the following dreamer was able to do.

> POOR FOUNDATION
> Vivian and I are strolling across the foggy moors. The fog rises and I can't see her. I hear a bell and turn to see a cow. I recognize Vivian in the cow and then it changes into a calico cat. Now I'm looking for a house for Vivian and I to share. I find one I like, but the owner says no one can live in the house because the foundation is poor. It begins to rain; I watch several bricks wash out of the foundation, and the house shifts. I'm glad I didn't rent the house.

Through this dream, I realized that I had been seeing Vivian through a thick fog of romantic fancies. I found her large frame and slow movements (portrayed by the cow) extremely appealing. I was also fascinated by her ability to live her life exclusively in the company of lesbians (symbolized by the calico cat, since calicos are always female). While it was a bit sad to let go of my cherished romantic myths built around these qualities, I saw that they were indeed a poor foundation for a relationship. Our relationship improved after I made more of an effort to see Vivian as she really was. •

Making Decisions and Commitments

A frequent, necessary decision in a serious intimate relationship is whether or not to make a commitment to that person. Deciding whether to pursue or end a budding relationship may not be easy; the clues for making the decision may not be readily noticeable in waking life. This is where dreams can be helpful in pointing out problem areas we need to consider in reaching our decision. The following dream alerted one woman to a problem that is of concern to many lesbians—whether or not to become involved with a woman who may still be attracted to men.

FLIPPERS

Jude is swimming with flippers on her feet. A man swims up behind her and tries to hold her legs so she can't swim, and this slows her down. She doesn't resist him.

This dream woke me up to Jude's continuing emotional dependence on men. After thinking about it, I decided to end our relationship. A few weeks later I met Jude in a cafe with her new lover—a man. I was glad my dream had alerted me to this possibility and saved me a lot of potential grief. •

Of course, not all dream messages are as direct as the one in "The Flippers," and they should be examined carefully in waking dreamwork before taking any action. Our dreams can inspire us, however, to think more about a problem, talk it out with the other person, or at least be aware of it before reaching any decision.

Structuring the Relationship

Once you commit yourself to another person, you still have to build a relationship that meets both of your needs. We each come with our own personal history, beliefs, and behavior patterns, and in spite of our romantic notion of "love everlasting," it takes work and dedication to make these mesh. Even if the "marriage" was "made in heaven," the structuring of it has to be done right here on Earth!

Defining a relationship means taking the time and effort to *make clear agreements* with your partner about the nature and boundaries of your relationship. It is especially important to be clear about what you need and want (or *don't* want) from each other. This is not so easy to do, and it is tempting to just fall into traditional patterns. You need not always follow tradition to find answers, however; you can follow your dreams! One woman received guidance in defining what she wanted from her fiancé in the following dream. Here, in the guise of a traditional business suit, a dream figure presents some very *non*-traditional solutions.

THE WEDDING RING

I'm walking along the street with a man wearing a business suit. Suddenly the man goes into a jewelry store and buys a wedding ring. I get mad and think, I don't want a wedding ring. He didn't even ask me about a wedding ring. The nerve of him! When he comes out I tell him this and he says, 'I'm not buying it for you, I'm buying it for me. I want to wear a wedding ring. If you want one, you can buy one.' I think, right on, that's exactly the kind of person I like![2]

Structuring relationships also means being clear with your partner about your expectations on important issues. If you don't do this, you risk feeling disappointed and angry when your own needs aren't met, or guilty and frustrated when you find yourself unable to meet your partner's needs. Once you become more aware of your expectations and those of your partner, you can begin to *negotiate* agreements in which each of you gets what you need. This process is *not* "giving in" or even "compromising." Negotiating leads to both partners feeling gratified and satisfied, and guards against compromising to the point of feeling bored or victimized.

Here, again, our dreams and structured dreamwork can be useful by spurring us to negotiate clear agreements with our partners, lovers, and friends. Our dreams can be particularly helpful in those situations where the traditional solutions available are not acceptable or workable. The following example shows how one woman used a dream to get clues for an agreement with her partner about how to share the space and responsibilities of their new home.

EIGHT TENNIS BALLS
Burt is going to be in a contest that involves doing something with eight tennis balls. There are only four balls in the can. I tell Burt that he doesn't have to worry about the other four balls because I already did those. That will make it easier for us to win.

At the time I had this dream, Burt and I were engaged and moving into a house we just bought together. We were still very much in the process of negotiating how much physical and psychological *space* we both needed as we made this new commitment. The house we bought had eight rooms in it, and we were in the midst of figuring out how to divide them up and share the responsibilities for the upkeep of the house. I knew that I wanted some of my own private space in the house and that I wanted to *share* the responsibilities for housekeeping, but I was still unsure of what seemed "fair." This dream helped me to realize that we could divide things up equally (both the physical space and the responsibility for chores) and that I could feel *good* about that—even though it was very different from what I had been taught and had done in the past. Burt liked this idea. We each got our own study and bathroom and took equal responsibility for the housekeeping chores. It took awhile for us to work out the details, but we had fun in the process and we both ended up feeling like we won something.●

INTIMACY

Despite our good intentions and best efforts, we are often perplexed and disappointed in our attempts to create fulfilling intimate relationships. Often we fall back into stereotyped roles, such as using tears or manipulation to get our way, or giving in to controlling men of the "strong, silent type." We need to find ways to overcome these culturally-induced, destructive patterns in order to achieve intimacy that is fulfilling for ourselves and our partners.

Self-Differentiation

Developing and maintaining our self-identity is perhaps the greatest personal challenge that confronts *all* women today. Because females have traditionally been denied opportunities to grow into full personhood, most women have had to seek their identities through their relationships with men. Even today, when our status in society is rapidly changing, many of us are so identified with particular relationships—or with our supportive and nurturing functions within them—that we depend on those relationships for our identity. Indeed, we often describe ourselves in terms of our relationships with others—as a wife, mother, sister, friend. This "other-identification" while having its roots in traditional sex roles, is not confined to heterosexual relationships. Many lesbians also struggle to discover their own identities apart from intimate partnerships.

Developing this sense of self apart from others is crucial if we and our relationships are to grow and mature. We must learn to respect our uniqueness and understand that personal growth is a "continuing process of self-differentiation . . . moving toward ever greater degrees of individual uniqueness."[3] Our dreams can give us clues for approaching and resolving this issue with our partners in our waking lives. The following dream shows

how one woman got a clearer sense of her need to differentiate herself
from her partner by making her own choices.

LITTLE GREEN APPLES
I'm waiting for James outside a small grocery store. He appears
and we embrace, then go inside the store to buy some apples.
There are many different kinds of apples. He gives me the biggest,
reddest one he can find. I thank him, but feel uneasy, because green
apples are my favorite, and he made the choice for me.

James likes to give me presents, but often he assumes he knows what I
want and makes choices for me. This dream alerted me to how much this
really bothers me. I was reluctant to discuss this with him, but this dream
gave me a clue: I began by thanking him, as I did in the dream, for the
things he gives me and does for me; from there I made him see that I need
to start making more of my own choices. After we talked about it, this
area of our relationship improved. ●

Dealing with Conflict

Conflict in a relationship is not only inevitable, it is necessary and even
desirable. If ignored, stored-up negative feelings can threaten the quality,
if not the survival, of a relationship.

Many of us are afraid of conflict, however. As women, we have
been socialized into the role of "peacemaker," the person who keeps
things going smoothly and peacefully at all costs—even if the price is our
own self-respect. In addition, many women fear conflict because they are
afraid of losing their partners, or of being hurt, physically, economically,
or emotionally. Yet, we must learn that when conflict arises, it presents
us with an opportunity to create new ways to meet the needs of both
partners.

The first step in resolving conflict is acknowledging or taking responsibility, *not blame,* for your part in the conflict. In the following
example, we see how one woman used a dream to see her own role more
clearly in a conflict over how much time she spent with her partner.

THE BLUEBIRD OF HAPPINESS
There is a tiny bluebird loose in my house. I think it is beautiful
and try to catch it so I can keep it. I finally grab it, and it struggles
to get away. One wing gets tangled and breaks. I have squeezed it
too hard and now blood is dripping from its mouth. It finally
flutters away, trailing drops of blood. I feel terrible and am afraid
it will die.

I love to travel but my partner is a homebody. Early in our relationship, I usually passed up travel opportunities because I felt guilty about spending time away from him. I resented "having" to stay home when I was eager to go away, and felt angry at him for "keeping" me there. When I used dream language to own each part of this dream, I saw that *I* was really the one responsible for trapping the free-as-a-bird part-of-me. I then asked my partner how he felt about my spending my free time away. He said he preferred that we spend it together, but that I should do whatever was best for me, and we could work it out together as we went.

Another important aspect of dealing with conflict is acknowledging feelings of anger, hostility, and aggression. Only by fully accepting and confronting these parts of ourselves can we learn to share our feelings in a constructive way. Our dreams can put us in touch with our negative feelings in a private context; then, after we have acknowledged and confronted these feelings, we can discuss the problem area more openly and effectively with our partners. One woman used a dream to help her accomplish this.

THE BROKEN RECORD
I'm at Fiona's and we are listening to music. I accidentally break one of her records and I apologize profusely for doing it, but I secretly feel gleeful at having done it.

This dream alerted me to some angry feelings I had about Fiona's habit of explaining everything over and over like a "broken record." After I dealt with this in my own mind, I was calm and caring in talking it over with her. Once she understood my feelings, she agreed to work on changing this aspect of herself. ●

A common source of negative feelings in a close relationship stems from feelings of jealousy. In addition to romantic involvements, we may feel jealous of many things that demand our partner's time or attention: jobs, hobbies, children, or other commitments. Jealousy can be an especially difficult issue to handle, as we may think our jealous feelings are silly, unjustified, or unbecoming; we may even hide them from ourselves. By confronting these feelings when they arise in our dreams, we can learn to accept them in a positive sense, as the following dreamer discovered.

THE SONG
My husband and Brenda go off to practice a song they plan to perform on the guitar. I notice that they're gone for three hours. I'm very angry. I fix dinner for myself and my son and clean up the

dishes. They're still not back, and I'm getting angrier and angrier. They come back and I tell them how I feel.

It seemed clear to me that this dream had something to do with jealousy, but I was unaware of the connection with my waking life. As I worked on the dream, I thought about my husband and the "triangles" in our lives. He had recently returned from a three-day business trip ("gone three hours") combined with a visit to his mother. It was the first time I had been alone for an extended period since the birth of our second child, and it had been difficult for me to manage everything alone. I didn't think it was "fair" to feel angry about it, though, since he was gone mainly for professional reasons. It was only after working on this dream that I realized my anger at being left alone to take care of the house and kids ("I fix dinner and clean up") while he went off and had a good time "performing" at a convention and visiting with his mother. The dream also brought up my concern about his mother's proposed move to our town and how that might take him away from me. I was used to having him "play his song" and his guitar for me alone (as he had always done in the past). •

When communicating negative feelings to our partners, it is important that we stay in the present and release pent-up feelings one step at a time, rather than dumping out a full "gunny sack" of past hurts. To stay on top of things, we need to share our negative feelings with our partners as soon as we become aware of them. This was the lesson conveyed to one woman by the following dream.

GETTING SHIT ON

I'm camping in a park with Matthew. It is raining and we are trying to pitch a tent, but the ground collapses, leaving a big pit underneath. The pit is some kind of maintenance center, and now instead of a tent peg I'm holding a long white pipe. Raw sewage is coming out, and I want to hook the pipe up to a drain down in the room. I tell Matthew to guide it in, and I slide down the pipe. Meanwhile, I'm hanging in midair becoming completely covered with excrement.

At this time Matthew was deeply involved with another woman and we were just trying to maintain our friendship. He was upset after an argument with her and had just come to me to talk about it. I was glad he did, but I also resented having to hear about her. After this dream I realized how much anger and resentment ("raw sewage") I still had stored up toward him and that, until I worked this through, on my own and with him, talks like this one would seem very cruel and insensitive, and I would feel "shit on." I had been holding in my anger because I wanted to maintain our friendship, just as I had tried to channel the sewage at the maintenance center. This dream helped me see that our friendship couldn't really begin until I took care of myself by airing my negative feelings. ●

Sharing of Caring

Just as we need to share negative feelings about our relationships, we also need to share the high points. This sharing of caring can foster intimacy during the peak times and strengthen our relationships when they are at low points. Our dreams can point to special areas of our relationships that we may not have noted consciously. Sharing these dreams with our partners—an expression of caring in itself—helps them understand what we value in the relationship, as in the following example.

> TICKLED PINK
> Allan is standing with his back to me, wearing a pink shirt. I sneak up behind him and throw my arms around his waist and lift him off the ground. He knows right away that it's me and begins to giggle. I start to tickle him and he giggles even more. He can't stop giggling.

This dream put me in touch with qualities I cherish in Allan—his childlike spontaneity and his overall ease with behavior atypical of males. I had taken it for granted that he was aware that I loved these qualities in him, but found that when I told him about the dream he was surprised and "tickled pink" (and giggled a lot!). ●

Sharing Sexual Feelings

One aspect of many intimate relationships that brings up intense feelings is physical and sexual contact. In recent years, women have become increasingly aware of their sexuality. As we become clearer about what we want physically and sexually from our partners, we can feel more at ease about asking for those things. Our dreams can help by giving us a way in which to share our sexual feelings and fantasies with our partners. Sometimes just sharing a sexual dream, particularly a sexually erotic one, with your partner, can be a useful (as well as stimulating!) way to overcome your inhibitions and increase your sexual enjoyment. Dreams can also be useful in making us aware of physical and sexual needs that we may be otherwise reluctant or unable to acknowledge, as in the following example.

MY BROKEN DOWN CAR

I am listening to a man giving a lecture. I remember that I have an appointment, so I decide to leave at the break. I go over to the man and tell him that I must leave. I feel very affectionate toward him and kiss him. He seems surprised but pleased. I go to try and find my husband. He comes in. I tell him I have a 5:00 appointment and my car is broken down. It is now almost 5:30 and I'm getting very upset.

I had been married for almost 5½ ("almost 5:30") years when I had this dream. Communicating my sexual needs and desires was often still difficult for me. This dream helped me remember that I had been more physically assertive before we were married, and that it had worked out well. Now that I was married, however, I depended more on my husband to take care of my sexual needs (symbolized by the broken down car, as cars are often symbols of sexual energy for me). This dream helped me be more direct with my husband about my sexual needs, which has improved our sex life considerably! ●

Balancing Intimacy and Autonomy

Intimacy takes a lot of energy, and we need regular opportunities to spend time away from it. These periodic reprieves from contact allow us to "refuel" and bring back more energy to the relationship. In order to have both intimacy and autonomy in a relationship, we need to establish a balance between contact and withdrawal. This balance is often difficult to achieve, particularly for women, who have been taught to submerge themselves in relationships to the point of ignoring their other needs. To take advantage of opportunities outside of our relationships, we must be willing to risk expressing our wishes to our partners and act upon them when we need to.

Often we are unsure of what kind of balance we need, for our needs change with the stages and circumstances of our lives. One woman used a dream to reach a decision about balancing her relationship needs with her other desires and commitments.

DONE LOVING

I have a job making evaluations of other people. I have a batch of evaluation forms to return, but my car isn't working and I have no way of distributing them. I tell the boss, Don Loving, that I will hire a taxi so that I can get them back to the people right away. He tells me not to worry, that it can be done later.

I had this dream when I was intensely involved with two lovers at the same time. I felt frazzled at dividing my time between them and also saving time to be alone. The best solution seemed to be to choose one relationship, but I didn't know which to choose. I used to work with a man named Don Loving, who had once quipped that his name could be spelled any way but with an "e," i.e., "Done Loving." This dream told me I was not ready to decide who I was "done loving," and that I should not try to make that evaluation now. It also made me aware of my state of physical and emotional exhaustion, symbolized by the broken car. I decided to take more time off from *both* relationships to be alone, and this turned out to be exactly what I needed to balance my life once again. ●

There is no pat, once-and-for-all decision we can make in balancing our intimacy and autonomy needs. We require both, and we will be constantly called upon to reevaluate the best ways of meeting those needs, for ourselves and for our partners.

BEING APART

In any intimate relationship, separation is an issue that both people must eventually confront. Even the best relationship may involve temporary separations due to illness, travel, or job relocation. The longer such separations last, the more each partner is likely to experience changes in routine or lifestyle, as well as emotional reactions to the loss, such as grief, anger, and depression. The separation need not be a long one to evoke such feelings, as one woman discovered.

THE ONION AND THE SHOE

I'm buying some shoes. A friendly woman waits on me. As I leave I notice someone trading in an old pair of shoes for a new pair. I go back and ask about that. The saleswoman tells me I can make a trade-in, but I have to put an onion in each shoe. I decide to do that and think about returning the pair I just bought.

I had this dream when I was out of town for a weekend workshop while my husband was home taking care of our baby. I had recently learned that my mother had a serious illness, and I had been dealing with my feelings about her mortality. This dream helped me realize how much more work I still needed to do around the issues of separation and loss, and how much they were brought up by being away from my husband and child. I would need to deal with these issues like an onion—a layer at a time. The onion image in the dream helped me acknowledge my need to cry and release the tension and sadness I felt about my mother's condition, something I had not done yet. While my old habits of avoidance and denial of pain were comfortable, like old shoes, they were no longer useful and could be traded in, like the shoes, for new and better ones.●

Creating New Patterns

When separation is permanent, the transition from being together to being apart is more difficult. Such a major change is almost always stressful, even where the change is seen as being for the better. An important relationship fulfills special needs and plays specific roles in our lives; partners usually pattern their lives around each other's daily routines and meeting one another's needs. After separation, new friends and activities may fill in the gap left by the absent partner, yet, more often than not, this transition forces us to confront ourselves and create new patterns. Our dreams can help us do this by suggesting ways to reshape our lives constructively. Such was the case with the following dreamer.

THE FOUND PART

I live in a huge house filled with many interesting people and several servants. I hear music in the street and run to my window. Below is a marching band. They need a clarinetist, so I hunt for my old band uniform and my instrument and run downstairs to join them.

I had this dream after I had broken up with my lover and was looking for ways to develop aspects of myself that I had neglected during our relationship. The dream pointed to my need for music again, something I had neglected because my lover had no interest in it. I found that getting back into my music again was a tremendous benefit, and it provided a vehicle around which I was able to make new friends and experience new things.●

The loss of a partner may be devastating and may require building an independent life from the ground up. This rebuilding process may seem particularly difficult if we feel lonely or depressed and, hence, inadequate to show the world the "better" side of ourselves. During such a period, our dreams can aid us greatly by validating our feelings and providing needed healing energy, as the following dreamer discovered.

HIGH AS A KITE

I am following Bruce on a suspension bridge across a bog. The bridge begins to sway violently, and I cling to the ropes for dear life. All of the bridge except the rope I am grasping dematerializes, and the breeze blows me gently skyward like a kite. Now the wind begins to die, setting me closer and closer to the surface of the marsh. Instead of falling into the morass, however, I stand on top of it, my feet not even wet or soiled. The breeze carries me aloft again, and I find myself on the opposite bank. I awaken feeling exhilarated.

Bruce and I had just separated to live on opposite coasts. Our parting was friendly, but we both knew it was permanent, symbolized in this dream by the "suspension" bridge. I had grown very fond of him, and I felt very sad at first about being separated from him. I was afraid of missing him and getting "bogged down" in depression; I wanted to feel good about the time that we had together while not regretting my decision to go my own way. This dream helped me to do this, as all I had to do was recall the imagery to lift myself above sadness, just as the exhilarating breeze lifted me above the marsh. Then I could recognize how much joy was there, too, in the memories of our relationship.

It is important to learn from our past relationships, so that when we move on, we take the positive aspects of the relationship with us and leave the negative ones behind. This is especially important to do if the relationship ended with bad feelings. In such cases, we may carry our feelings of vulnerability or defensiveness with us, making it difficult to establish more satisfying relationships in the future. Instead, we need to examine our contribution to the difficulties in the relationship. Once the problem areas of the old relationship are resolved, we are then free to pursue life from a fresher, wiser perspective, as this dreamer discovered.

THE WELL-FORMED TURD

I see a white hexagon figure, full of love. It indicates the best way to relate or act. It seems so easy. "Why don't more people do it?" I ask. Now I'm sitting on the toilet. I defecate a huge, round, well-formed turd. I feel good!!

I had this dream during a dream workshop in which I was working on feelings toward my ex-husband. We had been divorced over a year, but I was still angry about unresolved financial issues in our relationship. This dream helped give me a *physical* experience of what it was like to carry around all that "shit" and how good it could feel to get rid of it! Only after taking responsiblity for my anger and letting go of it in the dream, could I recognize and act on positive feelings I had for my ex-husband. The answer to my question about love in the dream was in taking responsibility for my own shit in the relationship. Shortly after this dream, my ex-husband and I settled our financial disagreements to our mutual satisfaction.●

Dreams, then, can help us deal with a wide range of complex issues that arise in our relationships. They are a ready source of information about unconscious feelings that need to be acknowledged and confronted. If we use our dreams constructively in this way, they can lead us to greater self-awareness and intimacy in our relationships.

chapter seventeen
We Are All
Each Other's Family

"FAMILY" IS A STATE OF MIND

We learn our most basic beliefs about who we are and how we should relate to others from our families. Much of this childhood learning runs so deep that we are not even aware of how it affects us. One of our tasks as adults is to sort through this legacy received from the family we grew up with—our family of origin—to keep and thank our family members for what was useful, and to grow beyond and forgive them for what limited us. This is how we earn our separate personhood. We all go through this process to some degree, playing out and seeking resolutions to childhood dramas in our relationships with friends and mates, and with our own children. Family dreamwork can help us to see this process more clearly, to work toward resolutions without forcing limiting roles and perceptions upon ourselves or those we love.

Family dreamwork may mean sharing dreams and working on un-resolved problems with your parents or siblings directly, if they are willing to join you in letting go of old patterns and beliefs in search of new ones. It can also mean sharing such dreams with friends, lovers, spouses, or children, and recognizing similarities—real or imagined—between the relationships with them and your relationship with someone in your family of origin. This kind of intimate sharing means shaking yourself out of old patterns that seemed safe and comfortable, exploring new possibilities, and taking risks that can pay off in personal growth and richer family relationships.

Family dreamwork can be useful to you, whatever your lifestyle. Many of us have close relationships outside of the traditional family structure that provide us with the kind of nurturing and support a traditional family might offer. Because such individually tailored networks include the people we turn to for meeting our family needs, these people can also share in our family dreamwork. In fact, dreamwork can be especially helpful in such situations. These nontraditional networks are often less stable than traditional families; dreams can help us cope with the uncertainties of relationships and commitments in which we are quite literally making up the rules together as we go along. They can also help us confront the potential or actual loss of someone important in our "family" as our networks rearrange themselves. Most of all, dreams can help us approach our family relationships creatively and openly, supporting one another in our personal growth.

The most powerful example of family dreamwork, in this broader sense, is that of the Senoi Indians, discussed in Chapter Three. Anthropologist Kilton Stewart claims that in their society, dreams and dreamsharing are a pathway to a peaceful, cooperative lifestyle in which each person, through the gifts from dreams, makes an important contribution to the common good of the family. Everyone is encouraged to transform anything negative or threatening in the dreamworld into a positive image, and to get something useful and creative from it to bring back with them into waking life. By resolving conflicts and fears symbolically in the dreamworld, and expressing these victories through dreamsharing and other daily activities, the Senoi are reported to have lived in harmony for generations. While we don't live in such a thoroughly supportive environment, we can use the Senoi as a model of what a family committed to dreamwork can do to help one another.

We also play important roles in the unfolding of those around us, not just with our immediate family members; thus, we are all each other's family. We have a responsibility to bring to each other the tools we need to grow, and the acceptance we need to recognize our faults and strengths. Women are often more aware than men are of this caretaking responsi-

bility, because it is part of our traditional role as the center of the family—
the childbearer, the nurturer, the peacemaker. Our task is to recognize
these roles as resources for bringing people together in all facets of our
lives. Perhaps someday we may all recognize our connection with each
other as a collective family. For now, such recognition can be achieved
in our dreams.

FAMILY OF ORIGIN

Separating ourselves from our family of origin is part of growing into
adulthood. Along with social and financial independence, we must also
achieve psychological independence. This last task is often the most difficult and prolonged struggle.

To win our psychological independence, or to become fully differentiated, we must come to see clearly the early messages we got from
our parents and siblings. Many of these are positive, helping us to grow and
encouraging us to develop our strengths. Some of these early messages,
however, limit us and our awareness of our own assets and virtues.

For women, the negative messages often assume the form of dis-
approval and discouragement of developing such traditionally masculine
traits as independence, assertiveness, and risk-taking. Furthermore, we are
often given mixed messages about the valuable characteristics we *are*
allowed to develop, such as emotional expressiveness, nurturance, intuition, and sensitivity to others. The message we often get is that such
qualities are really weaknesses that make us unfit for taking care of and
standing up for ourselves, or for doing anything but serving others.

As adults we can rework these negative messages into positive ones
that can serve as stepping stones toward a more confident and flexible
self-image. Though often difficult, this process contains promise even for
those of us with painful childhood memories, like the following dreamer
who was a victim of child abuse.

THE COINS
I'm walking through a store that my mother owns. I find some sand-
wiches and cakes. I take little bites, then wrap them up again so no
one can tell they were opened. I decide to buy something. As I'm
counting my currency, I realize some of the coins in my hand have
greater value than their face value. I keep these and spend the ordinary ones.

As a child, my mother often beat me and showed no consistency whatsoever in punishments and rewards. In the dream I'm taking nurturance (food), something I needed and never got. In keeping the valuable coins, I'm trying to extract something useful from my childhood. I think the "change" in my hand represents my desire to confront and deal with my past so I can *change* myself and my life for the better. My father is a coin collector, so maybe my knowledge of the hidden value of the coins represents things I learned from him that are more valuable to me than they appear at face value. ●

As influential as our childhood experiences may be, we are not at their mercy. Many of us never fully realize this and thus go on giving ourselves as adults the same old negative messages we received from others as children. Only by accepting our own part in perpetuating our destructive attitudes and behaviors can we come to recognize our power to change them. The dreamer of "The Coins" discovered this when she had the following dream, in which she began to take responsibility for her feelings of helplessness and victimization.

THE WILD RED HAIR

I see a man with wild red hair and wild eyes. He's wearing a military uniform and he's beating a dog, shouting "I'll teach you to behave yourself!" I cuss him, and tell him to stop. I say I hope the dog bites him good and hard. He sics the dog on me. The dog comes at me and I tell it, "You've got to get away from this man!" The dog sides with me and we run away together. The dog is wearing chains and harnesses, and as we run I start to break the chains off the dog's body. The man doesn't catch up with us, but it is a struggle to stay ahead of him.

The man represents my mother, who has red hair and wears a white uniform. My dream portrays a military uniform because of her violence, cruelty, and authority. In doing a fantasy ending for this dream, I had the dog go back and bite the man. It occurred to me later that I didn't take complete control and beat up the man myself. I haven't faced her yet, but I see myself moving toward someday confronting my mother more directly about my childhood. ●

Such confrontations are not always easy. Yet if you are willing to risk shaking up the old patterns of communication with the members of your family, dreamsharing can lead to greater closeness and understanding at many levels, as the following dreamer discovered with both her mother and brother.

THE FOREST OF NO RETURN

I'm standing on a beach with my parents and my younger brother. There are woods right behind the beach, and I run off chasing my little brother through them. They are dark and forbidding and remind me of "the forest of no return" in one of my favorite childhood movies. I'm running in effortless leaps, and my brother runs as fast as he can to stay ahead of me. I can hear my mother cautioning us not to go too deep into the woods, but already she sounds very far away.

Although by the time I had this dream I had grown up and moved off from the world of childhood (the beach) into the unknown and unexplored territory of adulthood ("the forest of no return"), there was a part of me (symbolized by my younger brother) that was still struggling (running "as fast as he can"). I still felt guilty when I asserted myself with my mother, even though I pretended to turn a deaf ear to her criticisms (Mother sounds "very far away"). After working on this dream, I was better able to talk to her about both my love for her and my need to live according to my own values.

This dream also made me more aware of my *brother's* struggle to grow up. As children, our relationship was marked by a lot of competition and teasing, and we fell into these old patterns whenever we were together again. I talked to him about this the next time I saw him, and we agreed to work to change this pattern. This resulted in the first closeness and real sharing we had ever experienced together. ●

FAMILY OF CHOICE

Your family of choice, whether a committed partnership, nuclear family, or non-traditional network, is a setting for two important life tasks or discoveries. First, it is in your family of choice that you play out, and hopefully resolve, the old "baggage" you carry with you from your original family. Second, in your family of choice, you explore and learn about yourself in new and unfamiliar roles such as career woman, breadwinner, lover, mate, or mother. In both these areas, we often use our own parents as models for our new adult roles. Even though we may not like some of the things our parents did, we often find ourselves repeating their mistakes. Paying attention to your dreams can alert you to how you may be carrying old patterns with you into other relationships. Dreamwork, especially with members of your family of choice, can help you create your own more realistic and adaptable ways of interacting with them and others in your life.

Having a source of insights such as dreamwork for dealing with family issues may be especially important for women, since we tend to maintain closer ties with our families of origin than men do, and are more likely to feel pressure from our parents concerning the way we manage our family life. Furthermore, because men often still think of the family as the woman's domain, a woman with a male partner may be expected to initiate all the changes in family interactions.

Dreamwork With Your Partner

Chapter Sixteen gave you an idea of how useful dreamwork can be in dealing with the significant relationship or partner in your life. Taking this a step further and doing dreamwork *with* your partner can help both of you become clearer about what your needs are and how to make them known to each other. It is thus a productive and creative way to involve your partner in the process of expanding the relationship with you, as one of the authors describes.

> THE STARLING
>
> I'm walking in the snow. I find a bird lying on the ground, frozen to death, and I pick it up. It is a starling. Its tongue is frozen to the roof of its mouth. I pry it loose. As it begins to warm in my hands, it starts breathing again—it isn't dead after all. I put it down expecting it to fly away. Instead it hops a few steps and begins to preen itself, surprisingly unafraid of me for a wild bird.

Right from the start of our relationship, my partner and I shared our dreams with one another. We started a dream shield of the most important symbols in our dreams, and talked about how we visualized these symbols and what they meant to us. I decided to incubate a dream to get a symbol for the focal point in the middle of the shield and had "The Starling" dream. ●

In a previous relationship I often dreamed of trying to catch a wild bird at times when I was feeling "caged," stifled, and unhappy in the relationship. Invariably the bird tried desperately to get away, and I always ended up hurting it, even though I meant well. Both my partner and I had many symbols of flight in our dreams, representing our "high" ideals for ourselves, our sexuality and sexual fantasies, freedom and independence, spiritual growth, even fears about the relationship and flight from confronting them. We came into our relationship with a lot of fears about becoming trapped or caged by the other's expectations and emotional needs—fears we found very difficult to talk about (the "frozen tongue"). Yet, by trusting one another enough to share our dreams and discuss our hopes and fears openly, difficult as it sometimes was, we set one another free, like the starling, to explore our relationship and be nurtured by its warmth.

Figure 17-1. Dream Shield: Images of Flight by E. Ann Hollier and Dick Delanoy

Dreamwork With and About Children

Dreams can also help us explore and improve our relationships with our children. It is hard to integrate the needs of another person into our lives no matter what the relationship. This is particularly true when that relationship is with a young child who is so dependent on us for caretaking. The issue for us as mothers and active women today is how to integrate mothering into our lives in new and balanced ways. This means acknowledging and meeting both our own needs and those of our children. This is easier said than done, of course, but vital nonetheless to our well-being and that of our children and families. Without this kind of balance, we risk either feeling hostile and angry as we martyr ourselves, or feeling guilty and selfish as we meet our own needs. The mother in the following dream dealt with both sides of this issue after the birth of her child.

> THE PLASTIC BAG
> I'm lying in bed. Samantha is on the floor next to me. I notice that she has a big plastic bag covering her face. I jump out of bed and try to pull it off of her but can't. She looks like she may not be breathing. I panic!

I was getting up during the night to nurse the baby and was often tired during the day. I had taken time off from my business, but felt selfish about taking naps, and felt guilty about "neglecting" both work and the baby. This dream helped me to relax some of my tension and resentment, and to look again at my "selfishness." I changed the ending of the dream in fantasy to see myself calmly taking the plastic bag off the baby so we could both breathe easier; I then gave myself the time to enjoy nursing my baby and to nurture *myself* by going to sleep and getting some rest. I still have trouble with this issue of my "selfishness," but working on this dream helped me feel better about my initial decision to take some time off from my job and my baby to meet my own needs.●

Women's opportunities are expanding as we enter the work force in increasing numbers to pursue careers. But liberation at home has failed to match this move toward liberation in the work force. Thus, many women find themselves working two full-time jobs, one at home and one at the office—often at the expense of their family life. In this new age of the liberated "superwoman," it is all too easy, as Betty Friedan points out in her book *The Second Stage,* to ignore the impact of our new found freedom on ourselves and our families.

> . . . in our reaction against the feminine mystique, which defined women solely in terms of their relationship to men as wives, mothers, and homemakers, we sometimes seemed to fall into a feminist mystique which denied the core of women's personhood that is fulfilled through love, nurture, home.[1]

We do ourselves and our families a disservice if we deny or play down the importance of family in our lives.

One way to stay in touch with our family needs is to pay attention to our children's dreams—to value and discuss them as a family. Because dreams reveal our innermost thoughts and feelings in a concise, symbolic way, they can be a convenient way of getting to the heart of matters in our families quickly but sensitively. A child's dream can be a "red flag," calling our attention to a dangerous or important turn in the road, and cautioning us to *slow down* and be aware.

It was a "danger signal" from her three-year-old son that called the attention of one of the authors to her family shortly before the birth of her second child. Through her son's dream, as follows, the whole family gained a new understanding of the feelings they were experiencing in anticipation of the forthcoming addition to their family.

> THE SCARY CLOWN
> Mommy is a scary clown, with a painted face and one big nipple on her neck. I say "Go away!" Daddy comes in and says, "Go away!"

My son woke up in the middle of the night and shared this dream. I was six months pregnant and growing larger quite rapidly now. He seemed to be responding to these changes in my body when he saw me in this dream as "scary" looking or deformed. This alerted me to the impact of my pregnancy on him, something to which I hadn't paid adequate attention. We started talking about the changes occurring in my body, and this seemed to alleviate some of his (and my own!) anxiety.

I suggested to my son later that perhaps the one nipple meant that he was afraid I wouldn't have enough "milk"—time, energy, or nurturance—available for him when the baby came. He taught me a thing or two when he immediately said, "No, I think there won't be enough for the *baby*!" This alerted me to his expectations about the baby's place in the family (especially when he said that the baby would have its *own* mommy and daddy!), and cued me in to some "scary" feelings we all needed to deal with in regard to the new baby—feelings of jealousy, confusion, and fear. As a result, my husband and I started talking to each other more about our feelings, needs, and fears as well. After the baby arrived, we continued to use this dream to help us all discuss and understand our feelings about having a new person in the family.●

One way to encourage your children to share their dreams with you is to tell them your own dreams. Sharing yourself with your children in this way conveys your caring and fosters intimacy with them. Even a very young, preverbal child will be able to pick up on the intensity in your voice and appreciate this shared experience at some level.

As with any story you would tell your children, you need to consider how appropriate it is for their age and level of maturity. Another important thing to remember in sharing your dream stories with your children—especially the younger ones—is not to leave them with any unresolved or scary feelings. You need to take time to discuss or work on the dream together, especially if you share an unpleasant dream. For example, you can make up a fantasy ending for it with your child that gives it a "happy ending."

If there is a message in the dream you want to share with your child, playing with the dream symbols can be a powerful way of communicating it; children—and most adults, for that matter—are more likely to listen to an interesting story than a lecture! Such was the experience of one mother in a dream she shared with her children about drowning.

THE DROWNING

I'm at a lake with my husband and two children. They're near the dock and I'm swimming. Suddenly they all jump in the water. The children sink. My husband gives me a shocked look and then goes down to get them. I dive down, too. I can't see anything—the water is cloudy and muddy. I'm scared but not panicking. I wake up suddenly.

I had this dream shortly after my son, age 3½, jumped in water over his head at the swimming pool; I had to dive in and pull him out, since he did not know how to swim. I had acted quickly, without panicking as in the dream—but I was quite upset by the incident. I had not really dealt with all my feelings and fears about it, as this dream made me realize. I needed to be clearer with my son and myself about the dangers of the water; I needed to think seriously about teaching both him and my infant daughter to swim—especially before we moved to our new house on a lake! Telling him this dream enabled me to share my fear with him in a concrete way. (My daughter was also in the room when I told the dream, and she watched and listened intently all the way through it.) I sensed my son's fear as I told him the dream and immediately added a new ending to it: I rescue my son and my husband saves my daughter. I then breastfeed the baby; she coughs up the water in her lungs, cries and goes on nursing. I felt competent and strong after doing this dreamwork with my children, and this feeling stayed with me the rest of the week. This was particularly helpful since my husband was away and I was home alone with both children for the longest stretch of time since they were born. ●

Once you start sharing your dreams with your children, they will often spontaneously begin talking about their own dreams more often.

You will need to be prepared to answer their questions and help them deal with whatever comes up in your dreamwork together. To this end, you can use many of the approaches you have already learned from working on your own dreams. The following dream was shared by the three-and-a-half-year-old son of the previous dreamer, shortly after he and his mother had worked on "The Drowning" dream together.

THE BAD BOY FAIRY
I'm lying in bed and a bad boy fairy puts something in my eye. I try to rub it out and can't. I'm mad and scared.

My son told me this dream in the car one morning on the way to school, about a week after we worked together on "The Drowning." I asked him if he wanted to work on it, and he replied, "Yes, and *change* it!" When I suggested he pretend to be the "bad boy fairy," he put his hands across his face, which he said was "putting on a mask." The bad fairy, who reminded him of a playmate, said he was "just teasing." I asked my son if the bad fairy had any message for him, and he had him say "I'm sorry." Then he took his "mask" off and was quiet for a while; before getting out of the car, he turned to me and said, "Mommy . . . I love you." ●

As you can see, sharing your dreams with your children and encouraging them to tell their dreams to you can be a very rewarding experience. Young children may not understand or be prepared to deal with the psychological interpretation of dreams; but they can still benefit from many of the other, more playful and intuitive approaches discussed in earlier chapters. They see dreamsharing as an exciting kind of storytelling, and they soon learn to look forward to it, blissfully unaware that it is also "good for them." Dreamsharing can also help you to understand your children better and make you more sensitive to their needs as they grow and change.

In addition to active dreamwork, you can help your children make their own special dream books. Write down their dream stories for them if they are too young to do so themselves, and encourage them to draw their own illustrations in space set aside for that purpose. Later these dream narratives can be expanded and used to make up stories together.

You can also use dreamwork with your children to help them exercise and enjoy their own imaginations. They can use their dreams as a rich source of materials for making up stories and drawings. Dreamwork can be used as a fun way of helping your children sharpen their writing or artistic skills, or even as a creative and educational alternative to television. Let their enthusiasm for such projects be your guide.

Helping your children explore their dreams in ways such as these can teach them to appreciate and nurture their inner experience. As they grow up in an environment that supports such exploration and takes the gifts of imagination and intuition seriously, they will be less hampered by many of the obstacles to growth and creativity that so many of us have had to overcome or unlearn as adults. Though not without its struggles, this process of sharing and learning from dreams can help everyone in your family stay on top of needs and changes as they arise, so that you can meet them in ways that will help all of you nuture, support, and learn from one another.

chapter eighteen
Aging
Is Becoming

YOUNG ADULTHOOD

For young girls and adolescents, getting older means becoming bigger, stronger, and more attractive. By age twenty, however, we are also concerned with what our aging will bring as we enter the strange and often frightening world of adulthood, as the following dream dramatically illustrates.

DIANA
I am standing with the goddess Diana in her temple. We are laughing and standing arm in arm on a balcony overlooking a courtyard within. Diana listens benignly to some people standing below us who have come to her with a petition. Now I am floating down a river. There is much merrymaking and music on the river banks. The ceremony ends and I wake up.

I had this dream on the night of my twentieth birthday. I had celebrated the day on top of a mountain and that, together with thoughts of entering a whole new decade, combined to make this birthday an almost spiritual experience, a rite of passage. I suppose that Diana, goddess of the hunt, the forest and wild animals, and of fertility, represents my awareness of having entered an age of new possibilities, of becoming an adult. ●

As we get older, we are forced to leave behind our familiar childhood identity and deal with dramatic changes in our self-concept. Rarely are we helped or prepared to deal with these age-related changes as they arise in our lives. Little attention has been paid until recently, even by psychologists, to the major states and issues of adulthood—"marriage, parenthood, career advancement and decline, retirement, widowhood, illness, and personal death."[1] Even less attention has been given to the particular patterns and needs of *women* in adulthood, which, as we shall see, are often very different than those of men.

Finding ways to cope with the imposing tasks of adult life is often difficult for us as women who, unlike men, are rarely encouraged to take an active responsibility in directing our own lives. Rather, we tend to rely on others, particularly men, to do the guiding for us. Paying attention to our dreams is a way of becoming more aware of the impact of these adult tasks on our lives. Working on these issues as they emerge in our dreams can help us take responsibility for doing the directing ourselves.

The main issues for women in their twenties relate to illusions and concerns about intimacy, commitment, and marriage. Until very recently, a young woman was told that the primary and proper goal for her was to marry "Mr. Right" who would "complete" her and take care of her and the children she would have. Even today, most of us would like the "perfect mate" who would solve all our problems—with little or no cost to the "perfect career" we may also hope to have! Then the fantasies of our twenties become the realities of our thirties: The expectations of our girlhood have not been and may never be realized. We may feel cheated, angry, or discouraged about the "mistakes" we thought we made and the choices we felt forced to make, like the following dreamer.

> BLOODY MURDER
> A man has stabbed a woman to death and leaves her body in the woods. I don't want him to get caught, so I roll the body into a ravine and try to cover the bloodstains in the dirt. I feel no remorse about her death.

I had this dream right after the man in my life told me he might be transferred out of state. After much discussion and soul-searching, I decided it would interrupt my career too much to go with him then. I felt this was the right decision, yet I still felt depressed and uneasy. This dream showed me how I had allowed my "masculine" ambitions for a career and professional competence to "kill off" my awareness of and openness to "feminine" relationship needs. Acknowledging these needs would be difficult, as they also brought up feelings of vulnerability and loss, yet it was important to recognize them and not pretend that they were dead. I know now that I will be confronted with such choices many times in my life and that I must learn to balance my career and relationship needs and be open to the feelings that arise from them. ●

Old illusions die hard, but more and more young women today are taking on adult tasks in ways that reflect new and original solutions. Many of us, for example, are devoting ourselves to careers earlier and having children later. This often upsets the familiar rhythms of life and aging. Unless we learn to bend and adjust, it can lead to tension and conflict in our lives—which will then be reflected in our dreams. Dreamwork helped the following dreamer resolve some of her concerns about aging by bringing the conflicting demands of parenthood and career up to consciousness.

LIFE AFTER FORTY
A young woman (in her twenties) is upset because she can't go out for the evening. An older woman (in her thirties)—me?—comes in and tells her that there are benefits to staying home.

I had this dream in my late thirties when I was eight months pregnant and home with the flu. I felt I was missing out on things (sports, social, and entertainment activities). It was also harder to give as much time and energy to my career, which made me feel even more frustrated and anxious. In working on this dream I had the older woman part-of-me describe the advantages of spending time at home: time to work with my plants, to cook, to write, to make love, to play music, to read, to rest, to enjoy the house inside and outside—fixing and organizing as well as playing, and finally time to do some "nesting," preparing for the baby's arrival in the house. Then I got a message from the younger woman part-of-me as well. This was most valuable in widening and balancing my perspective on spending so much time at home. She pointed out that there were still ways I could incorporate the parts of me that like to go out and work and "boogy" into my life. She pointed out that my husband and I can still go out and have a good time together with and without the children, that there is indeed "life after forty." ●

> ... Sometimes I'm surprised by an encounter with the mirrored image of the woman I've become when I wasn't looking. Curses! Snow White lives! And I am middle-aged, despite my youthful denial of such inevitability.[2]

As the words of this woman writer show, by middle age, we become increasingly aware of the distance and differences—physical, emotional, and cultural—between ourselves and the young. Most women first tend to notice the physical cracks in our mirrored image. From that point on, instead of measuring our age in terms of "time-since-birth," we tend to see our lives in terms of "time-left-to-live."[3]

Exactly when middle age begins is a very touchy and debatable question—one which many of us would rather ignore or delay. (It took one of the authors several weeks, even as she was working on this chapter, to realize that she was in fact entering middle age herself!)

For women, the age of 35 is a watershed—the age beyond which conventional wisdom says it is risky to bear a child. Many women may find themselves having dreams at this age about whether or not to have a child, or any more children (see Chapter Sixteen). Notions about delayed childbearing may be changing with women's new career orientations and the advances of medical science. Yet, for women, awareness of the approaching end of our childbearing potential often marks the beginning of what has been called the "Deadline Decade" or "My Last Chance."[4]

Most of the major dilemmas of our lives cluster between the ages of 40 and 60, and women are confronted with these issues, physically and mentally, somewhat earlier than men. Thus, somewhere between the ages of 35 and 45, we may find ourselves in the midst of a full-fledged midlife crisis; we know now that time is finite and our youth is behind us, but we are not at all sure how to cope with this startling realization.

It is certainly tempting to deny the awareness of our aging in a culture such as ours which reveres youth over age, particularly in the case of women: An older man is distinguished; an older woman is just "old." Working with dreams can give us some clues for dealing with this "double standard of aging"[5] in productive and creative ways. If we continually deny and reject the aging, older woman in us, we risk ignoring significant feelings, opportunities, and continued growth that can enrich our lives as we grow older. Our dreams can serve as a "mirror" to remind us that "Snow White lives," and we are getting older whether we like it or not.

While we are dealing with the sudden sense of our bodily decline at the onset of middle age, we are also reaching our sexual peak, which for most women occurs in the late thirties. At this stage, we often begin to fantasize and dream about having a new lover to restore our sense of physical and sexual attractiveness at a time when our rising sexual energies may no longer be met by our partners. We may also begin thinking and dreaming about new, more assertive ways to express and satisfy our sexual needs. The following dream shows how one middle-aged woman was able to use her dream message to revitalize her sex life with her husband.

THE SEX STORE
A woman (middle-aged) ushers me into her store. She leads me to a couch (examining table?) and prepares me to make love with a man who is coming (young, dark hair, moustache). At first I'm put off, then I get into it.

In working on this dream, the middle-aged woman part-of-me tells me that it's okay to be up front, direct, and assertive in "examining" or initiating the sexual part-of-me; it's nothing to be embarrassed, shy, or anxious about. She epitomizes the middle-aged woman at the peak of her sexuality. I'm impressed. The man who comes in looks like, or is, my husband. I remember that when we met and were dating I was very assertive with him physically and it worked out nicely—so why not do it *now!* ●

Another dramatic physical change that confronts the middle-aged woman is the climacterium, or *menopause,* from the Greek work signifying the end of the monthly cycle. Between the ages of 45 and 55, menstruation stops, and we can no longer get pregnant. While it may be final, however, the "change of life"—the awesome popular term for menopause— need not be as traumatic as many people seem to expect. Profound biological changes and some unpleasant physical discomforts occur during menopause; but the hormonal shifts are gradual, the discomforts are temporary, and neither these changes nor their symptoms need lead to depression or a mental breakdown as the "old wives' tales" might have us believe. As one post-menopausal woman said, it is necessary to "separate the old wives' tales from that which is true of old wives."[6] While many women should still go to their gynecologists to have the poorly understood "hot flashes" or other physical symptoms of menopause treated, the problems connected with this midlife transition in our female existence are as much social and psychological as they are biological.

The greatest emotional difficulty of the climacterium may be dealing with the loss of our reproductive capacity. Just as physical responses to menopause vary with the individual, so our reactions to becoming barren will depend on what being fertile has meant to us personally. Because it seems vague and mysterious, particularly to the younger woman, menopause and sterility may come to be associated with our fearful, unpleasant expectations of what growing old means, that is, the supposed end of our sexual desire and attractiveness.

Identifying the potential problems and fears of menopause helps us to control them as they come up—in our waking lives and in our dreams. The following example shows how one woman's menopausal "symptoms" disappeared after dreamwork when medical treatment failed.

MENOPAUSE
I'm going through menopause. I'm in the hospital having a hysterectomy. My husband leaves me because I had the hysterectomy. I wonder if he has another woman.

A middle-aged woman had this dream after she went to see her doctor about spotting and skipping her period. The doctor gave her pills for "nervousness." She talked with one of the authors about this dream at length, and it was suggested that she tell her husband about it. The next week she said that she had *stopped* the pills and *started* her period! Although her husband told her he thought her dream was "silly," she felt much better after their discussion. ●

Not all women have a difficult or negative reaction to menopause, however. Only ten percent of the women interviewed in one important study regretted the ending of their menstrual cycle.[7] In fact, most middle-aged women experience a "recovery" once menopause is over and feel "better, more confident, calmer, freer than before."[8] Rather than feeling run down, the post-menopausal woman may emerge with a burst of vigor and renewed energy. No longer preoccupied with procreating (or not procreating!), she can focus her reawakened powers of creativity on new pursuits.

Even before menopause, we may find ourselves becoming aware of the many new opportunities available to us in our middle years. This is a time for consolidating the experiences and learnings of our youth in order to reach a mature self-knowledge in what, for many of us, will be the most productive years of our lives outside the home. Now we have more time and freedom to focus on fulfilling *ourselves* as opposed to just caring for *others*. Our initial fears can be transformed into renewed energy. Interviews with both married and single women show that women consider this sense of increased freedom and confidence to be "the most conspicuous characteristic of middle age ... the beginning of a period in which latent talents and capacities can be put to use in new directions."[9]

While many middle-aged men are experiencing increased job pressures or even job boredom, we may be just discovering our hidden strengths and desires—and be feeling less guilty about acting on them! This is reflected in the dreams of middle-aged men who are having more daydreams about failing and guilt while women are focusing on success dreams.[10] Similarly, as they enter the middle years of life, men become more responsive to relationships and nurturant feelings, while women are more inclined toward and less guilty about aggressive and self-centered impulses.[11] These changes at midlife may permit more men to express their emotions and more of us to assert ourselves in creative and self-assured ways.

As we begin to assert ourselves at this mid-stage of our lives, we may feel exposed and "on the spot" in some new and challenging areas. Our dreams can be especially useful in helping us deal with this important transition point in our development. The following dream of a middle-aged woman artist, prior to her art opening in a major gallery, shows how paying attention to dreams can increase our sense of confidence in our newly found abilities.

SUCCESS

TV cameras and crews and a crowd of people roll up in front of me outside my studio. The spotlights and cameras light up and I am "on." Two men are pressing charges because they looked in my studio and saw boxes piled up there, stamped with the initials of the local community college. In my best lawyer-like style, I talk about what a great place the community college is and how they are always short of funds. Then I talk about how wealthy these two men are, and since they are both builders, that perhaps they could design and construct a storage addition as a gift to the college. That way the college wouldn't have to store boxes anywhere they could find—like they had done in my studio. As the TV cameras and lights swing over to the two men, I know I have won.

This certainly is a dream I couldn't have had earlier in my life. In fact, the conflict I won with these two men in my dream made me aware of how much more self-confident and forceful I am now than I ever used to be. This awareness led directly to my confidence at my gallery opening the following week.●

For the successful career woman, the jolt of mid-life is often experienced as a fear of time running out. Will there be enough time or energy to accomplish everything? Can all the demands be met before it's too late? Like the hurried rabbit in *Alice in Wonderland,* she may feel there's "no time to say hello . . . goodbye . . . I'm late, I'm late, I'm late!" Such were the concerns of a young career woman just entering middle age and in the midst of developing her own growing and demanding professional practice.

INTELLECTUALLY IMPAIRED

I go to my gynecologist's office. The nurse tells me that the delivery of my baby has left me "intellectually impaired"—still able to function "but not like a professor." I yell and get angry that the doctor didn't tell me about this before. I run out of the room . . . I run over to a woman who's standing near a podium talking to several people. I try to tell her something I want to have her announce at the business meeting. She's too busy to listen now. I leave . . . I see my friend Kathy. She's rushing—then she comes back. We lie down next to each other with my head in her lap. She kisses my forehead and says she loves me. I cry hard for a long time.

I had this dream when my daughter was about three months old. I had already gone back to work but didn't feel like I was functioning up to par ("like a professor"). I felt highly critical of my weaknesses and imperfections. Like the busy woman at the podium, I didn't take the time to listen to the "impaired" part-of-me. In fantasy I had this professional woman part-of-me announce: "You can do it! There's no rush. Take your time—and take care of yourself." I was glad to see that I could let the caring friend part-of-me (Kathy) accept me and take the time to care for me, if only in my dream. Hopefully, I will hear her message more clearly now in my waking life as well! ●

Middle-aged women who have stayed at home most of their young adult lives tend to have a somewhat different view of the time ahead than do men or career women. They may be overwhelmed by all the leftover time after the children go away to school, to work, or to marry, and they are faced with an "empty nest." This transition is especially felt by women for whom devotion to the home and family has been the primary source of their identity and self-esteem. Unlike men, women tend to define their roles and status in terms of events within the family life cycle. To lose this organizing force in her life is a tremendous blow to the mother for whom the nurturing role has been the raison d'être of her adult life.

Many men experience a similar loss of structure and meaning in their lives after retirement; but with a woman, especially the devoted caregiver, "retirement" can come a good twenty years sooner.[12] She may find herself feeling useless, rejected, scared, and lonely—and these feelings will be reflected in her dreams. (Middle-aged women have been found, in fact, to have the highest incidence of nightmares and sleep disturbances of any group.[13]) During this transition, she may have a difficult time accepting her children's increasing separation and independence from her; she may feel both responsible for the troubles that befall them and, at the same time, powerless to protect them from the pain and disappointment that is an inevitable part of their growing up. It is not surprising, then, to find many post-mothering, middle-aged women having dreams such as the one following.

THE BAY BRIDGE

I'm on the Bay Bridge with my husband and daughter. My daughter is in a red wedding dress, standing on the edge of the bridge. I reach out to her, but she falls and sinks into the water. My husband doesn't help. I wake up in tears.

I had this dream shortly after my daughter left home for California. She was having a lot of trouble making the adjustment there alone. This dream was an emergency call to me that she needed my help. It put me in touch with the pain I felt about being separated from her and about what she was having to struggle with on her own. I was aware that it was time for her to make a life of her own (in her "wedding dress") but that she was in danger and still needed her family at this "bridge" or time of transition in her life as well as in my own. It got me in touch with the fact that her predicament was not so much "my fault" as an issue for us all—my husband included. I took this dream as a message to go and get my daughter and get her some help. Subsequently, we all went into family therapy for awhile, and she returned to California with *all* of us feeling better about her leaving this time.●

In our middle years, as we permit the previously unknown parts of ourselves—both positive and negative—to emerge, we are inclined to spend more time taking stock of our lives, restructuring and redefining our ex-

periences and our very identities. It is in this period of increased introspection and self-evaluation that we confront a truth we have known but
feared and avoided facing all our lives: Each of us is ultimately alone. No
one, not even those closest to us—partners, friends, children, parents—can
know us or be there for us completely. This realization is a particularly
difficult one for women, who have been taught to depend on other people
and to serve others in order to feel worthwhile. As Gail Sheehy found in
her interviews with middle-aged women, the idea that "autonomy equals
aloneness" relentlessly pursues women at the crossroads into midlife.[14]

A major factor that can bring these realizations to the fore in middle
age is the aging or loss of our parents. For perhaps the first time since our
adolescence, we are sharply confronted with our ultimate separateness
from them. As children, we can feel secure and protected in our families;
and as long as our parents are alive and well, we may continue the illusion
that, whatever happens, there will always be someone who can take care
of us. With the illness and death of one or both of our parents, however,
we feel exposed, unprotected, and alone. Perhaps no other event in our
adult years has the emotional impact on our evolving self-image as the final
separation from our parents—their deaths—which for most of us occurs in
our midlife. Difficult as this loss is, it can provide us with the impetus to
turn to our inner strengths and resources and develop a new and deeper
trust in ourselves.

Our dreams can help us on this difficult and often lonely journey to
discovering the strength in our aloneness by helping us understand our
feelings and giving us a way to make sense of the confusion and pain we
may experience. One of the authors discovered this when her aging parents
both contracted serious illnesses.

TAKING CARE OF ME
I'm taking an exam in a small glassed-in room behind a classroom. I
can't concentrate, don't know the answers or understand the questions. I have my books and notes there and think of referring to
them but don't. My son is with me, distracting me. I'm getting
angry, frustrated, and upset. I give the exam to the professor. My
dad is next to me. He explains to the professor that I just had a baby
a few days ago and am not functioning well yet and shouldn't be
out. I feel foolish and stupid. I feel warmly toward my dad.

I had this dream shortly after the delivery of my second child and was
feeling very tired, isolated, and vulnerable ("glassed-in"). I wasn't at all
sure that I could pass the "test" of taking care of a house and two chil-

dren. My father offered to pay for a nurse or household help, and I agreed even though I felt I should be able to do it all on my own (without "books and notes"). Afterwards, I felt very grateful to him for "taking care of me" in this way. My father became ill and was hospitalized a short while later. I went back to this dream and worked on it then, focusing on my increased concern and need for him. I also re-worked the dream so that I took charge of dealing with the professor and the exam on my own. Working on the dream thus helped me to acknowledge my desire to be taken care of as well as my ability to function on my own. Being aware of these two sides of myself has helped me cope with both the birth of my child and the aging of my parents. ●

After the death of our parents, we may find ourselves thinking and dreaming more about losing our spouses and mates as well. The role that our partner may have filled to protect us from the fear of being alone in our middle years gradually ceases to provide us with security. As if in preparation for the likely solitariness of our old age, we begin to anticipate it in our dreams, as did this woman in her fifties.

LOST
I am lost. I look for Lowell but am unable to find him. I'm scared.

I have lived with my brother Lowell all my life. It is hard to imagine being without him. After the death of our parents, I began to have this "Lost" dream recurrently. Hopefully, paying attention to it now and acknowledging the feelings more openly will help me deal with my fears of being alone in the years to come. ●

OLD AGE

This is not a good society
in which to grow old or be a woman.[15]

The realities of growing old as a woman in our society today may seem harsh indeed. By their middle seventies, most older women are widowed, and almost half of them end up living alone. To complicate matters, women over age 65 are also much more likely to live below the poverty level than either younger women or men the same age.[16]

Most women are not prepared, psychologically or practically, to be alone and self-sufficient in old age. We have been so programmed to look and act as youthful as possible that old age often seems alien to us when it arrives—something that happens to other people. When we come face to face with the stark realities of old age, we must confront once again the need for finding out who we have become and what we are capable of in this new era of our life. Where can we turn as old women for answers to the difficult questions and trying situations we face in our old age? Are millions of us doomed to loneliness and poverty in our old age? As always, but perhaps more so in our old age, we need to cultivate and appreciate our connections with other women and with our dreamlife to give us support and guidance as we search for solutions to these challenges. The following example shows how one older woman worked with other women and her dreams to find new confidence and competence following her husband's death.

THE BREAD LINE

I'm standing in a bread line. When it comes my turn the woman serving soup tells me, "Oh you can have all the soup and bread you want." I eat but am still hungry, so I go back for more. I'm still hungry, regardless of how much I eat.

I dreamed this right after I lost my husband. My only job in life had been to look after the household and the family so that he could go out and earn a living for us. His life insurance provided me with enough money to live on, but now I was bored and didn't even know what I wanted to do. I felt like I was in that bread line, fed and clothed but unsatisfied. I wanted desperately to share my dream and my feelings with someone, so I joined a consciousness-raising group. I got a much better feeling there for my own life—what I liked and what I didn't like, things I had never thought about before. Through the group, I met a woman who hired me to help run her pet shop. Even though I could get by without the money, I really enjoyed my work, and let me tell you, that's a good feeling to have! ●

Like the woman in "The Bread Line" above, you may be faced with the illness or death of your mate or spouse in your old age. No other life event is considered as stressful as the loss of one's partner; and this event may be even more difficult for women who have been taught to depend on their mates for their identity and survival. Yet, as "The Bread Line" dreamer discovered, we can overcome this programming and choose to respond differently at this crossroad in our lives—finding new options and resources within ourselves to rely on. Turning to our dreams and to other women can be helpful and comforting in dealing with our aloneness after the death of a spouse or loved one. We have the power to transform our experience of loss by making our dreams *work for us* in both our waking and dreaming lives. One woman in her seventies whose husband had just died was able to do this by learning from a friend's negative reaction to a dream. Although her own dream experience was similar, she was able to use it positively in dealing with her own feelings of loss.

I had been speaking with a widow friend one evening who told me that her husband appeared to her regularly in her dreams, embracing her as he had when he was alive. She said she would wake up feeling sad that he wasn't really there.

I rarely remember my dreams except for an occasional nightmare, but the next morning I remembered the following dream:

TOGETHER AGAIN
I'm in bed and feel my husband's arms around me. I feel warm and content as we sleep together. I'm pleased and excited when I wake up.

My only regret when I woke up was that the dream didn't last longer! Now that I know it's possible for me to have such a pleasant experience with my husband in my dreams, I'm going to try to remember them more often. ●

In addition to the loss of our partners during old age, we must also face the reality of an increasingly shrinking social life in many other ways as well: Fewer and fewer people are around to interact with or to provide support; our children are involved in their own lives; other family members and close friends are dead or departed. Not all of us will rebound or reorient ourselves after these losses as effectively as the women dreamers in "The Bread Line" and "Together Again." Instead of greater self-awareness and flexibility in old age, many of us find increasing rigidity and despair. The loss of attachments and shrinking of our social life in old age can lead to severe depressions, states of panic, and even suicidal thoughts. While these reactions are possible, of course, in both sexes, they are more powerful for the older woman who suddenly finds herself without all the relationships she has depended on, and without the physical energy or preparedness to deal with the reality of this loss.

If we look to the dreams of older women, we will often find the intensity of these feelings presented in graphic form—to be confronted and worked through in constructive ways. Such was the case for an eighty-

year-old woman who had been depressed since her recent move to a
nursing home, and who was able to find reason for hope in the following
dream, even in the midst of her despair.

SWAN SONG
The river is in flood—flowing swiftly. Swans begin to come, carried
by the current. I grab them and collect them on the bank. Just as I
have them all, someone comes to say I can't do that and will have to
give them back. I do, except for two that a young man has taken. I
get in trouble because he took the swans away.

I am in a nursing home. I am going blind and I don't remember things
very well. I hurt all the time. I can't even get out of bed without help any
more. Sometimes I pray to God to let me die. There are so few things left
for me to enjoy. Most of the people and things that used to give me pleasure have been taken away from me, like the swans. I am so glad the man
hid two of the swans. I got in trouble, but I know he is saving them for
me. It took a long time, but I am learning that even in this place there is
beauty, and hope, and things to look forward to. ●

Another theme that frequently appears in our dreams as we near the
end of our lives is *reminiscence,* or a reviewing of the past. Many people
think of this kind of looking-back process in the aged as a psychological
ailment or "symptom" of old age. On the contrary, the *life review* has
been found to be "a naturally occurring, universal mental process . . .
prompted by the realization of approaching dissolution and death"[17]
While it may happen at any time in our lives, it is more likely to occur
in our later years because of the actual nearness of the end of our lives.

Rather than being dysfunctional, the self-awareness that comes with
reviewing our past can lead to a constructive reorganization and reintegra-
tion of our entire personality. It may even be a necessary part of our last
maturational task as we reach toward a realization of our integrity. This
integrity involves an acceptance of our origins as "the one and only life
cycle . . . that had to be."[18] This is a phase, then, of discovery, completion, and final consolidation. Our dreams can help us in this summing-up,
review process by pointing out the areas and relationships in our lives that
remain unresolved. For women, these issues often involve a review and re-
working of our relationships with our mothers. We may find ourselves,
like the sixty-three-year-old woman in the dream following, finishing argu-
ments and coming to understandings with our mothers in our dreams as
we never did in waking life.

MOTHER LISTENING

I'm with my mother explaining things to her. She's listening. I tell her, "I hope you understand why I did all those things."

After my mother's death I found myself having many dreams about her. After this particular one, I felt at peace about my mother as I never had before.

Like this woman, we may find our past coming up for review in our dreams naturally. We can also be more systematic about the task of our life review by using dream incubation or guided fantasy. One such fantasy from a dream workshop one of the authors gave for mothers and daughters is presented as follows. Her comments on her own mother's response to the fantasy show how meaningful life-review fantasies and dreams can be to both the older person and those around her.

MOTHER FANTASY

Imagine that you are with your mother . . . Notice where you are. See yourself there. Notice what you look like, what you are wearing, how old you are. Notice what she looks like, what she is wearing, how old she is. Now imagine that you start to argue. Hear what you say . . . Hear what your mother says . . . Now imagine that your mother is growing older and older, and that she won't be with you much longer—so that this may be your last chance to say what you need to say to her. Tell her now what you've always wanted to say. Hear the words. Notice how you feel . . . Now hear your mother saying what she needs to say to you. *Be* her speaking—and notice how she feels . . . Bring the conversation to an end . . . Now reach your arms out and embrace each other. Say goodbye for now . . . and come back into the present.

My mother tells me that she heard her mother in the fantasy tell her "I did the best I could." Tears come to her eyes. She tells me that she recalled how her mother protected her from everything—perhaps too much. Then she tells me that she did the best she could with me. She takes a pearl hair comb from her purse that belonged to her mother and gives it to me. I'm very touched since it's the only thing either of us has of my grandmother's. We both cry.

When she started telling me about her experience with the fantasy, my mother said she thought it was better not to bring those things up. I encouraged her to let out her feelings, that it might help her and that it was helping me. She continued on for several minutes—speaking of herself as a child, as a mother, and as a grandmother. Later that day I heard her reminisce about her mother in a carefree, joyous manner for the first time since her mother's death almost 20 years ago. ●

This fantasy shows how sharing dreams and fantasies in the course of the life review enables you to reveal untold or unknown truths to your loved ones that can increase intimacy and improve the quality of lifelong relationships. One older woman was able to do this with her two reluctant daughters by discussing the following dream with them.

LIFE PASSING BY

I'm sitting in a room talking to my two daughters. I tell them that life is passing me by, and that I want them to know that our life spent together was important to me. I tell them to remember those enjoyable times.

My daughters had been reluctant to talk with me about my feelings connected with my aging and death. Sharing this dream with them gave me a way to communicate to them my desire that they feel no regret or guilt about anything that happened between us. I feel much better and closer to them since I communicated this. ●

Like the two daughters in "Life Passing By," many of us are afraid to even consider the issue of death, viewing it as something negative and morbid. Fortunately, these attitudes are changing today. We see a growing awareness about death that is changing the way many of our institutions deal with death. Hospices are being set up so that dying persons can live out their last days with dignity and support. Courses in death and dying are now taught in schools, and specialized counselors are offering a safe environment in which dying people and their families can come to terms with death and its consequences.

Perhaps the most difficult aspect of dealing with death comes when we are confronted with the issue of our own mortality, as we must do in old age. Our dreams offer us a safe, private, and personal context in which to explore feelings about our own mortality. Following is a dream that helped a woman who had always feared death.

FIELD OF WHEAT

I am standing on a small hill looking at a field of golden wheat. I think what a shame it is that people are buried in boxes deep in the ground where their bodies cannot continue to nourish life. I think about the possible life forms that changed and became part of the soil that fertilized this beautiful crop of wheat, and how the wheat will be used to nourish people and animals. I decide that after I die

I want my body to be part of this cycle of life, death, and rebirth. For the first time, I think about dying and feel very good inside.

After I had this dream I checked into the burial laws of our state. I was disappointed and angry to find that the laws forbid any kind of burial where the body can decay and nourish plant life. In having my will drawn up, I dictated that my body be burned and my ashes scattered at sea, so that my body could become part of the ocean and help to nourish plant and animal life there. ●

Once we come to terms with our experiences from the past and with our death in the future, we are more free to live in the present. Those of us who have always avoided the present and put great emphasis on the future are especially prone to the anxiety and despair of old age, for with so little time left ahead, the future can no longer provide the hope it once did. It is in this final stage of our lives that we can perhaps finally choose, like the incomparable Katherine Hepburn, the "commonsense now." Rejecting the possibilities of an afterlife or prolonging her life in suffering, Hepburn queries unsentimentally in an interview with *Ms.* Magazine, "Life is very hard, isn't it? It does kill you, after all."[19] Maintaining such a positive, here-and-now view as we age allows us to live out our lives with increasing wisdom, integrity, vitality, and serenity. The following dream of a vibrant seventy-five-year-old woman educator shows how we can go on enjoying our lives productively even in old age.

NO BED, ONLY STANDING ROOM

A young student of mine has won a contest with the finals to be held in Chicago. She asks that I make her reservations. I call and do so. I am told they will have no bed, only standing room. I try to call again, but the alarm wakes me up.

This dream reminds me that I don't need to feel so old that I need to take to bed. I don't feel old—I have to look in the mirror sometimes and see my wrinkles to remember I'm not still 35 years old! I hope to keep on standing in the present as long as my legs will hold me. When people ask me how an old woman feels, I'll keep telling them to ask my Aunt Sue—she's 92! ●

As our dreams helped us throughout life, so too can they help us up to the very moment of death itself. If we trust them, our own dreams will provide the comfort and courage that, at the last moment of our lives, we can derive from ourselves alone. A poignant example is provided in the thoughts and dreams of the great-grandma on her deathbed in an intensely moving story by Ray Bradbury.

THE LEAVE-TAKING

A long time back, she thought, I dreamed a dream, and was enjoying it so much when someone awakened me, and that was the day when I was born. And now? . . . Ninety years . . . how to take up the thread and the pattern of that lost dream again? . . . Now, yes, now she saw it shaping in her mind quietly, and with a serenity like a sea moving along an endless and self-refreshing shore. Now she let the old dream touch and lift her from the snow and drift her above the scarce-remembered bed.

Downstairs . . . she could hear them living all through the house. 'It's all right,' whispered Great-grandma, as the dream floated her. 'Like everything else in this life, it's fitting.'

And the sea moved her back down the shore.[20]

Like Great-grandma above, we as women today, whatever our age, can learn to appreciate the wisdom of our gender and our age as they are reflected in our waking lives and in our dreams. Rather than feeling ourselves decline with age, as our culture would lead women to believe, we can *choose* to grow older—to seek out and savor the self-awareness, sense of urgent energy, focus and relish of life that come with age. By paying attention to the messages in our dreams, we can understand the wisdom of these words:

Old age is not an illness, it is a timeless ascent. As power diminishes, we grow toward the light.[21]

chapter nineteen
Out of the Sheets and into the Streets

THE POLITICS OF DREAMING

We have seen how dream insights help us by revealing the images we hold of ourselves—our *personal beliefs*. These beliefs can motivate us to change, or we can use them to perpetuate our personal status quo.

Our dreams can also reveal *cultural beliefs,* ideas that our society holds about itself. Cultural beliefs may be difficult to see, simply because we are so immersed in our culture that we do not often look at it objectively. Yet, the same "bird's eye view" that our dreams provide into our personal lives can also be applied to our cultural beliefs. This broader perspective is, in fact, a natural and necessary extension of our journey to self-discovery. Following is a dream that helped one woman discover both her personal and cultural beliefs about violence and dominance.

BOYS AND GUNS
The planet has been nuked, and everything is in ruins. I am with a group of survivors—men, women, and children, cooperating with one another to rebuild what has been lost. A bearded man, wearing a smock, is taking care of children. I have been given the task of fixing a motor vehicle.

Then some men wearing army uniforms hold their guns on us and say, "We're taking over. You're coming with us or we'll shoot you!" One woman says, "Don't you realize that what you're doing is what caused this in the first place?" We try to convince them that guns and force are harmful to human existence, but the men won't listen. I think to myself that they have the bodies of men but the minds of mere boys. I wonder what's going to happen to us.

As a blind person, I am used to dealing with all kinds of prejudices. In this dream, it felt good that *I* was the one doing vehicle repair, and no one seemed to think anything of it. I liked the fact that a gentle man was taking care of the children. The smock he was wearing symbolizes a nurturing, matriarchal attitude toward the world. It makes me sad that so many men are more like the army "boys" in my dream than that man. The dream seemed to be telling me that people have the potential to work together cooperatively, even though most people in our culture believe that guns and force are necessary to get things done.●

As this dream shows, dreams draw upon situations and events from both our inner and outer worlds. Thus, while a dream may reflect our weak spots, it may also point out flaws in the culture of which we are a part. Just as our dreams can heighten our awareness of ourselves and provide us with ways to improve our personal lives, they can also raise our consciousness about our world and show us ways to improve it. As we take control over our own lives through our dreamwork, we become more aware of the impact we can have on others as well. This is not as difficult as it may sound. The most ordinary events in your daily life—the products you buy, the electricity you use, the natural resources you waste or preserve, and so on—all have meaning and impact on the world around you. Thus, actions in your personal life can be *political* statements as well as personal ones. *The personal is political.*

Learning to look *beyond* the face value of our actions is vitally important to women. First, once we become aware of the wider influence our actions can have, we can exercise our personal choices to support those issues and beliefs vital to us as women. Second, as *many* of us withdraw our time, energy, and money from negative, prejudicial practices and spend them in positive, life-affirming ways, we will see a shift in the basic power structures and institutions that affect our lives. Our actions affect other actions, which affect other actions, and so on. Thus, we are all "political activists" whether or not we think of ourselves as such, just by the way we live our everyday lives.

As women, many of us are so accustomed to reacting to life situations in passive ways, that we may not see opportunities for taking action and effecting changes when they arise; or we may see them but fail to act on them assertively. Our dreams can help us see the potential value of our private actions in the public arena, and give us clues about where and how to put our energies to work. Such was the experience of one woman in the following dream:

> THE PICKLE JARS
> I go into the pantry to get a jar of pickles. The jars have fallen onto the floor. I pick them up and put them back on the shelf, but they keep falling off. I'm confused and frustrated because I don't know whether or not they should be on the shelf. I decide my grandmother would know, so I write to her and ask her what to do.

I had this dream while I was trying to get pregnant and reading a book on choosing the baby's gender. The book suggested buying a particular product and inserting it into the vagina to test for acidity. At the drugstore I ran into a salesman for the company that made the product. He said the product had not been tested for internal use and should definitely not be used that way. I thought about my dream and called upon the wiser, "grandmother" part of myself for advice, realizing that some action I might take could save a woman consumer from getting into a "pickle" by using this product inappropriately (it "shouldn't be on that shelf"). I then wrote to the book's author, as well as to the product's manufacturer, suggesting they publish a warning on the product.●

Many dreams offer information that you can use in a political or social setting. By learning to look at your dreams in this light and balancing your dream information with common sense judgments, you can bring the "politics of dreaming" into your life and put it to work changing others' lives as well as your own.

DREAMS IN THE SCHOOLS

Children often unconsciously adopt beliefs and attitudes from their parents and cultural surroundings which, if left unexamined, can limit their outlook and experience. Young people in particular need to be exposed to a variety of beliefs and value systems if they are to exercise their alternatives for structuring the future. They are confronted with a world in which the measures of personal worth, success, and the roles of women and men are no longer as clear as they once were. In the midst of this confusion, they must discover—or create—internal standards for judging themselves and others.

Looking at these standards and attitudes as they are expressed in dreams is a nonjudgmental way to help young people develop more open and tolerant views of themselves and the world. It can be more convincing to talk about the harmful effects of materialism, racism, or sexism, when children see these ideas reflected in their dreams. Using their own dreams, moreover, can help personalize such issues for students in a way that more traditional modes of education may not.

Public schools, with their emphasis on reading, writing, and arithmetic may seem like an unlikely place to put dream power to work. Yet, one of the authors used dreams as a source of material for teaching basic skills *and* educating students about their inner world at the same time.

During a junior high school workshop, students kept a dream journal and were given time at the beginning of class to record their dreams. Much of their academic work revolved around dreams: In science they learned about the characteristics of sleep and dreaming. In English they used their dream reports to study paragraph and sentence structure, grammar, spelling, and creative writing skills. In art they made dream drawings and collages. The students' own dreams were used to illustrate common dream themes, archetypes, and characters; in this way they learned basic concepts about the psychology of dreaming.

The students' dreams were also used as a way of helping them explore issues that were important to them. The following dream of a sixth-grade black girl in an integrated school, helped both black and white students air feelings about integration and racism.

THE BROTHERS

There are two monsters called gargantuas. They are brothers, one mean green one, and one brown one. They destroyed our city, even though the brown one didn't want to. He was trying to stop his brother.

Sharing this dream about brothers of different colors led to a class discussion of what it was like to go to an integrated school. Because the students had become accustomed to sharing important feelings with one another through dreams, this potentially explosive issue could be explored in a non-threatening way.•

Another dream, shared in a class of seventh-graders, led to a discussion of sex roles and sex-typing.

THE PACIFIST

A monster attacks me. I turn and confront it with a hold on its neck. My brother appears and tells me to break the monster's neck. I look in the monster's eyes and realize that I do not have the heart to kill anything ever.

Seventh-graders are often preoccupied with their budding adult sexuality and are very concerned with acting appropriately for their sex. Never again will many boys act so macho or girls so coy and helpless as they do at this age. This boy's dream was in striking contrast to other dreams he and his male classmates had, which were often violent and preoccupied with dominating or subduing others. Through discussion of the dream, both boys and girls were able to air some of their feelings of pressure to conform to roles and expectations that were sometimes constricting. They had an opportunity to explore the notion of being "womanly" or "manly" without exaggerated sex stereotypes.

Dreamwork, then, provides a creative way of extending education into the exploration of values and personal or cultural beliefs. It can help correct the imbalance that currently exists in schools toward competition and the mechanical learning of skills. By placing the tradition of reading, writing, and arithmetic in a meaningful context of personal experience through dreamwork, perhaps we can help our youth to apply their skills more effectively and live fuller lives as adults.

DREAMS IN WOMEN'S SPIRITUAL AND RELIGIOUS GROUPS

Because dreams often contain powerful personal images of our spiritual values and beliefs, we can use our dreams to guide us in relating to our religious and spiritual groups. Whether these groups are traditional religious institutions or informal groups with non-traditional beliefs and practices, our dreams can point the way to participation in the shared support, values, history, and rituals of the group in a way that enriches our own personal quest for spiritual enlightenment.

The histories of many religious and spirtual traditions are full of accounts of dreams and visions that had a profound effect, not only on the dreamer, but also on the spiritual community with which the dream was shared. You do not have to be a religious mystic, however, to use your dream insights to enrich your experience in a spiritual or religious group. Even though our society today does not generally regard dreams in this way, you can still experiment with using them as a focus for your own group explorations of spiritual symbols, values, and beliefs.

One structured exercise you might try requires each person in your group to choose and share three symbols from their dreams that represent some important aspect of their spirituality. One dreamer, an agnostic who had largely rejected conventional religion, had the following reaction to this exercise.

When I began to think about how my spiritual values were reflected in my dreams, three symbols immediately stood out:

- *The Goddess*—This powerful dream guide is a teaching figure, representing my awareness of and connection with the order, beauty, and wisdom of the universe, which some call God;
- *The White Eagle*—My perfect self in my dreams, a magnificent creature representing what I can become if I can free my spirit from earthly distractions and imperfections;
- *The Indian Dancers*—I feel a strong affinity for the Indians' search for spiritual awakening through an intuitive and mystical relationship to the forces of nature and the hidden forces within ourselves.

Realizing that my spiritual values are reflected in such a personal, daily experience as my dreams brought home to me the value of relating the experience of group worship to the rest of my everyday life in a meaningful way—something I had rejected as impossible before.●

An exercise such as this can help group members clarify their spiritual or religious identity and foster a sense of community through the exploration of shared values and beliefs. For example, the Indian dancers mentioned previously appear in "The White Armadillo," a dream discussed in Chapter Nine. The dream was shared during a dream workshop for Hadassah, a Jewish women's group, and members of the group reenacted the dance of the Indians. As the dreamer comments, "Acting out the dream was the culmination of what the dream was trying to express, bringing us together, putting us in touch with ... ourselves and one another." This coming together of the group through the dream dance was also significant for the dancer-participants, one of whom describes her experience saying, "As we went around, I felt more and more at one with the others. It was as though any motion I made was a part of the whole group's will." The shared experience of the dream dance helped the participants become more aware of their common bond as a group.

Dreams can also make you more aware of the impact you can have on your spiritual support group and the contribution you can make to the shared experience of a spiritual or religious ritual. The following example shows how one woman asked her dreams to help her contribute to a Hollowmass (Witch's New Year) ritual.

> CROSSED STICKS
> On my table I find two sticks, one crossed over the other, and a rock balancing on the center.

This dream reminded me of the Hawaiian custom of crossing two ti leaves and anchoring them with a stone when setting out walking on a trail, a practice that honored the goddess of the trails and made the path safe for the traveler. Since we were celebrating our chosen "paths" for the new year, this symbol of safe passage seemed an especially appropriate offering to bring to the Hollowmass. I went out to search for the things I wanted and quickly found two ti leaves but not the stone I wanted. I had had several dreams about Pele, the Hawaiian goddess of fire, destruction, and volcanoes, and I decided to ask Pele to help me find it. After meditating and invoking Pele, I felt myself being led to a dark area near a flower bed. I reached far back under a bush in the dark, and my hand came directly down upon a lava stone that was exactly like the one I had dreamt about.●

DREAMS IN BUSINESS AND GOVERNMENT

"How in the world," you may well ask, "can dreams affect business and government? Wouldn't I be laughed right out of the office if I suggested that dreams can make a useful contribution to executive decisions?"

We aren't suggesting that dream insights take the place of balance sheets, research data, and annual reports. Business and government executives constantly encounter, however, important policy decisions without enough hard facts to base them on. Further, their behind-the-scenes wheeling and dealing demands that they be wizards at interpersonal diplomacy. Anyone who can't handle tough decisions or deal with delicate interpersonal conflicts will not get very far.

Situations such as these require good "instincts," and the person who trusts and uses her intuition is way ahead of the game. Since dreams seem to be part of women's natural intuitive strengths, why not use them? We may find that our dreams contain useful information about ways we can influence our work situation, as in the following example.

WOMEN WORKING
Two women and I are all three playing the same guitar together. We are singing the song, "Women Working." We are having fun celebrating our joy in being women working together.

When sharing this dream at a dream workshop with two women present from my women's writing collective, it occurred to me that our collective was too task-oriented and could use more focus on feelings. Perhaps we could begin our work days with dream sharing, or set up a dream group so that we could get closer to one another. The two other women from the collective liked the idea, so we suggested to the rest of the members that we make dream sharing a regular part of our group activity. We now have a dream group that meets every week.●

These women were fortunate to work in a setting where they could openly use dreams to enhance the interpersonal side of their working relationships. In the following example, a dream warning showed one woman working in a more traditional work environment how to define her work responsibilities more clearly with her boss.

THE BRA
The boss hands me some money and tells me to go out and buy his wife a bra. I don't want to do it, but I take the money and say, "Yes, sir." I go to a department store but I can't choose one because I don't know what will fit her. I leave the store and go back to work, resolving to tell the boss that a bra is a very personal item, and he shouldn't have asked me to buy one for his wife.

I had this dream right after my boss had sent me out to buy perfume for his new girlfriend. I felt it was deceptive, yet I was working in the entertainment industry where employees were expected to be "flexible." I shared my dream with some of the other secretaries and asked them how they felt about it. One older woman said she resented that kind of thing, and had told the boss during her job interview that she wouldn't go out and shop for his wife or girlfriend. I decided she had the right idea, and that from now on, I was going to have a similar policy.●

In addition to helping you deal with other people wisely and diplomatically in your work, your dreams can help you make important administrative decisions. In Chapter Ten, you learned how to incubate dreams to solve specific problems; you can also use dreams for problem-solving of business or government decisions. Often, business managers and government officials must rely on intuition in judging how best to "sell" their ideas and projects to others. It is not always easy to tell from the "facts" whether to forge boldly ahead or wait patiently for a better time or circumstance in which to operate. Your dreams can help you become aware of information that you hadn't previously considered, or make you more aware of what your intuitive preferences are, as in the following example.

A ROOM OF ONE'S OWN

Lisa and I are to share an apartment together. We discover that it has a spacious living room and a bedroom with two twin beds. I am dismayed about the one bedroom, as I am anxious to have a room of my own. We discover there is a second bedroom after all, also with two twin beds. One side is open to the living room. Lisa volunteers to take it, and I offer her a set of blinds to hang across the open side to give it more privacy. I want her to be happy about her decision, but feel a little guilty as this also serves my selfish desire to have the more private room.

Lisa and I worked closely for a year on a large research grant. The staff had just quadrupled in size, and in addition to training our new people, we were also implementing a new computerized data management system. When I had this dream, I had begun to be very concerned about the demands on our time and feared that one of us would burn out from sheer exhaustion. The dream made it clear to me that we needed to divide up our responsibilities (have our own rooms). My dream also gave me clues as to how this should be done. I was the only person who understood the data management system and should focus on that more (which is exactly what I "selfishly" yearned to do), while Lisa's skills fit the more "public" (open to the living room) work of running the staff training program. I got in touch with my guilt about abandoning her to such a demanding task, and saw that I needed to help her devise ways of sometimes getting away from training. The fact that each room has two beds suggested we both needed to delegate responsibilities to (share our rooms with) other people. We immediately began training one of our new staff members to help us with administration, relieving us of some of the pressure we had been under.●

OUT OF THE SHEETS
AND INTO THE STREETS

You may recognize the need for changes in our society today, and you may want to do something to help bring them about. Actually, you may already be using your dream insights to do this, for as we pointed out earlier, you make political statements every day in the way you live your personal life. You have also seen how you can extend your "dream power" to influence others more directly by using dreams in public contexts such as education, religion and spirituality, business and government. These are only a few arenas where you can use your dreams to make political and social statements. You are constantly confronted in your daily life with these opportunities. They can arise when you least expect them, and your dreams can alert you to these hidden opportunities, nudging you into action—out of the sheets and into the streets! The following dream made one woman in New Zealand aware of something she could do to help women farmers.

> THE FARMERS
> I'm watching a parade go by. On one float is a group of women wearing working clothes. There are flowers along the side spelling out the words "Farmers' Wives." A dog runs past and rubs off some of the flowers, so that the float spells "Farmers." The women on the float can't see what the flowers say.

This dream gave me an idea for a contribution I could make to the New Zealand Women's Party, a third political party recently organized here. The dream reminded me of a newspaper article I saw, then forgot, describing how New Zealand women married to farmers were getting fed up with being unpaid, taken-for-granted, full-time labor. I wrote out my dream and outlined my ideas as to how the Women's Party could approach and organize this group of working women and educate them to the fact that they are farmers in their own right.●

It is often in the political arena that we meet with situations demanding fresh approaches to problems. We can look to our dreams for novel approaches that will help us bypass political bureaucracy and red tape, making our efforts for change more direct and effective. In the following example, we see how one woman used a dream to change smoking policies on public transportation.

THE MAYOR'S OFFICE

I'm in Italy. A messenger approaches me and says I'm wanted in the mayor's office. I tell him I've done nothing wrong. He pulls out a gun and forces me down some stairs to the mayor's office, and tells me to wait. I can see the mayor through the glass door, and he looks mean. I dread facing him, but also want to get it over with because the man next to me is puffing on a huge cigar and I feel like I'm suffocating.

I had this dream when I was living in a place where the bus system had no "NO SMOKING" signs, and people lit up whenever they felt like it. I complained to the bus drivers, but they ignored me, and I didn't know what else to do. Shortly thereafter I saw a man light up a cigar on the bus, and I suddenly remembered my dream—of course, the mayor's office! That night I drafted a letter to the mayor of the town. I received a prompt reply from her, assuring me that a no-smoking policy would go into effect immediately, and that any drivers refusing to comply with the policy would be reprimanded or removed from their jobs. After that, the air on the busses was clean for the first time, thanks to a terrific woman mayor and to my dream! ●

The possibilities for using dreams to improve public life are limited only by our imaginations and determination to put our dreams to work there. As more of us turn to the intuitive wisdom and creative insight of our dreams for guidance, we can help each other to create a more productive, humanistic, and socially responsible society, one that recognizes the importance and worth of inner knowledge and experiences, while protecting the rights and fostering the individual growth of both women and men. So take your dreams out of the sheets and into the streets *now!*

DREAM ON!

Women are freer now than ever before to choose from a variety of roles and lifestyles to meet their needs for personal growth, rewarding work, and satisfying intimate relationships. This change has also given men more freedom to explore their undeveloped capabilities and unrecognized needs.

Yet, no matter how closely your life and a man's life may come to resemble each other, you bring a different perspective to these experiences. Your social context—your natural propensities, weaknesses, strengths, upbringing, and expectations—will, on the average, be different from his. These differences will be reflected in your dreams, and because greater awareness of your inner, intuitive experience is one of women's natural strengths, you are especially well-equipped to use your dreams as a tool and ally.

You can use your dreams to help you make sense of your life, guiding you through the ever-changing kaleidoscope of roles, responsibilities, and choices. You can use your dreams to explore the frontiers of human consciousness, find practical solutions to problems, and to discover and develop creative abilities you never knew you had. As you bring your dream wisdom into your waking life, you will find you bring change not only into your own life, but into the lives of others as well, both in your intimate circle of family and friends as well as in the public context of work, social, and civic acitivities.

Yet, you must learn to "saddle your dreams before you ride 'em."[1] Throughout this book, you have discovered ways to harness your dreams and put them to work for you, enabling you to benefit from wisdom and insight that goes unheard and unused by many people in our culture, much to their detriment and ours. It is by paying attention to *all* of the levels of awareness available to you, bringing dreaming and waking knowledge together to complement one another, that you can lead the richest life, fulfilling your own potential and making an important contribution to the lives of others.

This book is written by women, for women, and about women, so that you can learn the private language of your dreams and apply it to the specific needs and situations that arise in your life as a woman today. As your waking life and dream life become meshed in this way, you will learn for yourself the truth in the words of Adrienne Rich who said,

> ... in breaking those silences, naming ourselves, uncovering the hidden, making ourselves present, we begin to define a reality which resonates to *us*, which affirms *our* being, which allows [women]... to take ourselves and each other seriously: meaning to take charge of our lives.[2]

So have fun and dream on. There is a whole world locked away inside of you, just waiting to be discovered.

Figure 19-1. Vision of Ezekiel Artist unknown

AFTERWORD

This book was made possible through the generous contribution of dreams and comments by friends, dream group members, and dream workshop participants. We have learned from each and every one of them and look forward to a continuing dialogue on dreams with our readers. We invite you to send us feedback on your experiences working with dreams, care of Spectrum Books, Prentice-Hall, Inc., Englewood Cliffs, New Jersey, 07632.

Notes

PART ONE INTRODUCTION

1. May Sarton, *Mrs. Stevens Hears the Mermaids Singing* (New York: Norton, 1965), 196. Reprinted by permission of W. W. Norton & Company, Inc., and Russell & Volkening, Inc.
2. Kay Deaux, *The Behavior of Women and Men* (Monterey, CA: Brooks Cole, 1976).
3. Jean Baker Miller, *Toward a New Psychology of Women* (Boston: Beacon Press, 1976), 88.
4. The term "gestalt" refers to the combination or organization of parts into a meaningful whole.
5. Mary Daly, *Beyond God the Father: Towards a New Philosophy of Women's Liberation* (Boston: Beacon Press, 1973).

CHAPTER ONE

1. Elizabeth F. Hailey, *A Woman of Independent Means* (New York: Avon, 1978), 4. Copyright © 1978 by Elizabeth Forsythe Hailey. Reprinted by permission of Viking Penguin Inc.
2. Adrienne Rich, *On Lies, Secrets and Silence—Selected Prose 1966–78* (New York: Norton, 1979), 193.
3. Kay Deaux, *The Behavior of Women and Men* (Monterey, CA: Brooks Cole, 1976), 64.
4. Jo Durden-Smith, "Male and Female—Why?" *Quest/80* (Oct. 1980), 19.
5. Deaux, *Women and Men.*
6. Carol Gilligan, *In a Different Voice—Psychological Theory and Women's Development* (Cambridge: Harvard University Press, 1982), 22.
7. Rich, *On Lies,* 35.
8. *Ibid.,* 48.
9 *Ibid.,* 193.

CHAPTER TWO

1. Rosalind Cartwright, "Happy Endings for Our Dreams," *Psychology Today, 12* no. 7 (1978), 66–76.
2. Dorothy Bryant, *The Kin of Ata are Waiting for You* (New York: Random House, 1971), 67.
3. See, for example, E. Hartmann, "Dreaming Sleep (The D-state) and the Menstrual Cycle," *Journal of Nervous and Mental Disease, 143,* (1966), 406–16; or P. Sheldrake and M. Cormack, "Dream Recall and the Menstrual Cycle," *Journal of Psychosomatic Research, 18,* (1974), 347–50.
4. Calvin Hall and Robert Van de Castle, *The Content Analysis of Dreams,* © 1966. Adapted by permission of Prentice-Hall, Inc., Englewood Cliffs, N.J.
5. Robert Van de Castle, *The Psychology of Dreaming* (Morristown, NJ: General Learning Press, 1971).
6. Robert Van de Castle, Director, Sleep and Dream Laboratory, University of Virginia, Charlottesville, VA, personal communication.
7. *Ibid.*

CHAPTER THREE

1. See, for example, "Dream Exploration Among the Senoi," in Theodore Roszak, ed., *Sources* (New York: Harper & Row, 1972), or "Dream Theory in Malaya," in Charles Tart, ed., *Altered States of Consciousness* (Garden City, NY: Doubleday & Company, Inc., Anchor Books, 1972).

PART TWO INTRODUCTION

1. Calvin Hall, *The Meaning of Dreams* (New York: McGraw-Hill Book Company, 1966), 12.
2. Jack Johnston, "Elements of Senoi Dreaming Applied in a Western Culture," *Sundance Community Dream Journal,* 2 no. 1, (Winter, 1978), 51.

CHAPTER SIX

1. John Weir, "The Personal Growth Laboratory," in Kenneth Benne, Leland Bradford, Jack Gibb, and Ronald Lippitt, eds., *The Laboratory Method of Changing and Learning: Theory and Application* (Palo Alto: Science and Behavior Books, Inc., 1975).
2. *Ibid.,* 305.
3. *Ibid.,* 306.

CHAPTER SEVEN

1. Joseph E. Garai, "The Progress of Art in Therapy," *Behavior Today,* (Feb. 14, 1977).
2. A mandala is a collection of symbols of religious significance, usually arranged symmetrically, enclosed in a circle. Mandalas are used in many Eastern religions as an aid to meditation.
3. Henry Reed, "Dream Shields," *Sundance Community Dream Journal, 1* no. 1, (Fall, 1976), 91–92.
4. Henry Reed, "Dream Shields: II–The Four Directions," *Sundance Community Dream Journal, 1* no. 2, (Spring, 1977), 184–89.

CHAPTER EIGHT

1. Kay Deaux, *The Behavior of Women and Men* (Monterey, CA: Brooks Cole, 1976).

CHAPTER NINE

1. Fritz Perls, *Gestalt Therapy Verbatim* (New York: Bantam Books, 1971).
2. Melinda Guttman, Associate Professor, City University of New York, personal communication.

CHAPTER TEN

1. Jack Johnston, "Elements of Senoi Dreaming Applied in a Western Culture," *Sundance Community Dream Journal, 2* no. 1, (Winter, 1978) 50-61.
2. Kilton Stewart, "The Dream Comes of Age," *Mental Hygiene, 46* (1962), 230-37.
3. Henry Reed, "Dream Incubation," *Sundance Community Dream Journal, 2* no. 1, (Winter, 1978), 9-26.

CHAPTER ELEVEN

1. This practice was suggested by John and Joyce Weir in their Laboratory in Self Differentiation, N. T. L. Institute, Bethel, Maine, July, 1976.

PART THREE INTRODUCTION

1. Sarojini Naidu, "Song of a Dream," *The Golden Threshold* (New York: John Lane Company, 1916).

CHAPTER TWELVE

1. Based on an exercise by Diane Mariechild, *The Womancraft Manual* (Quincy, MA: Diane Mariechild, 105 Elmwood Ave., 1976).

2. Based on a guided fantasy presented by Joyce Weir at the Laboratory in Self-Differentiation, N. T. L. Institute, Bethel, Maine, July, 1976.
3. Based on a case study in Steve Lankton, *Practical Magic* (Cupertino, CA: Meta Publications, 1980), 111-13.

CHAPTER THIRTEEN

1. Robert Louis Stevenson, "A Chapter on Dreams," *Memories and Portraits, Random Memories, Memories of Himself* (New York: Scribner, 1925), 172.
2. P. McKellar, *Imagination and Thinking* (New York: Basic Books, 1957).
3. Roy Dreistadt, "An Analysis of How Dreams are Used in Creative Behavior," *Psychology, 8* no. 1, (Feb. 1971), 24-50.
4. As quoted in Havelock Ellis, *The World of Dreams* (Boston: Houghton-Mifflin, 1911), 276.
5. Dreistadt, "An Analysis."
6. W. Kaempffert, Editor, *A Popular History of American Invention* (New York: Charles Scribner's Sons, 1924), II, 385. Copyright © 1924 Charles Scribner's Sons; copyright renewed. Reprinted with permission of Charles Scribner's Sons.
7. Melinda Guttman, Associate Professor, City University of New York, personal communication.

PART FOUR INTRODUCTION

1. Johann Wolfgang von Goethe, *Faustus, A Dramatic Mystery: Prelude at the Theatre. I.* 303 (1835).

CHAPTER FIFTEEN

1. Betty Friedan, *The Second Stage* (New York: Summit Books, 1981).
2. Adrienne Rich, *On Lies, Secrets and Silence—Selected Prose 1966-78* (New York: Norton, 1979), 193.
3. Carol Winget and Frederick Kapp, "The Relationship of the Manifest Content of Dreams to Duration of Childbirth in Primiparae," *Psychosomatic Medicine, 34,* (1972), 313-20.

4. Gina Luria and Virginia Tiger, *Everywoman* (New York: Random House, 1976), 89.
5. Norman Paul and Betty Paul, *A Marital Puzzle* (New York: W. W. Norton & Company, Inc., 1975), 226.
6. *Ibid.*

CHAPTER SIXTEEN

1. Adrienne Rich, *On Lies, Secrets and Silence—Selected Prose 1966-78* (New York: Norton, 1979), 193.
2. *Women's Choice,* (March, 1980).
3. George Bach and Peter Wyden, *The Intimate Enemy* (New York: Avon Books, 1970), 21.

CHAPTER SEVENTEEN

1. Betty Friedan, *The Second Stage* (New York: Summit Books, 1981), 86.

CHAPTER EIGHTEEN

1. Bernice Neugarten, "Adult Personality: Toward a Psychology of the Life Cycle," in Bernice Neugarten, ed., *Middle Age and Aging: A Reader in Social Psychology* (Chicago: University of Chicago Press, 1968), 139.
2. Hilma Wolitzer, "Life in the Middle: Parenting our Parents and Keeping Our Grown Children Young," *Ms.,* (Jan. 1982), 48.
3. Bernice Neugarten, "The Awareness of Middle Age," in Bernice Neugarten, ed., *Middle Age and Aging: A Reader in Social Psychology* (Chicago: University of Chicago Press, 1968), 95.
4. Gail Sheehy, *Passages: Predictable Crises of Adult Life* (New York: Bantam Books, 1976), 350.
5. Susan Sontag, "The Double Standard of Aging," *Saturday Review* (Sept. 23, 1972), 29-38.
6. Bernice Neugarten, U. Wood, R. J. Kraines, and B. Loomis, "Women's Attitudes Toward the Menopause," in Bernice Neugarten, ed., *Mid-*

dle Age and Aging: A Reader in Social Psychology (Chicago: University of Chicago Press, 1968), 200.

7. Avodah Kioffit, "Sexuality: The Facts of (Later) Life," *Ms.*, (Jan. 1982), 32.
8. Neugarten et. al., "Women's Attitudes," 199.
9. Neugarten, "The Awareness of Middle Age," 96.
10. Carol Kleinman, "New Sleep Research: Why Your Dream Life is Different from His," *Ms.*, (August, 1979), 29.
11. Neugarten, et. al., "Women's Attitudes," 140.
12. Maggie Scarf, *Unfinished Business: Pressure Points in the Lives of Women* (New York: Ballantine Books, 1980), 373.
13. Kleinman, "New Sleep Research," 29.
14. Sheehy, *Passages*, 488.
15. Kleinman, "New Sleep Research," 28.
16. *Statistical Abstract of the United States, 1981*, U. S. Department of Commerce—Bureau of the Census (Washington, D. C.: U. S. Government Printing Office, 1981), 41.
17. Robert N. Butler, "The Life Review: An Interpretation of Reminiscence in the Aged," in Bernice Neugarten, ed., *Middle Age and Aging: A Reader in Social Psychology* (Chicago: University of Chicago Press, 1968), 487.
18. Scarf, *Unfinished Business*, 521.
19. R. Morgan, "Katherine Hepburn: Getting on With It!" *Ms.*, (Jan., 1982), 73.
20. Ray Bradbury, *Dandelion Wine* (New York: Alfred A. Knopf, 1978), 209-10. Copyright © 1953 by Gourmet, Inc. Copyright renewed 1981 by Ray Bradbury. Reprinted by permission of the Harold Matson Company, Inc.
21. May Sarton, "The Family of Woman: Growing Toward the Light," *Ms.*, (Jan., 1982), 56.

CHAPTER NINETEEN

1. Mary Webb, *Precious Bane* (New York: E. P. Dutton & Company, Inc., 1929), 47.
2. Adrienne Rich, *On Lies, Secrets and Silence—Selected Prose 1966-78* (New York: Norton 1979), 245.

DREAM AND FANTASY INDEX

The plastic bag, 196
Poor foundation, 176
The psychology exam, 96–97
The punching bag, 158

The quarrel, 76

Ride home, 158–59
The ring of power, 148–49
A room of one's own, 227–28
Roses, 135–36
Rubber spiders, 32
Running for bus #30, 89–90

The sage, 31–32
The same body, 171
The scary clown, 197
Sea tortoise, 104–5
The sex store, 205
Shoveling leaves, 87
The silo, 63
The song, 181–82
The spray of salt, 139
The starling, 194–95
Success, 207–8
Suicide, 29
Swan song, 214

Taking care of me, 210–11
Taking charge, 157
The teacher, 125–26
The teacher fantasy, 126–27
Therapy, 163
There was a crooked house, 134–35
Tickled pink, 183
Together again, 213
Train ride, 88
Tree fantasy, 118–120
The triad, 9–10
The twins, 174
Two questionable things, 168–69
The two-story house, 94–95

Warning, 142–43
We burn you with our fire, 24
The wedding ring, 177–78
The whispering trees, 147–48
The white armadillo, 91
The wild red hair, 192
Women working, 226

SUBJECT INDEX